Norm Research in International Relations

Series Editor

Antje Wiener, Institut für Politikwissenschaft, University of Hamburg,
Hamburg, Germany

This book series offers an outlet for interdisciplinary research on norms in the context of international relations and global governance. It features scientific and scholarly studies which examine the way norms are created and re-created through interactions between actors at the international level, taking into account the reflexive nature of governance relationships and their impact on state behaviour through the re-constitution of norms.

Norms in international relations are defined as ideas of varying degrees of abstraction and specification that concern fundamental values, organising principles or standardised procedures. They resonate across states and global actors in the form of official policies, laws, treaties and agreements, while their meaning may be stable or contested.

Norm Research in International Relations (NRIR) welcomes proposals for research monographs, edited volumes and handbooks from a variety of disciplines that seek to advance theories and applied research in international relations and to arrive at a better understanding of the role and impact of norms. Relevant topics include, but are not limited to, issues of international justice, research on contestation, human rights, international treaties in areas such as energy, environment or security, and constructivist norm research in international relations theory, recognition theory and international law.

All titles in this series are peer-reviewed.

For further information on the series and to submit a proposal for consideration, please contact the Johannes Glaeser (Senior Editor Economics) Johannes.glaeser@springer.com.

Flavia Lucenti • Cecilia Ducci
Carmen Wunderlich • Jeffrey S. Lantis
Editors

Contestation in Prism

The Evolution of Norms and Norm Clusters in Contemporary Global Politics

Springer

Editors
Flavia Lucenti
Department of Political Science
LUISS Guido Carli University
Rome, Italy

Carmen Wunderlich
Department of Political Science
University of Freiburg
Freiburg, Germany

Cecilia Ducci
Department of Political and Social Sciences
University of Bologna
Bologna, Italy

Jeffrey S. Lantis
The College of Wooster
Wooster, OH, USA

ISSN 2522-8676 ISSN 2522-8684 (electronic)
Norm Research in International Relations
ISBN 978-3-031-83638-1 ISBN 978-3-031-83639-8 (eBook)
https://doi.org/10.1007/978-3-031-83639-8

This Springer imprint is published by the registered company Springer Nature Switzerland AG
The registered company address is: Gewerbestrasse 11, 6330 Cham, Switzerland

Acknowledgements

This edited book is the result of a collaboration between scholars at different stages of their careers who share a common interest in International Relations theory, with a particular focus on norm contestation. The project draws on an ongoing and intellectually stimulating dialogue between the editors and the authors. Given our different levels of professional development, along with diverse affiliations and wide geographical distribution (not to mention a global pandemic), participants met both online and in person during the stages leading up to the realisation of this volume. We are thus especially appreciative of the engagement that all the authors have committed themselves to this publication over time.

Some of our early discussions for this project began at the 2022 European International Studies Association (EISA) Pan-European Conference on International Relations (PEC) section on the theme of contestation in international politics, which was convened by the editors of this volume and in which most of its authors participated. Drafts of the chapters have been presented at numerous conferences, notably 2023 EISA-PEC, where we held the roundtable 'Contestation in Prism. Patterns of norm evolution, consolidation, and decay'. Our colleague Simon Koschut served as discussant for this roundtable, and we are grateful for his helpful feedback and input. We also hosted a virtual workshop in October 2023 to share and collect the ideas that allowed the volume to take its current shape, and in 2024, some of us participated in a panel at the annual meeting of the International Studies Association (ISA), titled "Norm Contestation in IOs: Towards Resiliency or Decline?" There, we benefited from the fruitful debate that took place among the panellists, and from the comments that Phil Orchard, Diana Panke, and Nicole Deitelhoff offered on our work.

We are indebted to Antje Wiener, who has believed in our project since the early stages of its development, and we appreciate her valuable and incisive comments throughout the life cycle of the manuscript. We thank her for her support of the book and for assembling this editorial team. We would also like to thank the publisher, Springer, and in particular the series editor, Niko Chtouris, for his support and guidance throughout the publication process. This volume exists because he first approached several of us at the EISA-PEC 2022 and encouraged us to turn the results of the various panels of the section we conveyed at that conference into a book. Furthermore, we cannot fail to mention the valuable insights we received from the anonymous reviewers, whose commentary helped us to improve our arguments and advance some of the innovative ideas in this volume related to the study of norm contestation.

Finally, we owe special thanks to Antonia Damm, a student assistant for Carmen Wunderlich at the University of Freiburg, for her meticulous work in the final editing and formatting of this edited volume.

Contents

About the Editors and Contributors

About the Editors

Flavia Lucenti, Ph.D., is Postdoctoral Research Fellow and Adjunct Professor at LUISS Guido Carli University, Department of Political Science. Her research interests include IR theory, China, Russia, technology, and norms. Previously, she worked as Research Assistant at the University of Oxford and as Postdoctoral Research Fellow and Adjunct Professor at the University of Bologna. She holds a Ph.D. in Political Studies and International Relations from the University of Roma Tre. She was a visiting Ph.D. candidate at the Hong Kong University, the Moscow State Institute of International Relations, and the European University Institute.

Cecilia Ducci, Ph.D. is Postdoctoral Research Fellow at the University of Bologna, Department of Political and Social Sciences. She earned a Ph.D. in Political Science and International Relations from the University of Bologna. She was a visiting Ph.D. candidate at Leiden University, Department of Political Science, and at the Peace Research Institute Frankfurt (HSFK). Her research interests include IR theory, norms, norm contestation, mass atrocities, and International Law.

Carmen Wunderlich is Interim Professor at the University of Freiburg, Germany, substituting the Chair of International Relations. Since 2018, she is *Akademische Rätin auf Zeit* (eq. to non-tenured Assistant Professor/Lecturer) at the University of Duisburg-Essen (currently on leave). She is also Principal Investigator of the research consortium "VeSPoTec – Nuclear Verification in a Complex and Unpredictable World," funded by the German Ministry of Science and Education, and an affiliate researcher at the Peace Research Center Prague. Her research focuses on global norm dynamics and practices of contestation with a specific focus on issues related to the control of weapons of mass destruction and nuclear disarmament. Wunderlich has published numerous articles and books on these subjects. Previously, she was a postdoctoral researcher at the Peace Research Institute Frankfurt and a visiting researcher at the WZB Berlin Social Science Center and the Vienna Center for Disarmament and Nonproliferation. She earned a Ph.D. from the University of Frankfurt.

Jeffrey S. Lantis is Professor of Political Science at the College of Wooster. His teaching and research interests include international security, constructivist norm theory, foreign policy analysis, and emerging technologies and international norms. Lantis has published numerous books and articles on these subjects in leading academic journals. He is co-editor of the journal *International Studies Perspectives* and past coordinator of the Innovative Pedagogy Initiative for the International Studies Association. He has previously served as Fulbright Senior Scholar in Australia and Visiting Scholar at Carleton University and the German Council on Foreign Relations. He earned a Ph.D. from the Ohio State University.

Contributors

Diego Badell Facultat de Ciències Polítiques i Sociologia, Autonomous University of Barcelona, Bellaterra, Cerdanyola del Vallés, Spain

Cecilia Ducci Department of Political and Social Sciences, University of Bologna, Bologna, Italy

Jonas Fritzler University of Amsterdam, Amsterdam, The Netherlands

Lukas Grundsfeld Freie Universität Berlin, Berlin, Germany

Hendrik Huelss Center for War Studies, Department of Political Science and Public Management, University of Southern Denmark, Odense, Denmark

Lucrecia García Iommi Fairfield University, Fairfield, CT, USA

Andrea Knapp University of Bologna, Bologna, Italy

Jeffrey S. Lantis The College of Wooster, Wooster, OH, USA

Pak K. Lee Conflict Analysis Research Centre (CARC) and Global Europe Centre, School of Politics and International Relations, University of Kent, Canterbury, UK

Flavia Lucenti Department of Political Science, LUISS Guido Carli University, Rome, Italy

Diana Panke Freie Universität Berlin, Berlin, Germany

Simone Tholens John Cabot University, Rome, Italy

European University Institute, Florence, Italy

Pawel Tverskoi Freie Universität Berlin, Berlin, Germany

Carmen Wunderlich Department of Political Science, University of Freiburg, Freiburg, Germany

Chapter 1
Contestation in Prism: An Introduction

Carmen Wunderlich, Flavia Lucenti, Jeffrey S. Lantis, and Cecilia Ducci

Introduction

The global political order is today under threat from many different actors and conditions, including serious international conflicts, intensified geopolitical tensions, mass atrocities and gross human rights violations, internal political divisions and an upsurge of populist sentiments, persistent inequalities, and new challenges from technological advances. These challenges and the evolution of international responses to them suggest that we may be witnessing realignments of guiding principles and norms that have shaped International Relations (IR) for decades. Institutions, norms, and principles that were once considered cornerstones of IR appear to be falling apart. For example, the so-called Liberal International Order (LIO) is being challenged both by external actors and actions and from within by erstwhile supporters, and contestation of underlying norms has taken various forms over the years (Adler-Nissen & Zarakol, 2021; Kornprobst & Paul, 2021; Lake & Wiener, 2025). Some norms have been debated and refashioned within

C. Wunderlich (✉)
Department of Political Science, University of Freiburg, Freiburg, Germany
e-mail: carmen.wunderlich@politik.uni-freiburg.de

F. Lucenti
Department of Political Science, LUISS Guido Carli University, Rome, Italy
e-mail: flucenti@luiss.it

J. S. Lantis
The College of Wooster, Wooster, OH, USA
e-mail: jlantis@wooster.edu

C. Ducci
Department of Political and Social Sciences, University of Bologna, Bologna, Italy
e-mail: cecilia.ducci2@unibo.it

F. Lucenti et al. (eds.), *Contestation in Prism*, Norm Research in International
Relations, https://doi.org/10.1007/978-3-031-83639-8_1

international organisations; others have been questioned or challenged directly through various types of contestation.

Contemporary IR theory has made significant progress in identifying and analysing norm contestation over the past two decades as a 'third move' in constructivist norm theory as a distinctive subfield (Orchard & Wiener, 2024, p. 8; Wiener, 2008, 2014). Today, there is greater attention to 'norms as processes' (Krook & True, 2012, p. 105) and a recognition that diverse actors can challenge norms in different ways and circumstances and '*in principle* at any time' during their development (Orchard & Wiener, 2024, p. 9). Scholars further recognise that contestation dynamics may work differently depending on the structural contexts, i.e., the level of institutionalisation and legalisation of a contested norm or to what extent norms are embedded in broader structures (for an overview, compare Deitelhoff and Zimmermann, 2019, p. 10).

This study embraces a multifaceted prismatic treatment of norm contestation as a process that has a wide spectrum of impact on norms and radiates in multiple directions—and chapters expand ideas about contestation processes, mechanisms, and implications that were undertaken with the third move in norm theory development. We can also situate the contributions of our chapter authors within Orchard and Wiener's (2024, pp. 15–18) interpretation-contestation framework: they describe different types of contestation including proactive contestation—typically present during norm construction or in the process of norm emergence, with actors seeking to improve extant norms; interpretive contestation—seen in contested compliance and critically revealing 'hidden norms'; and reactive contestation—which can occur with norm violations and normatively induced challenges of extant norms (Orchard & Wiener, 2024, p. 17). Chapters in this book predominantly explore variations of the interpretive and reactive forms of contestation, though they attend more directly to potential connections between contestatory dynamics and norm clusters and other structures. The chapters of this volume therefore directly speak to and build on recent norms research literature (e.g. Orchard & Wiener, 2024; Zimmermann et al., 2023), but further contribute to it by expanding on the relations between contestation dynamics and norm clusters. In this respect, the prismatic approach of this volume allows us to gain in-depth insights into not only different types of contestation dynamics and their effects on norms, but also in relation to other norms, by focusing on norm clusters.

Three distinctive contributions of this volume include, first, an examination of study of a wider array of types of contestation by addressing a gap in the literature regarding actual pathways or channels by which contestation can influence norms and how norm clusters might mitigate the effects of international challenges (Lantis & Wunderlich, 2018, 2022). Hence, we combine research on different types of contestation with studies on norm clusters to gain additional insights into the complexities of norm contestation dynamics. In this respect, past research on different forms and types of contestation—such as 'applicatory *vs.* validity' contestation (Deitelhoff & Zimmermann, 2020), 'reactive *vs.* proactive' contestation (Wiener, 2014, 2018), and 'discursive *vs.* behavioural' contestation (Stimmer & Wisken, 2019)—helps to inspire our work by both enriching and complexifying arguments about the impact of contestation on norms.

Second, this study draws norm clusters (Lantis & Wunderlich, 2018; Winston, 2018) into the broader conversation about contestation. Chapters speak to the debate between the robustness of—single—norms and the resiliency of the normative structures surrounding norms in the face of contestation. This acknowledges a definition of norm robustness that captures the strength of a norm based on its dual feature of validity and facticity (Deitelhoff & Zimmermann, 2019), but also adds a dimension by expanding on the concept of 'resiliency' in relation to norm clusters. In line with Lantis and Wunderlich, we consider robustness to be a more static notion compared to resiliency (2018, p. 571), which instead refers to the idea that 'norms embedded in […] clusters may be more resilient towards challenges and thus prone to survive contestation without significant damage to their validity' (Lantis & Wunderlich, 2018, p. 576). Chapters in the volume explore the effects of different types of contestation in different structural contexts, and the conclusion draws together the evidence in a structured, focused comparison of the results of this investigation and survey of the status of IR research on norms contestation, which is especially important and timely also given the current proliferation of academic works on contestation and their implications for norm life cycles, robustness, evolution, challenges, consolidation, or even decay (Arcudi, 2019; Deitelhoff & Zimmermann, 2020; Fehl & Rosert, 2020; Lantis, 2017; Lantis & Wunderlich, 2018, 2022; Orchard & Wiener, 2024; Percy, 2019; Percy & Sandholtz, 2022; Welsh, 2019; Wiener, 2014, 2018; Wunderlich, 2020).

Third, the editors and chapter authors for this volume offer contributions to norm theory from diverse perspectives and backgrounds. Established authors survey the existing literature on norm contestation, norm robustness, and norm cluster resiliency, as well as offer innovations in theory and the study of discrete policy subsystems. Other authors in this volume include early career researchers who bring diverse perspectives based on gender, identity, institution, and nationality to study contestation in prism. Together, these works yield an exciting mix of perspectives that can further promote dialogues across the field and outline new research programmes and avenues.

Norm Contestation in IR: Disentangling a Complex Concept

Constructivist research on norms is flourishing. Over the years, the field has seen a consolidation of support for norms as part of the canon of IR theory and further diversification of the research programme into sub-strands. The trajectory of norm research has traditionally been approached using a generational alignment, distinguishing the progression of studies through various 'waves' or 'generations' of scholarship (Cortell & Davis, 2000; Lantis, 2017; Widmaier & Park, 2012; Wunderlich, 2013). Early norm studies propagated an understanding of norms as shared standards of appropriate behaviour (Katzenstein, 1996, p. 5) and mainly focused their analyses on linear processes of norm development and diffusion (e.g. Finnemore & Sikkink, 1998; Katzenstein, 1996; Klotz, 1995). The ensuing models were based on the notion that norms, once internalised by a critical mass of states, become taken-for-granted. To Finnemore and Sikkink (1998, p. 904), once norms become 'internalised', they are simply 'not controversial'. Early work centred around the basic assumption that norms as ideational forces promote order and stability in the international system. This approach was quite formative in that it implied the absence of contestation and broad acceptance.

Since that time, however, scholars have advanced a series of theoretical moves that helped promote more critical analysis of contestation dynamics—and prompted the development of norms research as a distinctive IR subfield (Orchard & Wiener, 2024). More and more scholars have come to embrace the 'principle of contestedness' (Wiener, 2008, p. 47–50) in the past two decades, according to which norms are in constant 'latent' state of contestation, even after formal acceptance (Wiener, 2017, p. 4). Analytically, the concept of contestation is an ontological innovation that is used to critically examine the development, scope, strength, and resiliency of normative architectures. Contestation theory embraces processes of strategic, actor-driven social construction and deconstruction as well as challenges to the supposedly linear modelling of norm life cycles (Wiener, 2014). Critical constructivists challenge traditional understandings of norms as relatively stable and structuring devices. Wiener (2007) originally highlighted the problematic 'ontologisation' of norms and drew attention to their dual quality, while Krook and True (2012, p. 104) challenged conceptions of 'norms as "things"'. These and related works have advanced a more dynamic, processual understanding of norms.

Norm contestation theory has been greatly advanced by the work of Antje Wiener (e.g. 2007, 2008, 2009), who describes contestation as a 'range of social practices, which discursively express disapproval of norms' (Wiener, 2014, p. 1).[1] Contestation in the realm of norms concerns the normative core of international orders and refers to non-violent action taken to emphasise the constructive and intellectual nature of norm contestation (Wiener, 2014, p. 1). Central to this is an emphasis on the 'dual quality' of norms (Wiener, 2007, p. 49) as being simultaneously stable for a certain period of time and yet inherently contested, as they acquire specific meaning through interpretation and enactment in social contexts. Norms are and remain changeable 'works-in-progress' (Krook & True, 2012, p. 104), which gain significance in and through discursive practices—even after prior formal acceptance (Sandholtz, 2007, 2019; Sandholtz & Stiles, 2009; Van Kersbergen & Verbeek, 2007; Wiener, 2004, 2008). In a critical move, Wiener frames norms as both stable and flexible by acknowledging that contestation can occur at different stages of the

[1] In IR theory, the concept of contestation is used far beyond the field of norms studies, in particular in relation to challenges and critiques of the LIO, its early proponents and the institutional structures and processes on which it is based (see, e.g., Alcaro, 2018; Bettiza et al., 2023; Börzel & Zürn, 2021; Dian & Dugar, 2022). It also leads to the development of concepts such as 'deep contestation' (Checkel, 2023; Lake & Wiener, 2025), which seek to capture substantive disagreement with values, institutions, principles, and also norms.

norm life cycle, including norm constitution, negotiation, and implementation (Wiener, 2014, 2018). This interpretation dispenses with the idea of a cascading socialisation process of agents to norms, which has been criticised for upholding a liberal international normative order in support of US-led Western hegemony (García Iommi, 2020). According to this view, the meaning of norms is always subject to contestation and might even differ for agents belonging to the same normative community (Wiener, 2008; Wiener & Puetter, 2009). In sum, theories of norm contestation have evolved considerably over the past two decades, with scholars distinguishing different modes and types of contestation, both for descriptive and analytical purposes.

Types of Contestation

Consistent with the contemporary literature, we conceptualise contestation as 'a social practice of objecting to or critically engaging with norms' (Wiener, 2018, p. 2) that may be directed towards a norm's overall validity, its application in certain contexts, or its specific meaning (Wolff & Zimmermann, 2016, p. 518). This interpretation derives from the evolving conceptualisation of what constitutes norm contestation, which has evolved considerably from Wiener's (2004) seminal definition, which limited contestation to conflicts over the meaning of a norm.

Over time, scholars in the field have further differentiated modes and types of norm contestation, contributing to the advancement of knowledge and awareness of contestation dynamics. For example, later Wiener distinguishes 'reactive' forms of contestation, i.e., mere resistance or objection to norms, from more 'proactive' forms of contestation that are undertaken to critically engage with the global norms that are being challenged and in which the contesting agents have the capacity to do so (Wiener, 2018, p. 35). Proactive contestation refers either to influence on the formal procedure of norm negotiations on the global level, to habitual validation through 'social validation' within a specific social environment, or to cultural validation through 'expression of individual expectation mediated by individually held background experience' (Wiener, 2018, p. 43).

In an effort to trace the implications of norm contestation on norm robustness, Deitelhoff and Zimmermann (2020) identify two types of contestation discourses, namely 'applicatory' and 'justificatory'—or validity—contestation.[2] The two concepts play an important role in the saga of norm development and expand beyond the initial conceptualisation of norm contestation. Applicatory contestation opens up debates about whether a norm is applicable in a certain situation, what specific actions that norm requires its adherents to take and, if more than one norm is

[2] In a preliminary working paper Deitelhoff and Zimmermann (2013) used the definitions of 'applicatory' and 'justificatory' contestation. The authors then changed to the definition of 'validity contestation' rather than justificatory to indicate the form of contestation that is aimed at the general legitimacy of the core normative claim of a norm (Deitelhoff & Zimmermann, 2020).

applicable, which one should take precedence in the specific context under discussion (Deitelhoff & Zimmermann, 2020, p. 57). On the other hand, validity contestation touches on the general validity or legitimacy of a norm, i.e., whether its claims can be considered justified *at all* (Deitelhoff & Zimmermann, 2020, p. 59). Accordingly, validity contestation represents an objection and a challenge to the core of a norm, while applicatory contestation is a more limited type of contestation discourse that depends on the circumstances under discussion.

Validity contestation is believed to lead to greater undermining of the legitimacy of a contested norm, whereas applicatory contestation is viewed as even having a potentially positive impact on the norm, as it may subsequently lead to wider acceptance among recipient actors (Deitelhoff & Zimmermann, 2020, p. 58). Unless it becomes permanent, therefore, applicatory contestation may refine the parameters under which the norm applies and, consequently, contribute to its strengthening. Validity contestation, instead, invalidates the legitimacy of the norm itself. In this regard, Brunnée and Toope (2019, p. 74) draw out the difference between applicatory and validity contestation arguing that 'whereas validity contestation is rare in law, applicatory contestation is inevitable'. In other words, they consider applicatory contestation as inherent in the evolving 'meaning-in-use' of the norm (Wiener, 2009), especially when this is a legal one. It follows that, through applicatory contestation, a norm's scope of application is refined 'through processes of interpretation and justification' (Brunnée & Toope, 2019, p. 74). Conversely, if validity is contested, the norm may lose its efficacy.

Scholars have also begun to explore the emergence of more overt, i.e., direct, forms of contestation from more subtle ones, building on Wiener's (2014, p. 2) suggestion that contestation '[…] may be performed either *explicitly* (by contention, objection, questioning or deliberation) or *implicitly* (through neglect, negation, or disregard)' (emphasis added). In this vein, Drubel and Mende (2023) distinguish between 'open' and 'hidden' types of contestation, indicating by this last term the covert, implicit or disguised discursive contestation, while Schmidt and Sikkink (2019, p. 106) coined the term 'covert validity contestation' to refer to actions concealing deeper norm contestation. Similarly, Sandholtz (2019, p. 140) points out that applicatory contestation may conceal an 'indirect validity contestation' and that, once applicatory contestation becomes permanent, it establishes a wider range of 'exceptions' to the application of a norm, which can eventually 'reduce the scope of the broader norm'. Trenta (2021, p. 5) pushes these ideas further, introducing 'covert—or masked—applicatory contestation' aimed at a radical reshaping of a norm's meaning as the 'fourth dynamic of contestation'. More recently, Orchard and Wiener add the notion of 'interpretive contestation', which they subsume as a form of inadvertent contestation in which agents 'have *unknowingly* adopted different interpretations of what a given norm means' (emphasis in original) but 'believes that their understanding of the norm is the same as others' (Orchard & Wiener, 2024, pp. 15–16). Our volume recognises these different approaches but seeks to connect contestation with other multifaceted but well-defined related phenomena, including norm linkages and resiliency.

Along with types, the current literature also elaborates on the modes through which contestation can take place. While, in line with Wiener's initial indications, contestation takes place primarily through deliberation and discourse, non-discursive forms such as behavioural contestation have increasingly been taken into account. According to Stimmer and Wisken (2019, p. 521), this occurs 'when the actions of relevant actors imply the existence of conflicting understandings of the meaning and/or (relative) importance of a norm'. Importantly, as the authors note, behavioural contestation 'frequently occurs below the radar' (Stimmer & Wisken, 2019, p. 521) as actors do not directly and explicitly challenge the meaning or validity of the norm *expressis verbis*, i.e., on a discursive level. Behavioural contestation, hence, shows a lack of compliance, ineffective implementation, inaction or acts of sabotage (Stimmer & Wisken, 2019, p. 516), which represent a risk for the survival of the norm.

Agents of Contestation

For descriptive purposes, it also makes sense to elaborate on the different agents of contestation and arenas or levels of contestation, which are interlinked but distinct concepts. Particularly with regard to the wider usage of contestation in IR, scholars differentiate between contestation 'from within' and 'from outside' the LIO (Adler-Nissen & Zarakol, 2021; see also Bettiza & Lewis, 2020; Börzel & Zürn, 2021; Mukherjee, 2024; Newman & Zala, 2018). In norms research, this move is mirrored by scholars either focusing on instances of 'endogenous' contestation that comes from within a community of norm followers (Ducci & Lucenti, 2022; Schmidt & Sikkink, 2019; Trenta, 2021; Wiener, 2004) as opposed to contestation between different normative communities (Bode, 2019; Stefan, 2016), e.g., notions of norm localisation and subsidiarity (Acharya, 2011, 2014) or appropriation (Großklaus, 2015). While some scholarly literature concentrates on challenges to the LIO and normative agency by non-Western countries (e.g. Flonk, 2021; Glasius et al., 2020; Kolmašová & Reboredo, 2023; Wunderlich, 2020), it is equally important to acknowledge contestation practices and criticism towards the LIO's normative foundations from 'within' (Ducci & Lucenti, 2022, p. 283), even if it is often a more masked form of contestation (Schmidt & Sikkink, 2019).

Contestation may span different levels or arenas—local, national, regional, transnational, international—and involve a variety of actors, including not only states but also political leaders, international organisations, such as the European Union (EU) and other regional actors, as well as non-state actors. Agents can act for or against a norm through contestation, which, as we admit also in this book, does not necessarily negatively affect the norm but can also strengthen it or merely adapt it to the changing international environment.

In addition to examining the various agents of contestation, one could also assess the intentionality of contestation, which is inevitably related to the entrepreneurship of the agents. McKeown (2009, p. 11, emphasis in original) speaks of 'norm *revisionists*', who are defined as 'members of the state who actively seek to re-shape understandings of their country's relationship to the norm through changes in policy, practice, and/or discourse'. Their intent is to *challenge* the norm and, if their discourse resonates, their contestation may even lead to norm regress (McKeown, 2009, p. 11). When they have a chance to participate in norm negotiation processes, these actors may proactively, rather than reactively, engage with norms. In distinguishing between reformist and revolutionary norm entrepreneurs, Wunderlich (2020, p. 266) discusses their intentions relative to norm contestation. Reformist entrepreneurs, she argues, contest norms to reform and adapt the existing normative order. Conversely, revolutionary entrepreneurs intend to subvert the overarching, established order and its rules (Wunderlich, 2020, pp. 268–269). Similarly, Bettiza and Lewis (2020) understand contestation as either a 'counter-power' force that aims to undermine prevailing normative structures or as a 'corrective force' geared towards their reform. As such, they emphasise the power-laden nature of norm contestation as it forms 'part of the enduring battles for power and influence in world politics that, rather than occurring at the level of material capabilities, take place through the ideational realm' (Bettiza & Lewis, 2020, p. 560). While these authors point to the need to consider the overarching intention of the agents of contestation, Jose (2018, p. 7), instead, contends that actors may contest a norm not only with the specific intention of rejecting and challenging the interpretation of a norm, but also unintentionally 'by articulating their particular meanings of the norm's obligations'. Distinguishing between different types of agents and their respective intentions is therefore useful to better understand the trajectory of contestation dynamics, as well as gain a more comprehensive picture of the actors involved in such processes.

Theorising the Effects of Contestation on Norms

As noted above, contemporary norm contestation scholarship takes a more nuanced view of the effects of contestation, recognising them as contingent on a wide range of factors that help to determine its nature and impact. Our work is informed by these perspectives and challenges some studies that argue that contestation is necessarily detrimental or automatically produces a '*reverse cascade*' (e.g. McKeown, 2009, p. 11, emphasis in original) or even 'norm death' (e.g. Panke & Petersohn, 2016). Kutz (2014, p. 425), for example, explores how contestation can lead to the decay, or even death of those norms that 'once seemed well internalised and institutionalised'. Panke and Petersohn also examine conditions under which norms might die. They argue that whether a norm survives or not also depends on the strength of the contestant: 'if the norm challenger is strong, the norm may be replaced, significantly weakened or even completely abolished' (Panke & Petersohn, 2016, p. 4). In this respect, if the norm that is being contested is precise and thus cannot be adjusted on the basis of the contestation arguments advanced, the norm dies (Panke & Petersohn, 2016, p. 6). These authors thus offer a generally pessimistic view of the effects of contestation on norm robustness.

In contrast to these models, which suggest the regression, decay or death of norms in the face of contestation, other scholars have provided more nuanced visions and have advanced two general ways of thinking about how norms often survive challenges: norm robustness and norm cluster resiliency. Each is summarised briefly in the sections that follow.

Norm Robustness

Researchers often link the idea of contestation on norms to study the robustness or strength of an individual norm (e.g. Deitelhoff & Zimmermann, 2020; Hirsch & Dixon, 2021). Contemporary work in this area has also pushed beyond unidimensional understandings of norm strength as compliance and instead recognises the concept as much more complex. For example, Price (2006, pp. 254–255) claims that robustness encompasses not only the behavioural compliance with a norm but also its discursive acceptance. He focuses not only on states' compliance, but also on *opinio juris* and, therefore, the extent to which states believe that an action constitutes a legal obligation. Similarly, Brunnée and Toope (2019, pp. 75–76) stress the importance of 'reciprocity', meaning that norms are not merely imposed but must be socially accepted. This leads Deitelhoff and Zimmerman to the realisation—and here we follow them—that robustness encompasses validity and facticity. Hence, 'norm robustness is said to be "high" when its claims are widely accepted by norm addressees (validity) and generally guide the actions of the addressees (facticity)' (Deitelhoff & Zimmermann, 2019, p. 3). Accordingly, it combines both discursive acceptance of and behavioural compliance with a norm. Finally, Deitelhoff and Zimmermann (2019, p. 3, 2020, pp. 53–54) also specify that to analyse a norm's robustness, we should look into concordance, third-party reactions to norm violations, compliance, and implementation.

Deitelhoff and Zimmermann (2019, 2020) advance a detailed exploration of whether contestation has a positive or a negative effect on norm robustness in their recent work. They contend that above all the type of contestation, i.e., validity or applicatory contestation—rather than the relative power of contesting agents—significantly influences whether contestation has a negative or a positive impact on a norm's robustness. As indicated above, they argue that applicatory contestation can help refine norms' meanings and implementation, eventually fostering a consensus that lends legitimacy and robustness to a challenged norm (Deitelhoff & Zimmermann, 2020, p. 57). Even when applicatory contestation is used strategically, i.e., as a way to render a norm ineffective, it can still contribute to refining a norm's meaning and application because 'actors, by engaging in applicatory contestation, support a norm's general legitimacy and do not reject the idea that they are bound by a specific norm' (Deitelhoff & Zimmermann, 2020, p. 58). Similarly, in studying the US' contestation of the anti-torture norm under the Bush administration, Birdsall (2016, p. 192) states that the applicatory contestation over the anti-torture norm under the Bush administration actually 'reaffirmed the *absolute* prohibition of torture and clarified its application' (emphasis in original). In contrast, Deitelhoff and Zimmermann (2020) argue that justificatory or validity contestation could negatively impact norm robustness, as it invalidates the legitimacy of the norm itself. Wolff and Zimmermann (2016) similarly explore the level of intensity and depth of contestation in relation to norm strength. They claim that the degree of contestation is higher if contestation is meant to challenge the validity of a norm, whereas questioning the application of a norm constitutes a more modest form (Wolff & Zimmermann, 2016, p. 532).

These criteria for robustness bolster the idea that debate can be valuable for norm robustness in many circumstances. However, other scholars counter that contestation could have potentially negative effects on norm robustness, if it is prolonged (Ben-Josef Hirsch & Dixon, 2024; Panke & Petersohn, 2012, p. 723; Petersohn, 2014) or if the norm is challenged by powerful 'antipreneurs' (Bloomfield, 2016, p. 11; see also Heller et al., 2012; McKeown, 2009; Panke & Petersohn, 2012, 2016). Trenta's historical analysis of US foreign policy also challenges common wisdom and argues that 'applicatory contestation can be as "radical" as other forms of intervention. For this reason, actors often "covertly" called for applicatory contestation while settling for meaning contestation' (Trenta, 2021, p. 15). In this respect, he argues that applicatory contestation can intensify to the point of weakening the norm by 'shrinking the remit of the norm to allow previously prohibited policies' (Trenta, 2021, p. 5).

Following from these accounts is the assumption that different types and agents entail a different degree of intensity of contestation that concerns the impact on the norm in terms of application and validity of the norm and that varies from soft to hard (Johansson-Nogués et al., 2020, p. 8), where application, when not recurrent, is the softest while that affecting the validity of the norm is the hardest. This distinction between 'soft' and 'hard' is important because it opens up the possibility of considering as contestation also those forms that are not commonly seen as such. Like Johansson-Nogués, Vlaskamp and Barbé (2020, p. 10) explain 'Soft contestation is thus more a meanings-in-use contestation […] and occurs in cases where norms do not impose debilitating restriction on norm-takers, and hence most contesters feel no urgency in overturning or modifying the fundamental norm'. In contrast, '[h]arder contestation thus frequently leads to alternative norms being proposed, deliberative forums shifted to reframe the debate or the emergence of discourse and practice to prevent the effective implementation of the norm' (Johansson-Nogués et al., 2020, p. 10).

In summary, the literature on norm robustness shows that it is far from clear what exactly influences and affects norms, and how different types and modes often interact and overlap, affecting the impact and intensity of norm contestation dynamics. Our study argues that one key to help understand these different interpretations in empirical studies is to recognise that contestation dynamics may work differently depending on the structural contexts (see also Deitelhoff & Zimmermann, 2019 as well as Zimmermann et al., 2023 even though they do not explore the embeddedness of norms further), and the nature and scope of the relationship between contestation and structural contexts is worthy of much further exploration. Particularly interesting in this regard is the concept of norm clusters, which is central to this volume.

Norm Cluster Resiliency

Theories of norm linkages focus on the complex interrelationships between norms, including overlaps, linkages, and even collisions, and not just on single norms (Fehl, 2018, 2023; Fehl & Rosert, 2020; Gholiagha et al., 2020). Accordingly, scholars discuss that the effects of contestation cannot be analysed in isolation, since norms are embedded into broader normative architectures. As Lantis and Wunderlich (2022, p. 8, emphasis in original) put it: '[N]orms do not emerge *sui generis*, but instead enter a pre-existing normative structure consisting of different norms, rules, and social practices from which norms emerge. Those norms that diffuse most readily and gain legitimacy in the system more quickly are fostered in complementary normative "neighborhoods"'.

Lantis and Wunderlich (2018, p. 576) understand norm clusters as sets of norms that are similar in principles, values, and orientations within a given issue area. Specifically, norm clusters are defined as 'collections of aligned, but distinct, norms or principles that relate to a common, overarching issue area; they address different aspects and contain specific normative obligations' (Lantis & Wunderlich, 2018, p. 571). Individual norms remain significant as formalised statements of general principles, and norm cores display levels of facticity and validity (Deitelhoff & Zimmermann, 2020). But international norms are commonly grounded in broader clusters or networks of similarly aligned norms that are interlinked. Similarly, Wiener and True speak of a '"norm bundle" consisting of fundamental norms' (True & Wiener, 2019, p. 553) when analysing the Women, Peace, and Security (WPS) agenda, while Fehl and Rosert (2020, p. 8, emphasis in original) refer to 'norm complexes' to capture '*norm families, norm packages, and norm agglomerations*'.

Key factors that bind norms together in clusters are ideological or principled cohesion along with—strategically established—institutional linkages (Rhoads & Welsh, 2019). This coherency often follows a functional logic, where norms in clusters are 'understood to be an "appropriate" means of addressing the more general problem that motivates norm cluster adoption' (Winston, 2018, p. 647). Similarly, norm clusters are also entwined with institutionalisation and may, for example, be the result of negotiation processes in the context of international regimes (Lantis & Wunderlich, 2018; Percy & Sandholtz, 2022). Hence, norms that focus on common problems tend to foster complementary behavioural provisions, reflecting the mutually constitutive relationships between norms and institutions and legal prescriptions.

Fehl and Rosert (2020, p. 1) also address these complex relationships. They argue, '[i]nternational norms can hardly be understood without analysing their relations and interactions with other international norms. Inter-norm relations may be harmonious or conflictual, hierarchical or horizontal, clustered or separated'. Seen in this light, contestation is an integral part of norm development and stewardship. Wiener (2014, p. 1) asserts that norms effectively 'require regular contestation in order to work'. Regular engagement on normative meanings further involves norm networks, which depend upon critical re-evaluation to increase their legitimacy and implementation.

Whether the debates are about norm cluster foundations in broader institutional arrangements or the definition or implementation of a discrete norm within a cluster, norm cluster theory expects that synergistic linkages between norms will help mitigate or channel the effects of contestation of any form. Accordingly, norm clusters are considered to provide adaptive mechanisms for durability (Lantis & Wunderlich, 2018, p. 578). Percy and Sandholtz (2022, p. 935) argue convincingly that norms 'can survive even high levels of non-compliance' and they are 'resilient because they are embedded in larger normative structures'. Even if contestation may vary in terms of agency, intensity, and intentionality, norm cluster theory expects norm clusters to foster meso-level connections as a whole and trigger justification discourses, which can subsequently lead to the confirmation or even strengthening of the norm cluster. To Lantis and Wunderlich, norm clusters are not only 'common venues for contestatory debates, they may also be ideal' (Lantis & Wunderlich, 2022, p. 10), because it is within such institutionalised structures that actors are regularly 'forced' to (re-)negotiate their understanding of the contours of the norm cluster, the relative weighing and the relations between individual norms in a cluster (Wunderlich, 2023, p. 165). Institutionalised norm clusters may even offer procedures and standardised practices that help channel contestation (Zhang, 2024).

Yet, while there is convincing evidence for norm cluster resiliency, we still don't know exactly how contestation dynamics unfold therein. For example, is it just that norm clusters provide adaptive mechanisms for durability, or—and if so, under what circumstances—might interlinkages be able to channel the effects of contestation and thus prevent, for example, applicatory contestation from becoming permanent or escalating into validity contestation (Zimmermann et al., 2023, p. 28)? At the same time, Lantis and Wunderlich do not exclude the possibilities of conflicts resulting from norm interlinkages, such as instances over which norm in a cluster—or normative meaning—is to be given precedence over others in practice (Lantis & Wunderlich, 2022, p. 10; see also Gallagher et al., 2022). Some studies seem to indicate that disputes about the relative importance of individual norms in clusters can also lead to political blockades (Harris & Symons, 2013). Similarly, contestation dynamics in norm clusters could also reveal conflicts that result, for example, from different perceptions or interpretations of individual norms and their respective interrelations, thus leading to 'norm collisions' (Gholiagha et al., 2020). In a similar vein, referring to the US Supreme Court's decision on abortion, Mende (2024) analyses the strategic de-coupling of clustered norms with the aim to reinterpret them so as to advance altered normative understandings. Finally, the question of the extent to which contestation of a single norm can spill over to other norms in the cluster cannot be ruled out in theory, but has not yet been systematically researched in practice.

An alternative model of norm clusters developed by Winston (2018) focuses on the internal composition of norms themselves as being constituted by a distinct assemblage of problems, values, and behavioural rules. Winston (2018, p. 640–641) identifies these as core elements of a 'tripartite structure' of norms, including the problems a norm is supposed to solve, the values that contribute to identify and motivate actors to address these problems, and behavioural prescriptions or solutions. Winston's approach thus differs from that of Lantis and Wunderlich in that she conceptualises the cluster as *internal* to the norm, with reference to the intrinsic components, or principles, to which the norm is necessarily linked. These factors may further define compatibility or conflict in normative systems.

It follows that a norm cluster can be viewed as a multi-layered concept that can take place both within the norm and outside this, along with the interweaving of it with other norms. Collectively, these foundations serve as inspiration for our development of a framework that links norm contestation theory with norm clusters and linkages. If norm clusters are collections of similar, interwoven principles within and between norms that coalesce around a common substantive focus and/or principle, then we should reasonably expect these networks to be affected by multiple forms of contestation. It is this multidimensional, layered, or prismatic effect that this volume refracts and explores from different perspectives.

At first glance, the concepts of norm robustness and norm cluster resiliency may seem to contradict the principle of contestedness, which views norms as inherently contested and thus necessary for norms to obtain legitimacy (Wiener, 2007, p. 48). If contestation is 'the engine driving norm dynamics' (Müller & Wunderlich, 2018, p. 351), then why is resilience or robustness desirable at all? The answer lies in the norm-generative quality of practices of contestation, which may result in legal-constitutional orders based on foundational common values and in which contestation is channelled into regular contestation so that conflict be avoided (Wiener, 2014, p. 49; see also Krieger & Liese, 2023, p. 18). That way proactive contestation may even enhance resilience of a norm cluster if adequate channels for contestation are provided. Indeed, processes of contestation can contribute to a norm being discussed and reaffirmed or refined among a wider audience, enhancing the robustness of such norm. Similarly, contestation directed at a norm that is part of a wider cluster does not necessarily rest on the notion that contestation is normatively negative as it may strengthen and reaffirm the norm cluster as a whole. In other words, 'Contestation aimed at the underlying *principle* rather than at an individual norm could be particularly devastating because that would erode the whole cluster' (Zimmermann et al., 2023, p. 22).

Contestation in Prism: An Integrated Framework

Theories of norm contestation raise interesting questions about its impact on norm robustness and international cooperation, but most studies focus on the distinctive effects of contestation on discrete norms. Our investigation sets out to widen this lens by bridging insights from contestation theory with norm cluster theory, filling a gap in the literature on how norm contestation might impact norms embedded in and linked to broader normative-institutional structures. As noted above, one of the guiding arguments in the volume is that a norm's robustness must be studied in tandem with the concept of norm cluster resiliency, when addressing the type of contestation advanced, the agents and their intentionality, and the effect on the norms surrounding it. Thus, research paves the way for investigations into how the dynamics of norm contestation develop and influence norm and norm cluster evolution.

Research Program

The volume offers a platform for diverse and multidimensional studies of norm contestation and their effects on norms embedded in clusters. Based on the principle of *quod omnes tangit* and hence following Wiener (2018, pp. 27, 31–33), we assume that a contested norm remains a legitimate norm by definition, as long as contesting practices do not go so far as to undermine the norm's existence and a broad range of actors are included in the process of negotiation and contestation of a norm (Wiener, 2018, p. 71; Kurowska, 2019). But this collection of chapters also aims to explore important dimensions of how exactly norm contestation dynamics unfold and affect the robustness of a norm or the resiliency of a norm cluster. This volume features a diverse range of methodologies including both traditional and novel methodologies. Chapters employ interpretivist and qualitative methodology such as discourse, narrative, and content analysis (e.g. Yanow & Schwartz-Shea, 2015). Some of them also base their research on detailed data derived from intense fieldwork and interviews conducted to explain processes of contestation in the cases at hand. The volume also introduces other novel methodological approaches for researching norms and their contestation, such as practice theory.

Based on this framework, all chapters address a set of questions and integrate these theoretical perspectives into their contributions to different extent:

- What are the different forms of norm contestation that may be present in this issue area? How are these interlinked?
- What types of norms, norm clusters, or norm linkages are being contested in this issue area?
- How does contestation shape or affect the norms and state behaviour relative to the norms in this issue area? For example, what effects does applicatory contestation have on norm robustness, and is this mitigated by the linkages between norms in a cluster?
- Could contestation of a norm have a spillover effect on the norm or, on other similar norms, and if so, how does this impact the overall constellation of the norm cluster?

- What are the theoretical insights drawn from theory to case application, and what new research questions are generated from this exercise?

Organisation of the Book

The chapters in this volume feature expert commentary by scholars examining the presence and significance of norm clusters and norm contestation in issue areas including nuclear non-proliferation (Lantis, 2025, Chap. 2), Regional International Organisations (RIOs) (Panke et al., 2025, Chap. 3), the Responsibility to Protect (R2P) (Knapp and Fritzler, 2025, Chap. 4), the Responsibility to Prosecute (Lucenti et al., 2025, Chap. 5), Artificial Intelligence (AI) (Huelss, 2025, Chap. 6), gender equality norms and Sexual and Reproductive Health and Rights in the EU (Badell, 2025, Chap. 7), gender equality norms, non-impunity and norms regulating the use of force in international law (García Iommi, 2025, Chap. 8), and energy security in the Euro-Mediterranean cooperation (Tholens, 2025, Chap. 9). Focusing on these themes and related norms allows us to assess whether clusters of norms are more resilient in the face of contestation or, conversely, whether negative effects of contestation on a single norm's robustness may also affect principles that are constituent of the norm itself as well as other clustered norms.

In Chap. 2, Jeffrey Lantis builds on the opening conceptual framework and offers a novel contribution by extending the nascent theory of norm clusters by identifying three mechanisms by which networked norm clusters promote resiliency in the face of challenges: accountability, diffusion/dispersal, and regeneration/expansion. The chapter then conducts a plausibility test of the networked model of norm cluster resiliency by comparing mini-case studies of recent challenges to the nuclear non-proliferation norm cluster and the 'nuclear taboo'. Chapter 3, written by Diana Panke, Lukas Grundsfeld, and Pawel Tverskoi, provides yet a different perspective by focusing on RIOs and clusters of community norms. They distinguish analytically between the contestation of norms defining the rights or obligations of community membership in RIOs and the contestation of the substantive content or applicability of norms. On the basis of this heuristic framework, they then develop expectations about the frequency of occurrence of the different types of norm contestation with a specific focus on norm withdrawal. The case studies thus suggest that clusters of community norms define the rights and obligations of RIO member states and tend to lead to greater norm stabilisation, even when they threaten to withdraw their membership.

In line with the aim of the volume to deal with 'contestation from within', Chap. 4 focuses on the R2P norm cluster and its contestation on the part of Canada and Sweden. Using interviews and content analysis, Andrea Knapp and Jonas Fritzler examine Canadian and Swedish practices of applicatory contestation since 2000 and argue that the binary role descriptions of norm entrepreneurs and antipreneurs provided by agentic constructivism do not fully capture the attitudes of the two states. Canada and Sweden, they conclude, indeed, continue to pay lip service to their early role as R2P supporters, but at the same time engage in a form of soft contestation. This gradually affects the robustness of the R2P norms, while not affecting the norms of the wider human protection cluster. Still related to the humanitarian norm clusters, Chap. 5 discusses the contestation over the Responsibility to Prosecute as embedded in a norm cluster itself that consists of two juxtaposed founding principles, namely complementarity and universal jurisdiction. By investigating the conduct of Sri Lanka's post-civil war governments in prosecuting alleged atrocities the authors, Flavia Lucenti, Cecilia Ducci, and Pak K. Lee demonstrate how they prioritise complementarity over universal jurisdiction, thereby undermining the resiliency of the Responsibility to Prosecute as a cluster itself.

Moving on to highlight different forms of contestation, Chap. 6 draws on different normative agents and practices of contestation in the face of new emerging AI-driven technologies. Outlining an original insight into the meaning-*of*-use of norms, Hendrick Huelss addresses how the substance of norms is contested not only in application, but also as a result of practices. This perspective allows the author to introduce the discussion of how to deal with new challenges, such as AI systems, which may even turn into norm challengers or norm antipreneurs, without being guided by any human agency, as the theory has conceived so far, revealing new problems for normative research. The misuse of AI tools therefore has the potential of violating existing norms, with regard to their military use and the respect of certain norms, even if they are embedded in a norm cluster. Chapter 7 investigates the contestation of the gender equality norms and Sexual and Reproductive Health and Rights in the EU. In his contribution, Diego Badell reveals a remarkable shift in the EU's approach to gender and reproductive policies in recent years. For the first time, indeed, the EU's gender action plan failed to win unanimous approval, with Hungary and Poland openly questioning its validity. Chapter 8 by Lucrecia García Iommi discusses instead norm withdrawal with specific reference to the anti-impunity norm, in the context of the gender equality norm and the norms on the use of force. In her chapter, norm withdrawal is described as a type of contestation that leads actors, mainly states, to prioritise certain norms over others. In her view, norm clusters can potentially mitigate the negative impact of norm withdrawal on the contested norms, but also, in some more radical cases, amplify the effect of this type of contestation by making the state feel bound by a wider range of obligations. García Iommi's work therefore provides a critical insight into norm robustness and norm cluster resiliency, adding a layer of complexity to our research agenda on normative linkages.

Linking back to other theoretical debates, Chap. 9 explores the impact of covert, non-explicit contestation on international norms by examining various 'hidden transcripts' that oppose dominant narratives and normative policy frameworks. In her chapter, Simone Tholens asks when and how what the author sees as unarticulated normative configurations appear to be resistant to certain forms of contestation because they occur in a more covert and marginal dimension, rather than because they are inserted into a coherent normative structure. And finally, in the concluding chapter of the volume, we draw together the insights of the volume by reflecting upon the discussions raised in the introduction and throughout the chapters. In this respect, by recalling the main findings of the chapters, we illustrate the relevance of this discussion over how contestation influences a norm's robustness and cluster resiliency along what will emerge as the main theoretical dimensions underlying this volume.

References

Alcaro, R. (2018). Contestation and transformation. Final thoughts on the liberal international order. In R. Alcaro (Ed.), *The liberal order and its contestations* (pp. 152–167). Routledge.

Acharya, A. (2011). Dialogue and discovery: In search of international relations theories beyond the west. *Millennium, 39*(3), 619–637. https://doi.org/10.1177/0305829811406574

Acharya, A. (2014). Global international relations (IR) and regional worlds. A new agenda for international studies. *International Studies Quarterly, 58*(4), 647–659. https://doi.org/10.1111/isqu.12171

Adler-Nissen, R., & Zarakol, A. (2021). Struggles for recognition: The liberal international order and the merger of its discontents. *International Organization, 75*(2), 611–634. https://doi.org/10.1017/S0020818320000454

Arcudi, A. (2019). The absence of norm modification and the intensification of norm contestation: Africa and the responsibility to prosecute. *Global Responsibility to Protect, 11*(2), 172–197. https://doi.org/10.1163/1875984X-01102004

Badell, D. (2025). Gender equality norm cluster in action: The resiliency of sexual and reproductive health and rights in the EU. In F. Lucenti, C. Ducci, C. Wunderlich & J. Lantis (Eds.), *Contestation in prism: The evolution of norms and norm clusters in contemporary global politics* (pp. 125–142). Springer.

Ben-Josef Hirsch, M., & Dixon, J. M. (2024). Rethinking norm change: Content and strength in norm development. In I. P. Orchard & A. Wiener (Eds.), *Contesting the world: Norm research in theory and practice* (pp. 29–42). Cambridge University Press.

Bettiza, G., Bolton, D., & Lewis, D. (2023). Civilizationism and the ideological contestation of the liberal international order. *International Studies Review, 25*(2). https://doi.org/10.1093/isr/viad006

Bettiza, G., & Lewis, D. (2020). Authoritarian powers and norm contestation in the liberal international order: Theorizing the power politics of ideas and identity. *Journal of Global Security Studies, 5*(4), 559–577. https://doi.org/10.1093/jogss/ogz075

Birdsall, A. (2016). But we don't call it 'torture'! Norm contestation during the US 'war on terror'. *International Politics, 53*(2), 176–197. https://doi.org/10.1057/ip.2015.42

Bloomfield, A. (2016). Norm antipreneurs and theorising resistance to normative change. *Review of International Studies, 42*(2), 310–333. https://doi.org/10.1017/S026021051500025X

Bode, I. (2019). Norm-making and the Global South: Attempts to regulate lethal autonomous weapons systems. *Global Policy, 10*(3), 359–364. https://doi.org/10.1111/1758-5899.12684

Börzel, T., & Zürn, M. (2021). Contestations of the liberal international order: From liberal multilateralism to postnational liberalism. *International Organization, 75*(2), 282–305. https://doi.org/10.1017/S0020818320000570

Brunnée, J., & Toope, S. J. (2019). Norm robustness and contestation in international law: Self-defense against nonstate actors. *Journal of Global Security Studies, 4*(1), 73–87. https://doi.org/10.1093/jogss/ogy039

Checkel, J. T. (2023). *Identity politics and deep contestations of the liberal international order: The case of Europe* (EUI Working Paper). https://www.eui.eu/Documents/DepartmentsCentres/SPS/Profiles/Checkel/CwCWorkshopJune2023-CheckelPaper.pdf

Cortell, A. P., & Davis, J. W. (2000). Understanding the domestic impact of international norms: A research agenda. *International Studies Review, 2*(1), 65–87. https://doi.org/10.1111/1521-9488.00184

Deitelhoff, N., & Zimmermann, L. (2013). *Things we lost in the fire: How different types of contestation affect the validity of international norms* (PRIF Working Papers, 18). https://nbn-resolving.org/urn:nbn:de:0168-ssoar-455201

Deitelhoff, N., & Zimmermann, L. (2019). Norms under challenge: Unpacking the dynamics of norm robustness. *Journal of Global Security Studies, 4*(1), 2–17. https://doi.org/10.1093/jogss/ogy041

Deitelhoff, N., & Zimmermann, L. (2020). Things we lost in the fire: How different types of contestation affect the robustness of international norms. *International Studies Review, 22*(1), 51–76. https://doi.org/10.1093/isr/viy080

Dian, M., & Dugar, G. (2022). A post-western world in the making. The conceptual framework. *Interdisciplinary Political Studies, 8*(2), 233–245. https://doi.org/10.1285/i20398573v8n2p233

Drubel, J., & Mende, J. (2023). The hidden contestation of norms: Decent work in the international labour organization and the United Nations. *Global Constitutionalism, 12*(2), 246–268. https://doi.org/10.1017/S2045381722000259

Ducci, C., & Lucenti, F. (2022). 'Contestation from within': US escalating aversion to the international criminal court and the non-impunity norm in the Trump era. *Interdisciplinary Political Studies, 8*(2), 281–297. https://doi.org/10.1285/i20398573v8n2p281

Fehl, C. (2018). *Navigating norm complexity: A shared research agenda for diverse constructivist perspectives* (PRIF Working Papers, 41). https://nbn-resolving.org/urn:nbn:de:0168-ssoar-59468-2

Fehl, C. (2023). Protect and punish: Norm linkage and international responses to mass atrocities. *European Journal of International Relations, 29*(3), 751–779. https://doi.org/10.1177/13540661231158548

Fehl, C., & Rosert, E. (2020). *It's complicated: A conceptual framework for studying relations and interactions between international norms* (PRIF Working Papers, 49). https://nbn-resolving.org/urn:nbn:de:0168-ssoar-69733-0

Finnemore, M., & Sikkink, K. (1998). International norm dynamics and political change. *International Organization, 52*(4), 887–917. https://doi.org/10.1162/002081898550789

Flonk, D. (2021). Emerging illiberal norms: Russia and China as promoters of internet content control. *International Affairs, 97*(6), 1925–1944. https://doi.org/10.1093/ia/iiab146

Gallagher, A., Lawrinson, B., & Hunt, C. T. (2022). Colliding norm clusters: Protection of civilians, responsibility to protect, and counter-terrorism in Mali. *Global Responsibility to Protect, 14*(2), 204–231. https://doi.org/10.1163/1875-984X-14010015

García Iommi, L. (2020). Norm internalisation revisited: Norm contestation and the life of norms at the extreme of the norm cascade. *Global Constitutionalism, 9*(1), 76–116. https://doi.org/10.1017/S2045381719000285

García Iommi, L. (2025). Exceptions as contestation: Understanding norm withdrawal. In F. Lucenti, C. Ducci, C. Wunderlich, & J. S. Lantis (Eds.), *Contestation in prism: The evolution of norms and norm clusters in contemporary global politics* (pp. 143–161). Springer.

Gholiagha, S., Holzscheiter, A., & Liese, A. (2020). Activating norm collisions: Interface conflicts in international drug control. *Global Constitutionalism, 9*(2), 290–317. https://doi.org/10.1017/S2045381719000388

Glasius, M., Schalk, J., & De Lange, M. (2020). Illiberal norm diffusion: How do governments learn to restrict nongovernmental organizations? *International Studies Quarterly, 64*(2), 453–468. https://doi.org/10.1093/isq/sqaa019

Großklaus, M. (2015). Appropriation and the dualism of human rights: Understanding the contradictory impact of gender norms in Nigeria. *Third World Quarterly, 36*(6), 1253–1267. https://doi.org/10.1080/01436597.2015.1047206

Harris, P. G., & Symons, J. (2013). Norm conflict in climate governance: Greenhouse gas accounting and the problem of consumption. *Global Environmental Politics, 13*(1), 9–29. https://doi.org/10.1162/GLEP_a_00151

Heller, R., Kahl, M., & Pisoiu, D. (2012). The 'dark' side of normative argumentation—The case of counterterrorism policy. *Global Constitutionalism, 1*(2), 278–312. https://doi.org/10.1017/S2045381711000049

Hirsch, B., & Dixon, J. M. (2021). Conceptualizing and assessing norm strength in international relations. *European Journal of International Relations, 27*(2), 521–547. https://doi.org/10.1177/1354066120949628

Huelss, H. (2025). Contestation of normativity in military practices and the AI transformation. In F. Lucenti, C. Ducci, C. Wunderlich, & J. S. Lantis (Eds.), *Contestation in prism: The evolution of norms and norm clusters in contemporary global politics* (pp. 107–124). Springer.

Johansson-Nogués, E., Vlaskamp, M. C., & Barbé, E. (2020). *European Union contested.* Springer. https://doi.org/10.1007/978-3-030-33238-9

Jose, B. (2018). *Norm contestation: Insights into non-conformity with armed conflict norms.* Springer.

Katzenstein, P. J. (1996). *The culture of national security: Norms and identity in world politics.* Columbia University Press.

Klotz, A. (1995). Norms reconstituting interests: Global racial equality and U.S. sanctions against South Africa. *International Organization, 49*(3), 451–478. https://doi.org/10.1017/S0020818300033348

Knapp, A., & Fritzler, J. (2025). 'Soft contestation' of the responsibility to protect? Assessing Canada and Sweden's norm diplomacy. In F. Lucenti, C. Ducci, C. Wunderlich, & J. S. Lantis (Eds.), *Contestation in prism: The evolution of norms and norm clusters in contemporary global politics* (pp. 65–85). Springer.

Kolmašová, Š., & Reboredo, R. (2023). *Norm diffusion beyond the west: Agents and sources of leverage*. Springer.

Kornprobst, M., & Paul, T. V. (2021). Globalization, deglobalization and the liberal international order. *International Affairs, 97*(5), 1305–1316. https://doi.org/10.1093/ia/iiab120

Krieger, H., & Liese, A. (2023). Tracing value change in the international legal order: Perspectives from legal and political science. Oxford University Press. https://doi.org/10.1093/oso/9780192855831.001.0001

Krook, M. L., & True, J. (2012). Rethinking the life cycles of international norms: The United Nations and the global promotion of gender equality. *European Journal of International Relations, 18*(1), 103–127. https://doi.org/10.1177/1354066110380963

Kurowska, X. (2019). *The politics of cyber norms: Beyond norm construction towards strategic narrative contestation.* EU Institute for Security Studies. https://eucyberdirect.eu/content_research/the-politics-of-cyber-norms-beyond-norm-construction-towards-strategic-narrative-contestation/

Kutz, C. (2014). How norms die: Torture and assassination in American security policy. *Ethics & International Affairs, 28*(4), 425–449. https://doi.org/10.1017/S0892679414000598

Lake, D., & Wiener, A. (2025). Introduction: Understanding deep contestation. In A. Wiener, D. Lake and T. Risse (Eds.), *Deep Contestations of International Order*. Oxford: Oxford University Press (Draft 2.0, 14.04.23) (forthcoming).

Lantis, J. S. (2017). Theories of international norm contestation: Structure and outcomes. In *Oxford Research Encyclopedia of Politics*. Oxford University Press. https://doi.org/10.1093/acrefore/9780190228637.013.590

Lantis, J. S. (2025). Norm cluster resiliency in the face of contestation: Nuclear threats and international resolve. In F. Lucenti, C. Ducci, C. Wunderlich, & J. S. Lantis (Eds.), *Contestation in prism: The evolution of norms and norm clusters in contemporary global politics* (pp. 23–43). Springer.

Lantis, J. S., & Wunderlich, C. (2018). Resiliency dynamics of norm clusters: Norm contestation and international cooperation. *Review of International Studies, 44*(3), 570–593. https://doi.org/10.1017/S0260210517000626

Lantis, J. S., & Wunderlich, C. (2022). Reevaluating constructivist norm theory: A three-dimensional norms research program. *International Studies Review, 24*(1). https://doi.org/10.1093/isr/viab059

Lucenti, F., Ducci C. &. Lee, P. K. (2025). Conceptualising the responsibility to prosecute norm as a cluster: Impunity for war crimes in Sri Lanka. In F. Lucenti, C. Ducci, C. Wunderlich, & J. S. Lantis, (Eds.), *Contestation in prism: The evolution of norms and norm clusters in contemporary global politics* (pp. 87–105). Springer.
Mende, J. (2024). *Liberal-democratic norms under contestation: Norm relations and their decoupling in the US Supreme Court's decisions on abortion*. Global Constitutionalism, 1–25. https://doi.org/10.1017/S2045381724000004
McKeown, R. (2009). Norm regress: US revisionism and the slow death of the torture norm. *International Relations, 23*(1), 5–25. https://doi.org/10.1177/0047117808100607
Mukherjee, R. (2024). Hierarchy and endogenous contestation in the liberal international order. *Global Studies Quarterly, 4*(2). https://doi.org/10.1093/isagsq/ksae028
Müller, H., & Wunderlich, C. (2018). Not lost in contestation: How norm entrepreneurs frame norm development in the nuclear nonproliferation regime. *Contemporary Security Policy, 39*(3), 341–366. https://doi.org/10.1080/13523260.2017.1394032
Newman, E., & Zala, B. (2018). Rising powers and order contestation: Disaggregating the normative from the representational. *Third World Quarterly, 39*(5), 871–888. https://doi.org/10.1080/01436597.2017.1392085
Orchard, P., & Wiener, A. (2024). *Contesting the world: Norm research in theory and practice*. Cambridge University Press.
Panke, D., Grundsfeld, L., & Tverskoi, P. (2025). Regional organisations, exit threats, and contestation of community norms. In F. Lucenti, C. Ducci, C. Wunderlich, & J. S. Lantis, (Eds.), *Contestation in prism: The evolution of norms and norm clusters in contemporary global politics* (pp. 45–63). Springer.
Panke, D., & Petersohn, U. (2012). Why international norms disappear sometimes. *European Journal of International Relations, 18*(4), 719–742. https://doi.org/10.1177/1354066111407690
Panke, D., & Petersohn, U. (2016). Norm challenges and norm death: The inexplicable? *Cooperation and Conflict, 51*(1), 3–19. https://doi.org/10.1177/0010836715597948
Percy, S. (2019). What makes a norm robust: The norm against female combat. *Journal of Global Security Studies, 4*(1), 123–138. https://doi.org/10.1093/jogss/ogy044
Percy, S., & Sandholtz, W. (2022). Why norms rarely die. *European Journal of International Relations, 28*(4), 934–954. https://doi.org/10.1177/13540661221126018
Petersohn, U. (2014). Reframing the anti-mercenary norm: Private military and security companies and mercenarism. *International Journal: Canada's Journal of Global Policy Analysis, 69*(4), 475–493. https://doi.org/10.1177/0020702014544915
Price, R. (2006). Detecting ideas and their effects. In R. E. Goodin & C. Tilly (Eds.), *The Oxford handbook of contextual political analysis* (pp. 252–265). Oxford University Press.
Sandholtz, W. (2007). *Prohibiting plunder: How norms change*. Oxford University Press.
Rhoads, E. P., & Welsh, J. M. (2019). Close cousins in protection: The evolution of two norms. *International Affairs, 95*(3), 597–617. https://doi.org/10.1093/ia/iiz054
Sandholtz, W. (2019). Norm contestation, robustness, and replacement. *Journal of Global Security Studies, 4*(1), 139–146. https://doi.org/10.1093/jogss/ogy042
Sandholtz, W., & Stiles, K. (2009). *International norms and cycles of change*. Oxford University Press.
Schmidt, A., & Sikkink, K. (2019). Breaking the ban? The heterogeneous impact of US contestation of the torture norm. *Journal of Global Security Studies, 4*(1), 105–122. https://doi.org/10.1093/jogss/ogy036
Stefan, C. (2016). On non-western norm shapers: Brazil and the responsibility while protecting. *European Journal of International Security, 2*(1), 88–110. https://doi.org/10.1017/eis.2016.18
Stimmer, A., & Wisken, L. (2019). The dynamics of dissent: When actions are louder than words. *International Affairs, 95*(3), 515–533. https://doi.org/10.1093/ia/iiz019
Tholens, S. (2025). Hidden transcripts and normative transformations. In F. Lucenti, C. Ducci, C. Wunderlich, & J. S. Lantis (Eds.), *Contestation in prism: The evolution of norms and norm clusters in contemporary global politics* (pp. 163–181). Springer.

Trenta, L. (2021). Death by reinterpretation: Dynamics of norm contestation and the US ban on assassination in the Reagan years. *Journal of Global Security Studies, 6*(4). https://doi.org/10.1093/jogss/ogab012

True, J., & Wiener, A. (2019). Everyone wants (a) peace: The dynamics of rhetoric and practice on 'women, peace and security'. *International Affairs, 95*(3), 553–574. https://doi.org/10.1093/ia/iiz027

Van Kersbergen, K., & Verbeek, B. (2007). The politics of international norms: Subsidiarity and the imperfect competence regime of the European Union. *European Journal of International Relations, 13*(2), 217–238. https://doi.org/10.1177/1354066107076955

Welsh, J. M. (2019). Norm robustness and the responsibility to protect. *Journal of Global Security Studies, 4*(1), 53–72. https://doi.org/10.1093/jogss/ogy045

Widmaier, W. W., & Park, S. (2012). Differences beyond theory: Structural, strategic, and sentimental approaches to normative change. *International Studies Perspectives, 13*(2), 123–134. https://doi.org/10.1111/j.1528-3585.2012.00459.x

Wiener, A. (2004). Contested compliance: Interventions on the normative structure of world politics. *European Journal of International Relations, 10*(2), 189–234. https://doi.org/10.1177/1354066104042934

Wiener, A. (2007). The dual quality of norms and governance beyond the state: Sociological and normative approaches to 'interaction'. *Critical Review of International Social and Political Philosophy, 10*(1), 47–69. https://doi.org/10.1080/13698230601122412

Wiener, A. (2008). *The invisible constitution of politics: Contested norms and international encounters*. Cambridge University Press. https://doi.org/10.1017/CBO9780511490408

Wiener, A. (2009). Enacting meaning-in-use: Qualitative research on norms and international relations. *Review of International Studies, 35*(1), 175–193. https://doi.org/10.1017/S0260210509008377

Wiener, A. (2014). *A theory of contestation*. Springer. https://doi.org/10.1007/978-3-642-55235-9

Wiener, A. (2017). A theory of contestation – A concise summary of its argument and concepts. *Polity, 49*(1), 109–125. https://doi.org/10.1086/690100

Wiener, A. (2018). *Contestation and constitution of norms in global international relations*. Cambridge University Press. https://doi.org/10.1017/9781316718599

Wiener, A., & Puetter, U. (2009). The quality of norms is what actors make of it. Critical constructivist research on norms. *Journal of International Law and International Relations, 5*(1), 1–16.

Winston, C. (2018). Norm structure, diffusion, and evolution: A conceptual approach. *European Journal of International Relations, 24*(3), 638–661. https://doi.org/10.1177/1354066117720794

Wolff, J., & Zimmermann, L. (2016). Between banyans and battle scenes: Liberal norms, contestation, and the limits of critique. *Review of International Studies, 42*(3), 513–534. https://doi.org/10.1017/S0260210515000534

Wunderlich, C. (2013). Theoretical approaches in norm dynamics. In C. Wunderlich & H. Müller (Eds.), *Norm dynamics multilateral arms control: Interests, conflicts, and justice* (pp. 20–48). University of Georgia Press.

Wunderlich, C. (2020). *Rogue states as norm entrepreneurs*. Springer. https://doi.org/10.1007/978-3-030-27990-5

Wunderlich, C. (2023). Normcluster und Normkomplexität. Konzept, Mehrwert und Herausforderungen einer mehrdimensionalen Perspektive auf Normen. *Zeitschrift für Internationale Beziehungen, 30*(2), 160–171. https://doi.org/10.5771/0946-7165-2023-2-160

Yanow, D., & Schwartz-Shea, P. (2015). *Interpretation and method: Empirical research methods and the interpretive turn*. Routledge.

Zhang, Q. (2024). Prevention as a norm cluster? Mapping China's contestation on atrocity prevention. *International Affairs, 100*(1), 241–260. https://doi.org/10.1093/ia/iiad224

Zimmermann, L., Deitelhoff, N., Lesch, M., Arcudi, A., & Peex, A. (2023). *International norm disputes: The link between contestation and norm robustness*. Oxford University Press. https://doi.org/10.1093/oso/9780198873235.001.0001

Chapter 2
Norm Cluster Resiliency in the Face of Contestation: Nuclear Threats and International Resolve

Jeffrey S. Lantis

Six months after Russia began its illegal, full-scale invasion of Ukraine in 2022, western intelligence reports warned of a new threat: Russian leaders and generals were contemplating the use of tactical nuclear weapons to regain lost momentum on the battlefield. US government officials led a chorus of condemnations from around the world, describing the action as 'unthinkable' and warning that any use of nuclear weapons would be met with 'ultimate force' (Sanger & Tankersley, 2022). Russian actions violated numerous standing international norms, and members of the United Nations Security Council demanded that Russian leaders' threats to use tactical nuclear weapons stop immediately. The International Atomic Energy Agency also activated its emergency response plan in relation to fighting around the Chernobyl and Zaporizhzhia nuclear energy plants in Ukraine (Delanian et al., 2022). During the G-20 Summit in November 2022, President Joe Biden and Chinese President Xi Jinping agreed that 'nuclear war should never be fought and can never be won' and underscored their opposition to the use or threat of use of nuclear weapons in Ukraine (The White House, 2022).

The norm of non-use of nuclear weapons faced similar tests a few years earlier when presidential candidate Donald Trump began to discuss nuclear weapons proliferation and modernisation on the campaign trail. During meetings with foreign policy experts Trump reportedly asked about why the US could not use them (Neidig, 2016). Trump also tweeted that the nation 'must greatly strengthen and expand its nuclear capability until such time as the world comes to its senses regarding nukes' (Beauchamp, 2017). When pressed about the likelihood this could spark an arms race with Russia, Trump said simply, 'Let it be an arms race' (ibid). Once in office, President Trump ordered US withdrawal from two arms control agreements—the Intermediate-Range Nuclear Forces (INF) Treaty and the Iran nuclear

J. S. Lantis (✉)
The College of Wooster, Wooster, OH, USA
e-mail: jlantis@wooster.edu

F. Lucenti et al. (eds.), *Contestation in Prism*, Norm Research in International Relations, https://doi.org/10.1007/978-3-031-83639-8_2

deal—and suggested that other countries including Japan, South Korea, and even Saudi Arabia, should consider building their own nuclear weapons to guarantee security (De Luce & Windrem, 2019; Pengelly, 2022).

Both of these sets of challenges represent forms of antipreneurship and applicatory contestation of the nuclear non-use norm (Bloomfield, 2016, p. 311–312; Deitelhoff & Zimmermann, 2020), which were first discussed in Chap. 1 (see also Knapp & Fritzler, 2025, Chap. 4). While the provocations themselves were significant, this study focuses primarily on the agents and processes in normative networks developed to try to stop potential violations of the 'nuclear taboo', or the norm of non-use of nuclear weapons (Tannenwald, 1999, 2007). Specifically, this analysis advances a model of norm cluster resiliency that draws together insights from norm contestation theory and norm cluster theory to highlight pathways for the activation of norms in response to direct threats. Contestation theory explores agents, strategies of norm challenges, and potential outcomes for norm strength (Bloomfield & Scott, 2016; Deitelhoff & Zimmermann, 2020; Wiener, 2014, 2018), and norm cluster theory examines how clusters of norms constitute a flaw-tolerant systems that may help moderate the impact of even serious contestatory challenges to norms (Lantis & Wunderlich, 2018; Winston, 2018). This study identifies a set of action-channels or mechanisms, including activation for accountability, dispersal, and adaptation, which highlights the resiliency of norm clusters in the face of contestation by a variety of actors, including great powers. It details the two case studies of threats to use nuclear weapons highlighted above and draws conclusions regarding the activation of norm clusters and their ability to absorb, diffuse, and redirect the energy of contestatory challenges towards reinforcement of existing norms and even expansion of norm dimensions (Taleb, 2012).

Historical Contestation of the Nuclear Taboo

Political scientist Nina Tannenwald first described the norm of non-use of nuclear weapons as a 'nuclear taboo' or a 'bright-line' norm representing 'a de facto prohibition against the first use of nuclear weapons' (1999, p. 436). The norm captures and reflects sentiments against the use of nuclear weapons that emerged after World War II, including a general sense of revulsion or moral opprobrium associated with weapons of mass destruction that had induced restraint in global politics. Tannenwald contends that the taboo offers an important intersubjective, phenomenological dimension: a sense of 'prohibition' and 'danger' which 'involves expectations of awful or uncertain consequences or sanctions if violated' (2005, p. 8; Shamai, 2015). Looking back, Thomas Schelling (2005) called the non-use of nuclear weapons during the Cold War a 'stunning achievement' that demonstrated the consensus and restraint of the global community.

As a social norm, studies have demonstrated that an aversion to nuclear weapons has affected policy decisions (Tannenwald, 2007, 2018, 2022). Indeed, there is strong evidence of these dynamics in records of national security crisis decision-making in western countries during the Cold War, for example, and in international forums. Kütt and Steffek's (2015) fascinating analysis of diplomatic statements made during the NPT Review Process and the First Committee of the UN General Assembly—from 2000 to 2013—finds broad support for the norm of nuclear non-use. They suggest this discourse is further upheld by civil society actors like the International Campaign to Abolish Nuclear Weapons (ICAN), coalitions of like-minded states at NPT Preparatory and Review Conference meetings, and the UN Secretariat. Tannenwald asserted that nuclear weapons use has become so 'severely delegitimised' that the action would be 'practically unthinkable' (2005, p. 5).

However, even if one accepts that non-use is deeply entrenched in the normative system for sovereign state behaviour today, it nevertheless remains a subject of contestation and debate (Gibbons & Lieber, 2019; Press et al., 2013). Historically, contestation of the nuclear non-use norm has primarily taken the form of 'applicatory contestation' (Deitelhoff & Zimmermann, 2013). Government leaders have not publicly challenged the legitimacy of concerns about the use of nuclear weapons, for example. Rather, what we do see in the public record are occasional questions about whether the norm would be applicable in all situations. These were raised rhetorically, and indirectly, in debates about nuclear deterrence during the Cold War. And in the aftermath of the Cold War, world leaders took it on more directly. In 1994, the UN General Assembly asked the International Court of Justice (ICJ) 'urgently to render an advisory opinion on whether the threat or use of nuclear weapons in any circumstance would be permitted under international law'. At issue then was whether the non-use norm would apply in all circumstances—and whether even possessing, threatening to use, or using nuclear weapons represented a fundamental violation of the evolution of customary law. In its 1996 ruling, the Court tried to balance the norms of humanitarian law versus the norms of sovereign self-defence and deterrence. They recognised that the actual use of nuclear weapons would likely violate customary international humanitarian laws embedded in the 1907 Hague Convention and the 1949 Geneva Conventions—including the principle of distinction between combatants and non-combatants and the prohibition against causing unnecessary suffering to combatants—but they did not rule definitively whether the threat or use of nuclear weapons would be lawful or unlawful in an extreme circumstance of self-defence, particularly when faced with questions of survival of the state—in accord with Article 51 of the UN Charter (Turner, 1998).

This ruling was considered a victory by parties who drew very different conclusions: some state leaders saw their claims that the possession and even the possible discriminate use of nuclear weapons to defend their sovereignty as validated. US diplomats claimed that the 'opinion indicates that the use of nuclear weapons in some circumstances would be legal', while British lawmakers echoed that their position was validated: 'Like the Court, we believe that the use of nuclear weapons would be considered only in self-defence in extreme circumstances' (qtd. in Burroughs, 2016). However, many other states and nongovernmental actors saw victory in the ICJ's consideration of the assessment of customary international humanitarian law application to conflict as itself valuable. Proponents believed that nuclear weapons states were 'boxed in' by the ruling because their use could never truly be compatible with the rules of international humanitarian law (IHL). This interpretation later became the foundation of a challenge to the use of nuclear weapons that took the form of a Treaty on the Prohibition of Nuclear Weapons (TPNW) movement. The 2017 TPNW, or nuclear 'ban treaty' forbids the development, production, acquisition, possession, transfer, testing, use, and threat of use of nuclear weapons. The results, proponents argued, were a strengthening of the norm against the use, possession, and threat of use of nuclear weapons (Sauer & Reveraert, 2018).

Theorising Contestation and Norm Cluster Resiliency

Contemporary challenges to the nuclear taboo reflect similar patterns. Contestation of the nuclear non-use norm has involved strategic, actor-driven social construction and deconstruction of norm including rhetorical/discursive and behavioural challenges to the normative order. One way of thinking about these dynamics is as competition between norm entrepreneurs (Finnemore & Sikkink, 1998, p. 895) and norm antipreneurs (Bloomfield & Scott, 2016) that influences their meaning and acceptance. In a competitive ideational marketplace, norm supporters and challengers may include states, nongovernmental organisations, civil society actors, and even individuals who attempt to seize windows of political opportunity to convince others to agree to new standards of behaviour. For example, Wunderlich (2020, p. 3) identifies different 'agents of contestation' and their efforts to adapt norms on the basis of changing conditions. Other scholars (e.g., Heller et al., 2012; McKeown, 2009; Panke & Petersohn, 2016) similarly argue that 'norm challengers' can contest norms, with resulting effects on norm robustness. Bower and Lantis (2024) detail the processes of strategic social action of antipreneurial agency—including rhetorical, procedural, and behavioural strategies—and describe the mechanisms and scope conditions through which they operate (Bloomfield, 2016, p. 321).

The scope of this contest of ideas could not be more significant: Any use of nuclear weapons could kill millions of people, sicken millions more, irradiate vast areas, and fundamentally destabilise the world order. Violations of the norm, or even extreme threats of norm violations have the potential to unleash devastating nuclear strikes and reprisals that could lead to the extinction of most life on Earth (Van Munster, 2023; Vilhelmsson & Baum, 2023). Needless to say, these constitute incredibly impactful threats.

However, this chapter contends that norm clusters play a critical role in moderating the impact of contestation on individual norm robustness and the resiliency of the broader system. Even though the nuclear taboo is sometimes characterised as an individual norm (Tannenwald, 2007, 2018), it can also be viewed much more as an integral part of the broader nuclear non-proliferation norm cluster. The nuclear taboo is strongly linked to a broader network of nuclear non-proliferation norms in a cluster. Advocates for non-proliferation began to build momentum for a regime in the 1950s based on the conviction that the world should never again suffer the horrors of nuclear war. Non-use was the heavily implied centrepiece or connector among the key principles that were outlined in the NPT, including nuclear non-proliferation, the peaceful uses of nuclear technologies, and disarmament. The preamble to the NPT actually articulated the taboo as an assumption, and this cluster of norms gained support and became institutionalised in the 1970 NPT, which at the 1995 NPT Review and Extension Conference was extended indefinitely.

Finally, not only is the nuclear taboo at the heart of the non-proliferation norm cluster, its normative stigmatisation of nuclear weapons use informs all other dimensions of the cluster (Pescosolido & Martin, 2015; Shamai, 2015). In this sense the nuclear non-proliferation regime might be understood as creating a broad social frame that determines the development of nuclear weapons or the possible use of nuclear weapons by any country to be stigmatic, something that should be avoided. Such behaviour would be framed as 'deviant' or 'morally polluted', potentially delegitimising their development or use in any circumstances (Tannenwald, 2018).

Networks of Resiliency

How do norm clusters moderate the effects of contestation? Lantis and Wunderlich (2018) contend that two basic characteristics provide norm clusters with adaptive mechanisms for dealing with challenges. First, the degree of cohesiveness and synergistic linkages between the individual norms—as a function of norm clusters—can be developed to both tie together and balance the interests of different parties. The underlying logic or embeddedness in meta-governance principles helps to form a 'gravitational pull' of norms together, reflecting the synergy of beliefs and values between norms within a cluster (Lantis & Wunderlich, 2018, p. 576). Second, norm clusters that are grounded in larger international institutional and legal networks and have the foundation and support of international governmental organisations may be more robust and resilient. By providing fora for a priori 'regular contestation' they help fill the 'legitimacy gap between fundamental norms and standardised procedures' and tame 'the potentially conflictive outcome of political contestation' (Wiener, 2014, p. 3).

Yet, while these characteristics may be necessary to support structure in the international order, they are not themselves sufficient to overcome all contestatory challenges. Norm cluster networks provide the infrastructure that helps regulate and promote cooperative state behaviour, but the mechanisms and processes by which this occurs are worthy of further theoretical investigation. This study proposes a three-step process model in which challenges are processed by agents supporting norm clusters, the norm network becomes activated and mobilised to help respond to and disperse contestatory behaviours (Deitelhoff & Zimmermann, 2020; Wiener,

2014).[1] Taken together, these characteristics, steps, and processes help constitute a flaw-tolerant system that allows and adjusts for contestation while maintaining resiliency (Abbaspour et al., 2020; Bodó et al., 2021; Gao et al., 2022). Each of these steps is detailed further below.

Activation for Accountability

First, norm cluster networks provide the infrastructure that helps regulate and promote cooperative state behaviour. At the same time, they may also offer receptors that detect direct norm violations or indirect, potential threats to the system. This study posits that in the first stage of resiliency of norm clusters, evidence of norm violations, or potential norm violations, is reported by governmental or nongovernmental agents that operate within a larger network. While these characteristics are consistent with theories of norm robustness (e.g., Sandholtz, 2019), this study focuses on the power of networks — how supporters of the norm cluster mobilise to determine accountability and motivations. Much like the human immune system identifies antigens as a threat that induces an immune response, this system is likely to become activated by behaviour or rhetoric that does not conform to normative standards (Florini, 1996; Wunderlich, 2013).

The foundations of norm clusters in synergy and institutionalisation provide forums for norm supporters to address violations or potential violations when activated. Agents in the system—such as state, non-state actors, or international organisations—may call out challenges to normative standards and demand accountability. This principled frame for norm violations is further supported by stigmatisation processes, which Adler-Nissen (2014) and Zarakol (2014) describe as a process of calling out 'transgressive' or norm-violating behaviours to trigger action responses (Pescosolido & Martin, 2015). Ultimately, this study posits that the norm cluster serves as an innate system of resiliency that provides a general defence against norm violations or potential norm violations (see Fig. 2.1).

Norm Cluster Dispersal

Much like the activation and accountability process isolates the potential threat, dispersal mechanisms offer ready networks that can help absorb and diffuse challenges or tensions across the cluster (Sandholtz, 2016). Foundations for the study of norm cluster connections are grounded in theories of complex systems and international and polycentric governance (Morin & Richard, 2021; Orsini et al., 2020).

[1] Activation for accountability is necessary in order to qualify a norm cluster and its supporters as responsive to *stimuli*, but the additional dynamics may occur concurrently and synergistically.

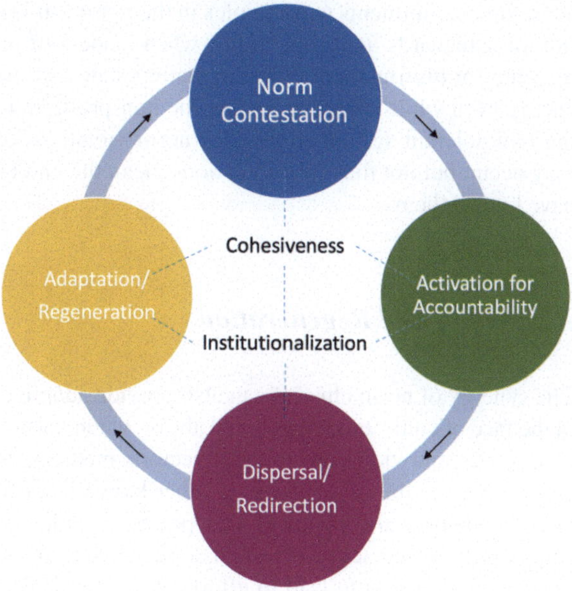

Fig. 2.1 A norm cluster resiliency system model

Here we assume that if activation does not suffice to end transgressive behaviour, norm clusters and synergies are likely to be employed to help to disperse the energy across the system. This reinforcement means that contestatory challenges may be received, absorbed, and processed through ideational pathways of coordination, resulting in a diminished impact of violations or potential violations of the system. Indeed, a system of dispersal mechanisms could be highly flaw-tolerant and responsive to external stimuli, as well as promote resiliency.

This study posits that dispersal mechanisms work as follows: Once a norm cluster becomes activated, agents in the system employ to disperse and re-channel the energy of the challenge by reinforcing basic normative visions of the cluster. These actions typically include diplomatic statements, challenges, resolutions, and actions taken by individual norm supporting states or, more often, through discourse in international organisations. Because normative systems are often 'integrated within hierarchies of increasing abstraction and comprehensiveness' (Müller, 2013, p. 5), their synergistic connections allow agents to disperse or absorb the blow of norm violations of potential norm violations. When norm clusters face non-compliance and violations in some sectors, an activated response involves shifts in focus and energy by supporters to other bulwarks of the norm cluster or regime. Not only do supporters call out contestation and potential violations of discrete norms, they tend to emphasise the value of those and related norms through diplomatic discourse.

The process of dispersal of contestatory energy across norm clusters may be either 'horizontal', as leaders shift their focus and resources to supporting norms within norm clusters, or 'vertical', as agents attempt to contextualise challenges within larger meta-governance normative foundations. In the case of the threat of nuclear weapons use, for example, dispersal mechanisms can be witnessed in the shore-up commitments to principles in the non-proliferation regime, such as activation of safeguards and inspections, when leaders of nuclear weapons states resist pressure for disarmament. Some signatory states promote peaceful uses of nuclear energy even while others challenge the non-proliferation commitment. The resulting flaw-tolerant system allows that norm violations or threats of norm violations may occur, but not that such violations mean the end of normative standards as we have known them.

Adaptation and Regeneration

The synergy of norm clusters can also provide adaptive and regenerative properties in the face of contestation. As noted above, when norm clusters or regimes face non-compliance and violations in some sectors, members are likely to shift their focus and energies within the clusters to other bulwarks of the regime. Actions that provoke challenges are identified and potential violators are held accountable, and energy is dispersed across the often dense network of norm clusters. However, those challenges also tend to lead to efforts at institutional and legal adaptation that can result in generation of new dimensions for the norm cluster.

This study posits that adaptation is a relatively constant process that results from contestation and responses to new stimuli, threats, or opportunities. But, as Wiener (2014, 2018) argues, contestation can also be healthy: it can help to highlight some areas for further attention and, through discourse, promote legitimacy of norms and norm clusters. This study expects that adaptation and regeneration can occur when diplomats and NGOs become actively engaged in the task of shoring-up or adapting the normative system to respond to the challenge. An energised norm cluster that faces serious potential threats. If, for example, a norm like the nuclear taboo is blatantly violated through nuclear weapons use, we might expect that the system would shift its focus to limit and isolate the transgressor, but also to develop an adaptation of the norm frame for the greater good. Adaptation might take the form of establishing norms against the use of certain thresholds of the power of nuclear weapons to be used or reinforcement or expansion of nuclear weapons free zones or no-first-use agreements (Taleb, 2012).

Challenges may also create the impetus for new norm development within clusters. The most likely pathway for this is through what Price (1998) called norm 'grafting'. As norm discourses typically foster discussions of 'crystallised growth both between and among different norms and norm clusters, through creative re-combinations of pre-existing normative meanings' (Lantis & Wunderlich, 2022, p. 12), agents may also strategically create normative congruence. New norms may be advanced to fill serious gaps in the broader normative architecture and to help shore-up problem areas identified by contestation. These are most often fostered within existing networks, and their development can quickly become entwined with institutionalisation, and international law, as well as discursive struggles in historically contingent environments (Großklaus, 2017; Holzscheiter et al., 2016; Sandholtz & Stiles, 2008).

Research Design

This study offers a timely investigation of norm contestation and adaptive mechanisms in relation to the nuclear taboo. It examines the utility of this three-step model of norm resiliency in which contestatory challenges are processed through deductive, exploratory analysis of norm discourses and policy process-tracing (Casula et al., 2021; George & Bennett, 2005; Gerring & Cojocaru, 2016). This approach is designed to help order and frame rich qualitative research, investigate activity and engagement in contested policy processes, and illuminate political actors and processes surrounding these debates (e.g., Casula et al., 2021). The two case studies presented here highlight different dimensions of applicatory norm contestation by contemporary norm antipreneurs, and they feature variance across the research design in terms of norm advocacy and different possible outcomes. Both cases reflect great power, high stakes antipreneurial challenges where applicatory contestation represents punctuations of agreed principles, and as such we would expect them to garner international responses that can be traced in the diplomatic record.

Trump Era Nuclear Threats

After decades of international support for the non-use of nuclear weapons, a confluence of events in the 2010s significantly increased fears that nuclear weapons might be used in anger or by accident. The election of US President Donald Trump, coupled with a wave of populism in the United States, contributed to rising tensions with Russia, North Korea, China, and Iran. Notably, Trump himself offered the strongest rhetorical challenges to the nuclear taboo and the American orthodoxy of nuclear restraint of any elected president in decades. During his campaign, he supported a proactive nuclear weapons posture and the build-up of the US arsenal, and he even encouraged countries like Japan, South Korea, and even Saudi Arabia to consider developing their own nuclear weapons (De Luce & Windrem, 2019). President Trump reportedly told his national security advisors that he wanted a nearly 'tenfold increase in the US nuclear arsenal' (Kube et al., 2017). Critically, the Trump administration's 2018 Nuclear Posture Review (NPR) also described a rapidly deteriorating security environment, called for nuclear weapons modernisation, and even detailed 'extreme circumstances' in which the United States might use nuclear weapons (Garamone, 2017). These included vague references to nuclear responses to cyber-attacks and discounted the US commitment to existing nuclear weapons conventions (Sanger & Broad, 2018, p. A1).

Activation

The non-proliferation regime and the nuclear taboo may have bowed under the pressure of Trump administration initiatives and the president's antipreneurial rhetoric from 2016 to 2021, but they did not break. On the contrary, the international community appeared to rally in support of the nuclear taboo and began to isolate and challenge Trump's actions and those of American diplomats. In response to Trump's threats early in his presidency, for example, European leaders spoke out against American unilateralism and 'national egoism' and stressed that only international solutions to common challenges would promote security and prosperity (Sengupta & Specia, 2017). Supporters immediately called for greater recognition of the potential harm of nuclear weapons use and sought to strengthen the synergy, or cohesion, among the founding principles of the regime that explicitly spoke to the humanitarian and moral aspects connected with nuclear weapons and the three normative pillars of the NPT (Thakur, 2018).

Norm supporters in the international community also tried to stigmatise and challenge American leaders' statements (Kurosawa, 2018). By identifying weapons development and use as stigmatic, activists and policymakers alike were discursively framing the connective tissue of the non-proliferation regime—they were helping to make the implicit more explicit. NGOs enlisted concerned diplomats in a broader effort to socially construct and frame regime parameters. By reframing how to understand nuclear weapons, challengers of Trump actions sought to emphasise that use would be illegitimate and unacceptable. For example, prominent figures from the UN Secretary General to the Pope publicly expressed support for the elimination of nuclear weapons and the illegitimacy of nuclear threats (Sauer & Reveraert, 2018, p. 1).

Other institutions were also activated in the face of the challenge. For example, the international law community argued that Trump's actions violated the spirit of the NPT and went against rulings by the International Court of Justice. The UNGA First Committee regularly discussed security concerns in relation to new threats to nuclearise, along with diplomatic discourse at Review Conferences and Preparation Committee meetings for the NPT (Gibbons, 2018). The UN also established an Open-Ended Working Group (OEWG), which eventually recommended the UNGA to hold a conference in 2017 to formulate a nuclear weapons prohibition treaty (Kurosawa, 2018; Løvold, 2021). Meanwhile, leading diplomats from the European Union, the African Union, and many others spoke out against Trump's provocations regarding nuclear weapons.

Dispersal and Rechanneling

The non-proliferation norm cluster appeared to work effectively to disperse contestatory challenges to help sustain the system. Once again, the resiliency of the norm cluster appeared to help mitigate the effects of these challenges. The dispersal mechanisms included cooperation between the UN and NPT regime supporters, further strengthened by the emergence of a new humanitarian movement in the

2010s. Indeed, perhaps the most significant advancement of cohesive principles that facilitated more ready dispersal of the energies of threats from the Trump administration actually pre-dated it: the development of a social movement focused on the humanitarian impact of nuclear weapons. Starting in the 2014, diplomats from around the world, along with experts and delegates from hundreds of civil society organisations, issued the 'Austrian Pledge'—later called the Humanitarian Pledge—designed to fill the legal gap for the prohibition and elimination of nuclear weapons (Vienna Conference on the Humanitarian Impact of Nuclear Weapons, 2014).

Trump's nuclear threats became the embodiment of the types of challenges that the international community viewed could undermine the norm cluster. Just a week before the US presidential election in 2016, the UNGA First Committee adopted a resolution to convene negotiations on nuclear weapons ban in the coming months. Negotiations took place that spring and summer, and the delegates finalised a Treaty on the Prohibition of Nuclear Weapons (TPNW) in July 2017. The TPNW was designed to push beyond the NPT regulations calling for negotiation of disarmament and move towards the complete elimination of nuclear weapons. By reframing how to understand nuclear weapons, ban supporters sought to change the narrative and establish nuclear weapons as illegitimate and unacceptable on both moral and legal grounds (Borrie, 2014, p. 631).

Adaptation and Regeneration

International responses to the Trump administration's threats also demonstrate the adaptability of the non-proliferation norm cluster and the nuclear taboo to rhetorical pressure. Trump's challenges first triggered a reinforcement of the principle that nuclear weapons should never be used. Evidence also suggests that new challenges to the norm of non-use and the broader non-proliferation regime were also substantially mitigated by institutional and legal commitments, including the UN First Committee and the UNGA's High Level Meeting on Nuclear Disarmament (Pretorius & Sauer, 2019).

While the humanitarian movement pre-dated the rise of Donald Trump to the US presidency, the record suggests that his rhetoric and the resulting international tensions served as a catalyst and focal point for an equal and opposite reaction: great momentum for new norm development through grafting the prohibitionary norm onto the non-proliferation norm cluster. Indeed, this may represent an excellent case study of norm grafting at work: world leaders identified a serious challenge associated with nuclear possession and threats, and they worked with a larger epistemic community and grassroots movement to graft a prohibition norm onto the existing framework. As noted earlier, possession and non-use were always referred to implicitly by the non-proliferation regime, but they were never explicit in legal language. But when the international community observed the brazenness of Trump's actions, they seemed even more motivated to identify the problem and push for normative solutions. In short, Trump's actions and statements seemed to provide a catalyst for even greater support for stigmatisation of nuclear weapons (Michaels & Williams, 2017).

Outcome

This case illustrates the evolution of responses to provocations by Trump and others regarding potential use of nuclear weapons. Efforts to disallow and stigmatise nuclear weapons possession also had the effect of drawing together the strands of the non-proliferation regime into a more cohesive whole. Negative framing of nuclear weapons possession through discourse enabled agents to strengthen the regime (Borrie, 2014; Gibbons, 2018). By identifying weapons development and use as stigmatic, activists and policymakers alike were discursively framing the connective tissue of the non-proliferation regime—norm supporters were helping to make the implicit explicit. NGOs enlisted concerned diplomats in a broader effort to socially construct and frame regime parameters. By reframing how to understand nuclear weapons, ban supporters sought to change the narrative and establish nuclear weapons as illegitimate and unacceptable on both moral and legal grounds (Borrie, 2014, p. 631). The very legitimacy of weapons possession was questioned because of its potential to lead to the unthinkable—and this discourse further highlighted the connective tissue in the non-proliferation norm cluster.

Vladimir Putin and Nuclear Threats in the War on Ukraine

Russian President Vladimir Putin's order for the invasion of Ukraine in February 2022 violated international law and challenged a wide range of international norms. More than 100,000 Russian troops began pouring into Ukraine with the goal of taking control of the capital and overthrowing a government that had grown increasingly hostile to them. In the process, Russia violated numerous international norms, including sovereignty and territorial integrity as defining principles of the United Nations system and norms against targeting civilians embedded in the Geneva Conventions. Russian troops were accused of war crimes in areas that they occupied, as well as genocide, and they carried out regular, indiscriminate attacks on civilians and the civilian infrastructure throughout the country (Blinken, 2022a). The International Criminal Court opened a war crimes investigation of Russian actions just weeks after the start of the war.

However, 6 months later when Ukrainian forces launched successful counterattacks against the Russians, western signals intelligence captured warnings of a new threat: Russian generals began to discuss the possible use of tactical nuclear weapons to regain advantage on the battlefield. In September 2022, leaders in Moscow made these threats more overt: President Putin said that his government would use 'all means available' to secure what he called 'the territorial integrity of Russia' (Mollman, 2022). Former President Medvedev also warned that Russia had the right to defend itself with nuclear weapons if pushed beyond its limits and said it was 'not a bluff' that Russia could use nuclear weapons to defend annexed territory in Ukraine (qtd. in Shapero September 27, 2022b). These developments were especially ironic because Russian authorities tried to use international law and the principle of self-determination as a normative wedge to defend their illegal annexation of the Ukrainian territories of Donetsk, Kherson, Luhansk, and Zaporizhzhia. And when their hold on these territories was challenged by a new Ukrainian military offensive, Putin was willing to threaten to violate the nuclear taboo—an illegal action—to defend his illegal claim on annexed territory. Taken together, these events appeared to raise prospects for a violation of the nuclear taboo through the possible use of lower-yield tactical nuclear weapons on the battlefield.

Activation

Governments and nongovernmental organisations around the world rallied to call out this threat and challenge Russian strategic calculations, prompting a renewed discourse on the meaning of responsible nuclear stewardship in a world of conflict. They identified Russian actions and threats as a direct challenge to the norm cluster. Western leaders requested an emergency UN Security Council meeting a day after the conflict began where they advanced an unsuccessful resolution that called on Russia to immediately stop its attack and withdraw all troops from Ukraine (United Nations, 2022). Within a week, general concerns about the spread of the conflict became much more focused and manifest, as Russian troops conducted an artillery attack on Ukrainian forces dug-in around the Zaporizhzhia Nuclear Power Plant. The war had come to the front stoop of Europe's largest operating nuclear plant, and there were widespread fears that this fighting might trigger a nuclear accident. Diplomats held another emergency UN Security Council meeting where many decried the recklessness of Russian forces. The International Atomic Energy Agency activated the organisation's emergency response plan and briefed members of the UN Security Council on the heavy fighting around the plant (Stahl, 2022). UN officials made clear that the attacks on the plant violated Articles 53 and 56 of the Additional Protocol to the Geneva Conventions, which outlaw attacks on civilian infrastructure and especially sensitive targets critical to meeting human needs. US Ambassador Linda Thomas-Greenfield described the attack as a 'dire threat to the world' that threatened a 'nuclear catastrophe' (Face the Nation February 27, 2022).

Months later, when news emerged of the threat of tactical nuclear weapons use, US government officials led a chorus of condemnations from around the world, describing Russian threats of tactical nuclear weapons use 'unthinkable' and warning that any use of nuclear weapons would be met with 'ultimate force'. US leaders raised the alarm about the potential Russian action, much like they had done before the pending Russian invasion 6 months earlier. At a UN Security Council meeting in September 2022, Secretary of State Antony Blinken warned that Putin had 'doubled down' on the invasion and demanded that the Russians end their 'reckless nuclear threats'. He continued, 'The very international order that we have gathered here to uphold is being shredded before our eyes. We cannot, we will not allow President Putin to get away with it' (Blinken, 2022b). President Biden pressed for accountability in bilateral and multilateral diplomacy, warning of the threat of a nuclear 'Armageddon'. US Defence Secretary Lloyd Austin similarly issued public warnings against Russia, calling its invasion an 'invitation to an increasingly insecure world haunted by the shadow of nuclear proliferation' (Shapero, 2022a). Drawing connections between the norm cluster, he warned that it incentivised would-be proliferators to try to get 'a hunting licence of their own. And that could drive a dangerous spiral of nuclear proliferation' (Shapero, 2022a).

The international diplomatic community believed that it had successfully coordinated warnings to Putin in the fall of 2022 when there was serious alarm in western governments that Russia was preparing to use a tactical nuclear weapon in Ukraine (Sanger & Barnes, 2024).

Dispersal and Rechannelling

Supporters of the non-proliferation norm cluster sought to re-channel and disperse Russian contestatory challenges and absorb the problems to help sustain the system. The dispersal mechanisms in this case included challenges in multilateral organisations and international legal institutions and activation of nuclear safety protocols, backed by support from the humanitarian movement that had been activated in the creation of the TPNW. Diplomats met the threats of the Russian government in a variety of nodes of the norm cluster, allowing them to effectively try to disperse the contestatory energy. For example, they used more than a dozen meetings of the United Nations Security Council along with emergency sessions of the General Assembly and General Assembly First Committee meetings to advance their concerns. For instance, the UN General Assembly called an emergency session in February 2022 under the auspices of the Resolution 377A—also known as 'Uniting for Peace'—and diplomatic discourse led members of the international community to double-down on related norms, including nuclear safety. Similarly, the United Nations, the European Union, and the International Atomic Energy Agency also provided support for nuclear safety measures and inspection programs as part of the non-proliferation norm cluster.

International legal institutions also created forums for dispersal of contestatory energy. For example, the International Criminal Court opened an investigation in the spring of 2022 into whether Russian forces had committed war crimes. They dispatched teams to gather evidence of genocide and war crimes including torture and sexual violence. In addition, the ICC became a forum for the dispersal of the challenge and labelling of potential Russian actions as war crimes during the 21st session of the Assembly of States Parties to the Rome Statute in The Hague in December 2022. In an appeal by the International Campaign to Abolish Nuclear Weapons (ICAN), activists argued that the humanitarian movement meant that 'the use of nuclear weapons [in Ukraine] would be a war crime', and that leaders responsible would be subject to international review and prosecution (ICAN November 9, 2022).

Adaptation and Regeneration

International responses to Russian threats also demonstrate the adaptability of the non-proliferation norm cluster and the nuclear taboo to rhetorical pressure. Efforts to disallow and stigmatise nuclear weapons possession also had the effect of drawing together the strands of the non-proliferation regime into a more cohesive whole. Negative framing of nuclear weapons use through discourse appears to have enabled agents to strengthen the regime (Borrie, 2014; Gibbons, 2018). By identifying weapons use threats as stigmatic, activists and policymakers alike were discursively framing the connective tissue of the non-proliferation regime—they were helping to make the implicit explicit.

In many ways, the escalation of Russian threats to use nuclear weapons served as yet another wake-up call for the international diplomatic community, and diplomats and NGOs ramped up their communication, discursive framing, and dissuasion tactics. By the late fall of 2022, for example, UN diplomats were citing the Russian action as impetus for greater non-proliferation initiatives. In October 2022, the President of the General Assembly Csaba Kőrösi from Hungary said that the situation created an opportunity to 'flip the paradigm' by reversing the global trend to acquire weapons of mass destruction (UNGA First Committee 2022). Ukrainian diplomats stressed that their government had forsaken nuclear weapons through the Budapest Agreement of 1994 and that this demonstrated the potential value of arms reductions. Once again, diplomats articulated the linkages of the non-proliferation norm cluster, including the First Committee's responsibility to address updates to conventions on biological and chemical weapons, safeguard the NPT, and bring the Comprehensive Nuclear Test Ban Treaty fully into force, as evidence of how synergistic connections could promote resiliency of norm clusters. Finally, the war created renewed momentum for expanding support for the TPNW to further codify the legal and normative frame that the threat of use of nuclear weapons constituted a violation of the prohibitionary norm.

Outcome

The international community rallied in response to Russian actions in Ukraine. Most members of the United Nations, along with all members of the European Union, and many other diplomats around the world condemned Russia's illegal invasion of Ukraine. They cited numerous standards of international law and norms that had been violated by the action, and they demanded that Russia be held accountable for this. When the Russian military faced setbacks and generals began talking about total war, diplomats again condemned even the hint that Russia might consider the use of tactical nuclear weapons to regain advantage on the battlefield. And while it may be impossible to draw direct causal linkages between these circumstances and outcomes, it is the case that in the spring of 2023—at this writing—, those nuclear threats did not materialise. Putin continued to issue threats about the escalation of western involvement in armaments for Ukraine, but those were perceived as increasingly empty threats that did not generate dramatic international responses. In the end, it appears that the catalyst of Russian actions helped serve as a reminder of the need for vigilance and constant efforts to find normative and legal limits to dangerous state behaviour.

Conclusion

This chapter has highlighted the value of understanding norm dynamics within larger constellations. It advances a new three-stage model of norm cluster resiliency in the face of contestation and conducts a plausibility probe that highlights areas for further development and exploration. Real-world applications help to bolster the claim that norms are better understood as clustered together within a wider constellation of international norms, and that one cannot fully understand how discrete challenges might impact norms without acknowledging the importance of international normative, legal, and political interconnections.

This study suggests several lessons for additional theory refinement. First, it suggests that norm clusters may represent some of the most dynamic and engaging areas for further inquiry. Viewing norm clusters as interconnected helps to explain their development, maintenance, and resiliency. Second, this approach challenges linear and empirical conceptions of norm strength and weakness. While such arguments remain popular (Ben-Josef Hirsch & Dixon, 2021; Bower, 2019; Deitelhoff & Zimmermann, 2019), a multidimensional framework suggests that assessments of norm strength are better understood as a function of norm connectedness and prominence in broader normative constellations. Because social constructs are necessarily intersubjective—they are perhaps best characterised as representing a dynamic collective consciousness (Orchard & Wiener, 2024). Third, this paper raises an interesting question about how to 'measure' the resiliency of norm clusters given that this may vary over time. If cohesiveness is determined by the long history of the regime, then does it vary for any modern challenge to individual norms? Is there a time period when the cluster was weaker or stronger, and individual norms more or less able to withstand challenges?

These questions naturally lead to consideration of how norm clusters may represent flaw-tolerant systems that allow for and adapt to contestatory challenges while maintaining resiliency. Consistent with Wiener's (2014, 2018) assertions about contestation and reinforcement of the legitimacy of norms, this model suggests that clustering helps to bolster the impact and longevity of individual norms. From the natural world to social and political realms, we see evidence of systems that have evolved to withstand damage and overcome or repair it without severely compromising their integrity. Studies of fault tolerance from biology, engineering, computer science, and other areas remind us of the value of trying to understand the cohesive properties and systems that can work best in the social world. Similar to

Taleb's (2012) conception of regimes as anti-fragile systems, this study imagines that through combinations of institutionalisation, legalisation, and normative discourse, the non-proliferation norm architecture and other norm clusters have the potential to not only adapt to difficult situations but even to thrive. If norms rarely die (Percy & Sandholtz, 2022), then the dynamics of their survivability are well worthy of further social scientific inquiry.

Finally, this model may also have applications to understand international responses to a wide range of challenges, from North Korean nuclearisation and the Covid-19 pandemic to the future of Ukrainian sovereignty and prospects for war in space. Discrete norms that some observers might characterise as 'under assault' by real-world events may in fact be facing a process of contestation that ultimately strengthens their global impact. In other words, compliance may fluctuate and antipreneurs may challenge normative standards, but norm cluster resiliency often perseveres.

References

Abbaspour, A., Mokhtari, S., Sargolzaei, A., & Yen, K. K. (2020). A survey on active fault-tolerant control systems. *Electronics, 9*(1513). https://doi.org/10.3390/electronics9091513

Adler-Nissen, R. (2014). Stigma management in international relations: Transgressive identities, norms, and order in international society. *International Organization, 68*(1), 143–176. https://doi.org/10.1017/S0020818313000337

Beauchamp, Z. (2017, January 18). Donald Trump's very confusing thoughts on nuclear weapons, Explained. *Vox*. Retrieved March 8, 2025, from https://www.vox.com/world/2017/1/18/14310168/trump-nuclear-policy-inauguration-explained

Ben-Josef Hirsch, M., & Dixon, J. M. (2021). Conceptualizing and assessing norm strength in international relations. *European Journal of International Relations, 27*(2), 521–547. https://doi.org/10.1177/1354066120949628

Blinken, A. J. (2022a, March 23). *War crimes by Russian forces in Ukraine*. Press Statement from the U.S. Department of State. Retrieved March 8, 2025, from https://www.state.gov/war-crimes-by-russias-forces-in-ukraine/

Blinken, A. J. (2022b, September 20). *United Nations Security council ministerial meeting on Ukrainian sovereignty and Russian accountability*. U.S. Department of State. Retrieved March 8, 2025, from https://www.state.gov/secretary-antony-j-blinken-at-the-united-nations-security-council-ministerial-meeting-on-ukrainian-sovereignty-and-russian-accountability/

Bloomfield, A. (2016). Norm antipreneurs and theorising resistance to normative change. *Review of International Studies, 42*(2), 310–333. https://doi.org/10.1017/S026021051500025X

Bloomfield, A., & Scott, S. V. (2016). *Norm antipreneurs and the politics of resistance to global normative change*. Taylor & Francis.

Bodó, B., Brekke, J. K., & Hoepman, J. H. (2021). Decentralisation: A multidisciplinary perspective. *Internet Policy Review, 10*(2), 1–21. https://doi.org/10.14763/2021.2.1563

Borrie, J. (2014). Humanitarian reframing of nuclear weapons and the logic of a ban. *International Affairs, 90*(3), 625–626. https://doi.org/10.1111/1468-2346.12130

Bower, A. (2019). Contesting the International Criminal Court: Bashir, Kenyatta, and the status of the non-impunity norm in world politics. *Journal of Global Security Studies, 4*(1), 88–104. https://doi.org/10.1093/jogss/ogy037

Bower, A., & Lantis, J. S. (2024). Contesting the heavens: US antipreneurship and the regulation of space weapons. *European Journal of International Security, 9*(1), 1–22. https://doi.org/10.1017/eis.2023.2
Burroughs, J. (2016). *Looking back: The 1996 advisory opinion of the international court of justice*. Arms Control Association. Retrieved March 8, 2025, from https://www.armscontrol.org/ACT/2016_07/Features/Looking-Back-The-1996-Advisory-Opinion-of-the-International-Court-of-Justice
Casula, M., Rangarajan, N., & Shields, P. (2021). The potential of working hypotheses for deductive exploratory research. *Quality & Quantity, 55*(5), 1703–1725. https://doi.org/10.1007/s11135-020-01072-9
De Luce, D., & Windrem, R. (2019, June 4). Trump admin gave green light to nuclear permits for Saudi Arabia. *NBC News*. Retrieved March 8, 2025, from https://www.nbcnews.com/news/world/trump-admin-gave-green-light-nuclear-permits-saudi-arabia-after-n1013826
Deitelhoff, N., & Zimmermann, L. (2013). *Things we lost in the fire: How different types of contestation affect the validity of international norms* (PRIF Working Papers, 18). https://nbn-resolving.org/urn:nbn:de:0168-ssoar-455201
Deitelhoff, N., & Zimmermann, L. (2019). Norms under challenge: Unpacking the dynamics of norm robustness. *Journal of Global Security Studies, 4*(1), 2–17. https://doi.org/10.1093/jogss/ogy041
Deitelhoff, N., & Zimmermann, L. (2020). Things we lost in the fire: How different types of contestation affect the robustness of international norms. *International Studies Review., 22*(1), 51–76. https://doi.org/10.1093/isr/viy080
Delanian, K., De Luce, D. & Kube, C. (2022, June 13). What will Biden do if Putin goes nuclear?. *NBC News*. Retrieved March 8, 2025, from https://www.nbcnews.com/politics/national-security/will-biden-putin-goes-nuclear-experts-say-nuclear-response-unlikely-no-rcna32756
Finnemore, M., & Sikkink, K. (1998). International norm dynamics and political change. *International Organization, 52*(4), 887–917. https://doi.org/10.1162/002081898550789
Florini, A. (1996). The evolution of international norms. *International Studies Quarterly, 40*(3), 363–389. https://doi.org/10.2307/2600716
Gao, C., He, X., Dong, H., Liu, H. &, Guangran L. (2022). A survey on fault-tolerant consensus control of multi-agent systems: Trends, methodologies and prospects. International Journal of Systems Science, 53(13), 2800–2813. https://doi.org/10.1080/00207721.2022.2056772
Garamone, J. (2017, August 21). *President unveils new Afghanistan, South Asia strategy*. U.S. Department of Defense, DOD News. Retrieved March 8, 2025, from https://www.defense.gov/News/News-Stories/Article/Article/1284964/president-unveils-new-afghanistan-south-asia-strategy/
George, A. L., & Bennett, A. (2005). *Case studies and theory development in the social sciences*. MIT Press.
Gerring, J., & Cojocaru, L. (2016). Selecting cases for intensive analysis: A diversity of goals and methods. *Sociological Methods & Research, 45*(3), 392–423. https://doi.org/10.1177/0049124116631692
Gibbons, R. D. (2018). The humanitarian turn in nuclear disarmament and the treaty on the prohibition of nuclear weapons. *The Nonproliferation Review, 25*(1), 11–36. https://doi.org/10.1080/10736700.2018.1486960
Gibbons, R. D., & Lieber, K. (2019). How durable is the nuclear weapons taboo? *Journal of Strategic Studies, 42*(1), 29–54. https://doi.org/10.1080/01402390.2018.1529568
Großklaus, M. (2017). Friction, not erosion: Assassination norms at the faultline between sovereignty and liberal values. *Contemporary Security Policy, 38*(2), 260–280. https://doi.org/10.1080/13523260.2017.1335135
Heller, R., Kahl, M., & Pisoiu, D. (2012). The 'dark' side of normative argumentation – The case of counterterrorism policy. *Global Constitutionalism, 1*(2), 278–312. https://doi.org/10.1017/s2045381711000049

Holzscheiter, A., Bahr, T., & Pantzerhielm, L. (2016). Emerging governance architectures in global health: Do metagovernance norms explain inter-organizational convergence? *Politics and Governance, 4*(3), 5–19. https://doi.org/10.17645/pag.v4i3.566

Knapp, A., & Fritzler, J, (2025). Soft contestation' of the responsibility to protect? Assessing Canada and Sweden's norm diplomacy. In F. Lucenti, C. Ducci, C. Wunderlich, & J. S. Lantis (Eds.), *Contestation in prism: The evolution of norms and norm clusters in contemporary global politics* (pp. 65–85). Springer.

Kube, C., Welker K., Lee C. E., & Guthrie, S. (2017). Trump wanted tenfold increase in nuclear arsenal, surprising military. *NBC News*. October 11. Retrieved March 8, 2025, from https://www.nbcnews.com/news/all/trump-wanted-dramatic-increase-nuclear-arsenal-meeting-military-leaders-n809701

Kurosawa, M. (2018). Stigmatizing and delegitimizing nuclear weapons. *Journal for Peace and Nuclear Disarmament, 1*(1), 32–48. https://doi.org/10.1080/25751654.2017.1419453

Kütt, M., & Steffek, J. (2015). Comprehensive prohibition of nuclear weapons: An emerging international norm? *The Nonproliferation Review, 22*(3–4), 401–420. https://doi.org/10.1080/10736700.2016.1157246

Lantis, J. S., & Wunderlich, C. (2018). Resiliency dynamics of norm clusters: Norm contestation and international cooperation. *Review of International Studies, 44*(3), 570–593. https://doi.org/10.1017/S0260210517000626

Lantis, J. S., & Wunderlich, C. (2022). Reevaluating constructivist norm theory: A three-dimensional norms research program. *International Studies Review, 24*(1). https://doi.org/10.1093/isr/viab059

Løvold, M. (2021). The future of the nuclear taboo: Framing the impact of the TPNW. *Journal for Peace and Nuclear Disarmament, 4*(1), 100–106. https://doi.org/10.1080/25751654.2021.1940701

McKeown, R. (2009). Norm regress: US revisionism and the slow death of the torture norm. *International Relations, 23*(1), 5–25. https://doi.org/10.1177/0047117808100607

Michaels, J., & Williams, H. (2017). The nuclear education of Donald J. Trump. *Contemporary Security Policy, 38*(1), 54–77. https://doi.org/10.1080/13523260.2017.1291206

Mollman, S. (2022, September 30). Putin vows to use 'all means available' to defend annexation, Ukraine intel warns of 'very high' nuclear threat. *Fortune Magazine*. Retrieved March 8, 2025, from https://fortune.com/2022/09/30/putin-russia-ukraine-annexation-nuclear-weapons-nato-biden/

Morin, J. F., & Richard, B. (2021). Astro-environmentalism: Towards a polycentric governance of space debris. *Global Policy, 12*(4), 568–573. https://doi.org/10.1111/1758-5899.12950

Müller, H. (2013). Introduction. Where it all began. In C. Wunderlich & H. Müller (Eds.), *Norm dynamics multilateral arms control: Interests, conflicts, and justice* (pp. 1–19). University of Georgia Press.

Neidig, H. (2016, August 3). Scarborough, Trump asked adviser why U.S. can't use nuclear weapons. *The Hill*. Retrieved March 8, 2025, from https://thehill.com/blogs/ballot-box/presidential-races/290217-scarborough-trump-asked-about-adviser-about-using-nuclear/

Orchard, P., & Wiener, A. (2024). *Contesting the world: Norm research in theory and practice*. Cambridge University Press.

Orsini, A., Le Prestre, P., Haas, P. M., Brosig, M., Pattberg, P., Widerberg, O., & Gomez-Mera, L. (2020). Complex systems and international governance. *International Studies Review, 22*(4), 1008–1038. https://doi.org/10.1093/isr/viz005

Panke, D., & Petersohn, U. (2016). Norm challenges and norm death: The inexplicable? *Cooperation and Conflict, 51*(1), 3–19. https://doi.org/10.1177/0010836715597948

Pengelly, M. (2022, October 26). Trump bragged about new U.S. nuclear weapons, Woodward tape shows. *The Guardian*. Retrieved March 8, 2025, from https://www.theguardian.com/us-news/2022/oct/26/trump-nuclear-weapons-boast-woodward-tape

Percy, S., & Sandholtz, W. (2022). Why norms rarely die. *European Journal of International Relations, 28*(4), 934–954. https://doi.org/10.1177/13540661221126018

Pescosolido, B. A., & Martin, J. K. (2015). The stigma complex. *Annual Review of Sociology, 41*(3), 87–116. https://doi.org/10.1146/annurev-soc-071312-145702
Press, D. G., Sagan, S. D., & Valentino, B. A. (2013). Atomic aversion: Experimental evidence on taboos, traditions, and the non-use of nuclear weapons. *American Political Science Review, 107*(1), 188–206. https://doi.org/10.1017/S0003055412000597
Pretorius, J., & Sauer, T. (2019). Is it time to ditch the NPT?. *Bulletin of the Atomic Scientists*. Retrieved March 8, 2025, from https://thebulletin.org/2019/09/is-it-time-to-ditch-the-npt/
Price, R. (1998). International norms and the mines taboo: Pulls toward compliance. *Canadian Foreign Policy Journal, 5*(3), 105–123. https://doi.org/10.1080/11926422.1998.9673152
Sandholtz, W. (2016). Treaties, constitutions, courts, and human rights. In C. A. Smith (Ed.), *Globalizing human rights* (pp. 17–32). Routledge.
Sandholtz, W. (2019). Norm contestation, robustness, and replacement. *Journal of Global Security Studies, 4*(1), 139–146. https://doi.org/10.1093/jogss/ogy042
Sandholtz, W., & Stiles, K. (2008). *International norms and cycles of change*. Oxford University Press.
Sanger, D. E., & Barnes J. E. (2024, February 17). U.S. fears Russia might put a nuclear weapon in space. *The New York Times*. Retrieved March 8, 2025, from www.nytimes.com/2024/02/17/us/politics/russia-nuclear-weapon-space.html
Sanger, D. E., & Broad W. J. (2018, February 4). To counter Russia, U.S. signals nuclear arms are back in a big way. *New York Times*. Retrieved March 8, 2025, from https://www.nytimes.com/2018/02/04/us/politics/trump-nuclear-russia.html
Sanger, D., & Tankersley, J. (2022, September 22). U.S. warns Russia of 'catastrophic consequences' if it uses nuclear weapons. *New York Times*. Retrieved March, 8 2025, from https://www.nytimes.com/2022/09/25/us/politics/us-russia-nuclear.html
Sauer, T., & Reveraert, M. (2018). The potential stigmatizing effect of the treaty on the prohibition of nuclear weapons. *The Nonproliferation Review, 25*(5–6), 437. https://doi.org/10.1080/10736700.2018.1548097
Schelling, T. C. (2005, December 8). An astonishing sixty years: The legacy of Hiroshima. *The Nobel Prize*. Retrieved March 8, 2025, from https://www.nobelprize.org/prizes/economic-sciences/2005/schelling/lecture/
Sengupta, S., & Specia, M. (2017, September 23). How world leaders reacted to Trump at the U.N. *New York Times*. Retrieved March 8, 2025, from https://www.nytimes.com/2017/09/23/world/americas/world-leaders-trump-un.html
Shamai, P. (2015). Name and shame: Unravelling the stigmatization of weapons of mass destruction. *Contemporary Security Policy, 36*(1), 104–122. https://doi.org/10.1080/13523260.2015.1012352
Shapero, J. (2022a, November 19). Austin warns Russian war on Ukraine could lead to a dangerous spiral of nuclear proliferation. *The Hill*. Retrieved March 8, 2025, from https://thehill.com/policy/international/3743416-austin-warns-russian-war-on-ukraine-could-lead-to-a-dangerous-spiral-of-nuclear-proliferation/
Shapero, J. (2022b, September 27). Putin nuclear threat not a bluff, Medvedev says. *The Hill*. Retrieved March 8, 2025, from https://thehill.com/policy/international/3662868-putin-nuclear-threat-not-a-bluff-medvedev-says/
Stahl, L. (2022, November 20). IAEA head on preventing a nuclear disaster in Ukraine and around the world. *CBS News*. Retrieved March 8, 2025, from https://www.cbsnews.com/news/zaporizhzhia-rafael-mariano-grossi-iaea-60-minutes-2022-11-20/
Taleb, N. N. (2012). *Antifragile: Things that gain from disorder*. Random House.
Tannenwald, N. (1999). The nuclear taboo: The United States and the normative basis of nuclear non-use. *International Organization, 53*(3), 433–468. https://www.jstor.org/stable/2601286
Tannenwald, N. (2005). Stigmatizing the bomb: Origins of the nuclear taboo. *International Security, 29*(4), 5–49. https://www.jstor.org/stable/4137496
Tannenwald, N. (2007). *The nuclear taboo: The United States and the non-use of nuclear weapons since 1945*. Cambridge University Press.

Tannenwald, N. (2018). How strong is the nuclear taboo today? *Washington Quarterly, 42*(3), 89–109. https://doi.org/10.1080/0163660X.2018.1520553
Tannenwald, N. (2022, July 1). Is using nuclear weapons still taboo?. *Foreign Policy*. Retrieved March 8, 2025, from https://foreignpolicy.com/2022/07/01/nuclear-war-taboo-arms-control-russia-ukraine-deterrence/
Thakur, R. (2018). Nuclear turbulence in the age of trump. *Diplomacy & Statecraft, 29*(1), 105–128. https://doi.org/10.1080/09592296.2017.1420531
The White House. (2022, November 14). *Readout of President Joe Biden's meeting with President Xi Jinping of the People's Republic of China*. White House Briefing Room Statement. Retrieved March 8, 2025, from https://www.whitehouse.gov/briefing-room/statements-releases/2022/11/14/readout-of-president-joe-bidens-meeting-with-president-xi-jinping-of-the-peoples-republic-of-china/
Transcript: UN Ambassador Linda Thomas-Greenfield on 'Face the Nation'. (2022). February 27. Retrieved March 8, 2025, from https://www.cbsnews.com/news/transcript-linda-thomas-greenfield-un-ambassador-face-the-nation-02-27-2022/
Turner, R. F. (1998). Nuclear weapons and the world court: The ICJ's advisory opinion and its significance for US strategic doctrine. *International Law Studies, 72*(1), 165. https://doi.org/10.1093/bybil/68.1.165
United Nations. (2022, February 26). *Russia blocks security council action on Ukraine*. UN Press and Information Office. Retrieved March 8, 2025, from https://news.un.org/en/story/2022/02/1112802
Van Munster, R. (2023). Nuclear weapons, existentialism, and international relations: Anders, Ballard, and the human condition in the age of extinction. *Review of International Studies, 1–19*, 813. https://doi.org/10.1017/S0260210522000638
Vienna Conference on the Humanitarian Impact of Nuclear Weapons. (2014). Retrieved March 8, 2025, from https://www.bmeia.gv.at/en/european-foreign-policy/disarmament/weapons-of-mass-destruction/nuclear-weapons/vienna-conference-on-the-humanitarian-impact-of-nuclear-weapons/
Vilhelmsson, A., & Baum, S. D. (2023). Public health and nuclear winter: Addressing a catastrophic threat. *Journal of Public Health Policy, 1-10*, 360. https://doi.org/10.1057/s41271-023-00416-7
Wiener, A. (2014). *A theory of contestation*. Springer. https://doi.org/10.1007/978-3-642-55235-9
Wiener, A. (2018). *Contestation and constitution of norms in global international relations*. Cambridge University Press. https://doi.org/10.1017/9781316718599
Winston, C. (2018). Norm structure, diffusion, and evolution: A conceptual approach. *European Journal of International Relations, 24*(3), 638–661. https://doi.org/10.1177/1354066117720794
Wunderlich, C. (2013). Theoretical approaches in norm dynamics. In H. Müller & C. Wunderlich (Eds.), *Norm dynamics in multilateral arms control: Interests, conflicts and justice*. University of Georgia Press.
Wunderlich, C. (2020). *Rogue states as norm entrepreneurs: Black sheep or sheep in wolves' clothing? Norm Research in International Relations*. Springer. https://doi.org/10.1007/978-3-030-27990-5
Zarakol, A. (2014). What made the modern world hang together: Socialisation or stigmatisation? *International Theory, 6*(2), 311–332. https://doi.org/10.1017/S1752971914000141

Chapter 3
Regional Organisations, Exit Threats, and Contestations of Community Norms

Diana Panke, Lukas Grundsfeld, and Pawel Tverskoi

> Let me make this official (…). If they convict us in the OAS [Organization of American States] or any of its bodies, Venezuela is pulling out, because it would make no sense to be there. (Hugo Chávez as cited in AFP, 2007)

In the early 2000s, Venezuelan President Hugo Chávez reacted strongly to an unfavourable report by the Organization of American States' (OAS) Inter-American Human Rights Commission on the human rights situation in Venezuela. Dissatisfied with what he perceived as the unequal condemnation of human rights violations by the organisation, Chávez used the threat to withdraw from the OAS to contest the organisation's application of human rights norms, which form an integral part of broader community norms of the OAS. Regional Organisations (RIOs), such as the OAS, are constitutively interlinked with clusters of community norms, which both enable them to function and are reproduced through enactment in organisational practices.[1] A RIO's cluster of community norms defines the rights and duties of RIO members and constitutes a regional identity by defining standards of legitimate

The paper is part of a research project 'Should I stay or should I go? State Exits from Regional Organizations' funded by the German Research Foundation (DFG; PA 1257/10–1) and the authors are grateful for the financial support. We thank the editors and Simon Koschut for valuable comments on an earlier version of this paper. We also thank Léonie Berton, Antonia Damm, Lisa Hartmann, Luise Hartmann, Luise Kienel, Dagmar Kohlmeier, Fenna Kreuz, Hanne Oldenhof, Moritz Pohlner, Tim Rauschenberger, Mirjam Schellinger, Martin Stoll, Tim Vent, Chira Walke, and Lukas Weißenberger for excellent research assistance.

[1] Following Panke et al. (2020, p. 1), we define RIOs as 'organisations that are based on a set of written legal rules—primary law—as well as headquarters or a secretariat in which at least three states cooperate with one another on the basis of geographic criteria in more than one narrowly defined issue area'.

D. Panke (✉) · L. Grundsfeld · P. Tverskoi
Freie Universität Berlin, Berlin, Germany
e-mail: diana.panke@fu-berlin.de; lukas.grundsfeld@fu-berlin.de; p.tverskoi@fu-berlin.de

F. Lucenti et al. (eds.), *Contestation in Prism*, Norm Research in International Relations, https://doi.org/10.1007/978-3-031-83639-8_3

membership in the RIO community (Slocum & van Langenhove, 2005; Spandler, 2018; Thomas, 2017). However, these norms are not static or given but rather constantly contested (Linsenmaier et al., 2021; Wiener, 2018) due to internal incoherencies (Sandholtz, 2008), contingent contexts of application (Sandholtz & Stiles, 2009), and complex processes of localisation (Acharya, 2018).

This chapter analyses contestations of RIOs' community norms through member states' threats to exit RIOs. While previous research has studied withdrawal threats as attempts by states to induce institutional reforms in International Organisations (IOs) (von Borzyskowski & Vabulas, 2023), this analysis is one of the first to investigate exit threats in the context of norm contestation. These ideas also speak to those in another chapter in this volume on norm withdrawal by Lucrecia García Iommi (2025, see Chap. 8).

In line with this volume's framework, we define 'contestation as practices of objecting to or critically engaging with norms' (Wiener, 2018, p. 2, as also cited in Chap. 1, p. 5). Contestations of RIOs' community norms can take different forms and differ in severity. Threatening to withdraw its membership represents a member state's 'nuclear option' of contestation concerning RIO norms. The broad majority of norm contestation within RIOs takes place during the normal day-to-day operation of the organisation and involves constructive or destructive discursive critique as well as behavioural contestations, without pressuring the RIO and fellow members through exit threats. Yet, while not every exit threat is directly related to discursive contestations of RIO community norms, this is the case in about two-thirds of the threats to leave. These exit threats represent valuable focal points for analysing the most severe, salient, and contentious instances of norm contestation within RIOs.

In this chapter, we distinguish different types of RIO community norms and modes of contestation and assess theoretical expectations concerning the frequency of occurrence and outcomes of contestation through a set of explorative case studies of contestations of RIO community norms through exit threats. Bringing together research on norm contestation and regional and international organisations, this chapter contributes to our understanding of broad dynamics of cooperation and contestation. In particular, this chapter makes the following contributions to the core questions put forward in this edited volume. Concerning the question of which different forms of norm contestation can be evidenced, we differentiate between two forms of discursive contestation, related to a norm's scope of application—applicatory contestation—and substantive content—validity contestation—(Deitelhoff & Zimmermann, 2020; Panke & Petersohn, 2012). We argue that the former is more prevalent than the latter with regard to community norms. Furthermore, concerning the second question of the edited volume we contend that community norms can be contested with respect to membership rights as well as membership duties, with contestation of the latter being only slightly more common.

This analysis also provides insights into the effect of contestations, thereby addressing the edited volume's third question. We show that in most instances, contestations of RIOs' community norms result in the norms' stabilisation. Most strikingly, stabilisation occurs not only when the challenger state uses withdrawal threats to stabilise the community norm in question, but also when it pushes for modification or replacement of the norm. This suggests that RIOs' clusters of community norms tend to be rather resilient and rarely changed by individual instances of member states threatening to withdraw from the RIO. Thus, even in cases when member states succeeded in modifying specific community norms—as did Russia in the Council of Europe (CoE)—these changes are not necessarily permanent and can be potentially reversed. However, this also reveals that temporary modifications of RIOs' community norms, although rare, are most likely following instances of validity contestation. Our contribution ends with theoretical conclusions and outlines avenues for future research.

RIO Community Norms

As 'complexes of rules and norms identifiable in space and time' (Keohane, 1988, p. 1), all IOs are constitutively interlinked with norms. This both enables the IO to function and is reproduced through their enactment in organisational practices. While this applies to all IOs, due to their regional character, RIOs are interconnected through more specific clusters of norms. Understanding regions as 'socially constructed, spatial ideas, which follow concepts of community and society' (Goltermann et al., 2012, p. 4), RIOs are based on clusters of community norms that they seek to uphold, which can relate to shared histories, cultures, or challenges as well as a common purpose or destiny (Deutsch et al., 1957). Accordingly, community norms are clusters of norms that explicate who can join RIOs, which core objectives the organisation seeks to pursue, which institutions and instruments the RIO is based upon and can use to further the community of members, as well as core cooperative principles including solidarity and respect of sovereignty amongst the members. RIOs' community norms thus define appropriate behaviour within the region and constitute a regional identity by setting standards of legitimate membership in the RIO (Finnemore & Sikkink, 1998; Spandler, 2018; Thomas, 2017). This also involves the othering of those not belonging to the region (Linsenmaier, 2015; Slocum & van Langenhove, 2005). RIOs' community norms are derived from and at the same time represent more fundamental normative structures of regional order (Reus-Smit, 1999), which they uphold by distinguishing legitimate from illegitimate deviations (Reus-Smit, 2017, 2018).

Scholars offer various ways to differentiate between norms, including according to their constitutive or regulative function (Searle, 1995), their level of abstraction, ranging from fundamental norms and organising principles to standardised procedures (Wiener, 2017), or their spatial dimensions (Lantis & Wunderlich, 2022). For our purpose, we heuristically distinguish two types of norms entailed in sets of RIO community norms according to the fundamental functions they fulfil: (1) norms defining membership rights, and (2) norms defining membership duties (Milewicz, 2020, pp. 44–48). The first addresses the question of what a member state can legitimately expect from the RIO, e.g., in terms of material support, solidarity, or freedom. How much support of what kind and in which circumstances can the state demand from the community, and regarding which issues the state can insist on not being challenged by the RIO? Examples of norms regulating membership rights are the norm of non-interference, norms demanding economic support or collective defence, or norms regulating access to certain roles and positions within the RIO. The second revolves around the question of what the RIO and the other member states can expect from the member state. Which conduct can the community legitimately demand the member state to adhere to? Which degree of solidarity—e.g., in terms of material contributions—can the RIO legitimately expect from the state in which situation? Examples are norms of human rights, democracy, and good governance, as well as norms regulating—exceptions to—states' payments of membership fees or contributions to RIO activities such as field missions.[2]

Exit Threats as Contestations of RIO Community Norms

Community norms are not static background conditions but are continuously contested (Linsenmaier et al., 2021; Wiener, 2008, 2018). This ongoing contestation results from three different processes and the interplay among them. First, an RIO's set of community norms is never perfectly aligned and coherent. Instead, there are always tensions and contradictions within and between norms. Contradictions may come to the forefront during the process of application, for example, leading to contestations about which aspects of a norm—or norms within a set of norms—take precedence over others (Sandholtz, 2008; van Kersbergen & Verbeek, 2007). Second, the potential contexts of norms' applications are diverse and conditional. In every case of application, they require a translation from the abstract to the specific. While less abstract organising principles and standardised procedures require less translation, they are also more limited in their applicability. In contrast, fundamental norms, which have the widest range of applicability, require the most translation and thus leave the most space for contestation (Sandholtz & Stiles, 2009; Wiener, 2014). Third, the contestation of norms occurs in the context of their localisation into specific contexts, as actors reinterpret and reformulate RIOs' community norms according to local normative standards (Acharya, 2018; Zimmermann, 2017).

[2] While norms determining RIO members' rights and duties form closely intertwined clusters (Lantis & Wunderlich, 2018, 2022; Winston, 2018), we argue that it is possible to heuristically distinguish different norms according to their function as primarily opening up rights for members—such as having access to funds—or calling them to adhere to specific duties—such as paying membership contributions.

Threatening to withdraw its membership is a state's 'nuclear option' of contesting RIO norms, potentially endangering the organisation's prosperity, standing, and political influence. We define exit threats as public statements by state officials indicating the state's intention to terminate its membership in the RIO (see also von Borzyskowski & Vabulas, 2023). Thus, in contrast to a notification of withdrawal, which is a matter-of-fact statement of a state's already taken decision, a withdrawal threat is an expression of dissatisfaction with the organisation and/or fellow member states linked to the possibility of exiting the organisation in the future. While RIOs' community norms are constantly contested, we assume that the broad majority of norm contestations within RIOs take place below the threshold where states feel required to threaten to leave the RIO. In effect, while not all exit threats are connected to contestations of RIO community norms, the cases in which they are represent valuable focal points to analyse state agency and the most severe, salient, and contentious instances of norm contestation within RIOs (Bloomfield, 2015; Schneiker, 2021; Wunderlich, 2020).[3]

Our study applies contemporary norm theory insights on the different forms of contestations a norm can face, including: (1) contestation of the scope of its application and (2) contestation of the validity of its substantive content (Deitelhoff & Zimmermann, 2020; Panke & Petersohn, 2012, 2016). In the former case, contestation revolves around the norm's applicability in a specific situation: that is whether the situation falls within the realm of instances governed by the norm. The latter case involves two issues. On the one hand, what can be contested are the specific substantive consequences or implications that follow from a norm in a concrete situation.[4] On the other hand, more fundamentally, contestation can address the moral righteousness of the norm's content as such.

Combining the two types of RIOs' community norms and the two forms of norm contestation, we analytically differentiate four ways in which exit threats can contest RIOs' community norms (cf. Table 3.1).

The upper left quadrant in Table 3.1 captures cases in which member states contest the applicatory scope of norms defining membership rights. For example, this

Table 3.1 Four different types of contestation of RIOs' community norms

		RIO's Community Norms Defining:	
		Membership Rights	Membership Duties
Contestation of:	Applicatory Scope		
	Substantive Content		

[3] For a different perspective on norm withdrawal, see García Iommi (2025, Chap. 8).

[4] Trenta (2021) labels as 'meaning contestation' attempts to '(re)shape the intersubjective expectations set by the norm, by redefining the concept at the centre of the norm and/or challenging expectations as to the behaviour the norm requires from its addressees', repre Deitelhoff and Zimmerman's (2020) broader conception and subsume all contestations of norms' substantive content under validity contestation.

could occur if a state considers the RIO to unjustifiably interfere more severely in its domestic affairs compared to those of other member states. In the lower left quadrant, member states contest the substantive content of membership rights. This entails, for instance, a state contesting whether the reasons for the RIO's interference in its domestic affairs are covered by the norm's substantive focus and aim or the norms regulating the distribution of roles and positions within the RIO. The upper right quadrant contains cases in which member states contest the application of membership duties. This would, for example, include states seeking to achieve exemptions from the payment of membership fees, or states arguing that the RIO's good governance standards do not affect a specific domestic political practice. Finally, in the lower right quadrant, states contest the substantive content of membership duties. This can involve cases in which states contest the righteousness of human rights or good governance standards as such, or whether they must make financial contributions to the RIO at all.

This framework allows the explication of expectations concerning contestations of RIO community norms. First, while norm contestations take place in all four quadrants, we expect differences concerning the *frequency of occurrence*. On the one hand, we anticipate that in all RIOs scope contestations are more frequent than contestations of the content of a norm. Scope contestations do not target the purpose of a norm, but its applicatory scope. Such low-threshold contestations are less severe and have fewer far-reaching implications for the future of the RIO and should occur more frequently. By contrast, appealing for a new interpretation of a norm's core or calling the very purpose of a norm into question, content contestations are more severe and more likely to affect the core identity or central function of an RIO. Hence, they should occur less frequently (see also García Iommi, 2025, Chap. 8). On the other hand, we also expect the prevalence of contestations to differ depending on whether they address norms defining membership rights or duties. Given that under conditions of sovereign equality all states—could—equally benefit from rights provided to RIO members, the issue of membership rights in RIOs has the potential to create a positive-sum situation. In contrast, as norms defining membership duties impose costs and constraints on every individual member state, the possibility of a positive-sum situation is precluded. In effect, while '[r]ights are the correlatives of duties' (Milewicz, 2020, p. 45), we nonetheless expect that RIO norms defining membership duties should be more frequently contested than those defining membership rights.

Second, we expect different *effects* to follow from the respective forms of contestation. Following contemporary work by Percy and Sandholtz (2022), we conceptualise the possible effects of contestation on norms in terms of (a) stabilisation, (b) modification, and (c) replacement. Stabilisation refers to instances in which a norm's scope and substance are not changed but reaffirmed. Modification means that the applicatory scope and substantive content of a norm change in a way that preserves the original norm but defines it in a more specific way, thus either weakening or strengthening the norm. In contrast, replacement involves the shifting of a norm's content, and potentially also the scope of its application, in such a fundamental manner that the old norm is de facto replaced by a new one (Percy &

Sandholtz, 2022; Sandholtz, 2019). Notably, exit threats can seek to stabilise norms in the wake of modification attempts by other member states, or they can strive to achieve changes. Thus, during processes of contestations of RIO community norms, exit threats can be deployed to achieve any of these three possible outcomes. Concerning the occurrence of these outcomes, we expect the following: on the one hand, as contestations of applicatory scope can more easily be accommodated by compromises, we expect that they are more likely to lead to incremental modifications of norms. Being reflective of the more fundamental challenge they represent, contestations of norms' substantive content are more likely to result either in stabilisation or more radical norm replacement (Panke & Petersohn, 2012).[5] In these cases, if exit threats are used to induce or prevent the replacement of a norm through the contestation of its validity, failures to achieve the respective goal might trigger actual exits. On the other hand, we expect the potential positive-sum character of norms defining membership rights to exert a stabilising influence on them, primarily leading to norms' stabilisation. In the absence of the possibility of achieving a positive-sum situation, norms defining membership duties should be less stable. Accordingly, contestation of RIO norms defining membership duties should be more likely to lead to modification or replacement. In these constellations, failures to achieve or prevent the respective outcome might lead to the realisation of exit threats. We empirically examine these expectations in the next section.

Empirical Analysis

To further illuminate the pattern of norm contestations through exit threats and discuss which of the formulated expectations are empirically plausible, we search for cases of exit threats that relate to RIO norms and place them into the '2×2 matrix'. The Regional Organisations' Competencies (ROCO) 2.0 dataset (based on Panke et al., 2020) covers 73 RIOs in Africa, the Americas, Asia, and Europe between 1945 and 2022 and was extended to include the years 2021 and 2022. A threat to exit an RIO is not a formal measure of RIO member states, but a verbal or written discursive act in which the state communicates its dissatisfaction with the organisation and fellow member states and links this to the possibility to withdraw from the RIO in the future. As such verbal or written discursive acts are not formally reported in annual RIO reports or other official documents, data on threats to withdraw from RIOs can only be systematically collected on the basis of a LexisNexis newspaper

[5] Panke and Petersohn (2012, p. 723) argue, 'Incremental change is brought about by actors' attempts to limit the applicatory scope of a norm while they do not openly challenge its legitimacy, its prescriptive status or even its aim as such. In such contexts, driving agents typically argue that a particular norm, such as the non-intervention norm, is generally good and valid, but cannot be applied to a particular circumstance—e.g., if a state violates fundamental international human rights standards. This curbing mechanism reduces material or cognitive compliance costs step by step. If it continues, the norm's applicatory scope becomes increasingly limited'.

analysis (see also von Borzyskowski & Vabulas, 2023). A search of all 73 RIOs between 1945 and 2022 in the LexisNexis database[6] established the universe of possible threats. It reveals a total of 123 cases of exit threats, whereby 71 instances—about two-thirds—relate to community norms as they concern the rights or duties of RIO members.

We observe several patterns pertaining to the *occurrence of different types of exit threats*. In line with the expectation concerning scope and content contestations, the comparative analysis of exit threats that are linked to RIO norms shows that most instances of contestations concern the applicatory scope of a norm. In fact, of the total 71 exit threat cases related to norm contestations, 50 contest the applicatory scope and 21 the substantive content of RIO norms. In line with our expectation, this suggests that states tend to opt for low-threshold contestations rather than forms of contestation that have the potential to call into question the identity or core function of an RIO. In other words, discursive and behavioural contestations from within, such as critique, constructive re-negotiations, public protest, or non-compliance are more often than not directed towards issues that can be resolved without questioning the core of the RIO and its community norms as such. While conflicts of applicatory scope allow for relatively easily attainable compromises, quick fixes hardly exist for validity contestations, as they concern the substantive content of RIOs' community norms that address the core of RIOs' self-understandings. Furthermore, 32 withdrawal threats contest RIO community norms defining membership rights, whereas 39 question those defining membership duties. This tends to align with our expectation that by entailing the possibility for a positive-sum situation, norms defining membership rights should be less frequently contested than those defining duties. Yet, the contrast between rights and duties is considerably less pronounced compared to the one between applicatory scope and norm content.

Contestations and Their Effects

In order to examine the second expectation on the *effects of contestations*, we select one empirical illustration from each quadrant in a manner that encompasses temporal variation, contestations by smaller and bigger states, and contestations taking place in RIOs from different regions of the world (see Table 3.2). Qatar and the Gulf Cooperation Council (GCC) represent an instance of membership rights contestation with respect to norms' applicatory scope. To illustrate contestations of the applicatory scope of membership duties, we consider Zimbabwe in the Southern African Development Community (SADC). In the lower two quadrants, the focus is on contestations of the substantive content of RIO norms. Concerning membership

[6] The search included the terms 'exit' and 'withdraw*', respectively, combined with the name and abbreviation of each of the 73 RIOs in turn, for each year of RIO existence.

Table 3.2 Case selection for qualitative analysis

		RIO's Community Norms Defining:	
		Membership Rights	Membership Duties
Contestation of:	Applicatory Scope	GCC—Qatar	SADC—Zimbabwe
	Substantive Content	EAEU—Kazakhstan	CoE—Russia

rights, we examine Kazakhstan in the Eurasian Economic Union (EAEU). Finally, with regard to the contestations of the substantive content of membership duties, we focus on Russia in the CoE. For the qualitative analysis of these cases, we rely on official RIO and member state documents, newspaper articles, and secondary literature, in order to portray the norm contestation dynamics and the possible effects of these exit threats for the states concerned and the RIO as a whole.

Contesting the Applicatory Scope of Membership Rights (Quadrant 1)

The GCC, established in 1981 by the Arab dynastic monarchies located in the Persian Gulf (Beck, 2015; Ramazani, 1988), focuses primarily on economic and monetary integration as well as cooperation on technology and infrastructure among its members (Al-Khodiry, 2012; Panke et al., 2020). In 2017, long-standing conflicts about Qatar's foreign policy culminated when Bahrain, Saudi Arabia, the United Arab Emirates, as well as non-GCC member Egypt—the 'Quartet'—imposed a land, sea, and air blockade on Qatar, expelled Qatari nationals, and suspended economic and diplomatic relations with the country (Negri, 2018). Simultaneously, the Quartet presented Qatar with a list of demands, which included terminating its support for terrorist groups, suspending its contacts with the Muslim Brotherhood, shutting down the Al Jazeera media network, expelling Turkish troops, and ending all diplomatic and economic relations with Iran (Al-Eshaq & Rasheed, 2022; Keating & Abbott, 2021). In effect, these demands represented the attempt to alter the applicatory scope of the membership right to conduct an independent foreign policy. While not denying that Qatar had the sovereign right to conduct its foreign policy, the Quartet sought to achieve significant modifications concerning the norm's application. They defined far-reaching exceptions linked to rationales that could potentially destabilise the regimes of the Quartet. A spokesman of the Qatari government noted that the blockade 'is about limiting Qatar's sovereignty […] and outsourcing our foreign policy' (Financial Times, 2017).

In response, Qatar threatened to withdraw from the GCC unless the 'siege' (TNS, 2017) was lifted, thereby using the threat to stabilise the norm defining member states' sovereign right to conduct an independent foreign policy and preventing its modification or replacement. Qatar's Minister of Foreign Affairs stated that the blockade represented 'an intervention in the internal affairs of another country…We will not negotiate on our sovereignty…[I]t is unacceptable that a Persian Gulf State make the decision [sic] for other countries' (TNS, 2017). Not complying with the Quartet's main demands, Qatar blamed the coalition for 'violating the GCC principles' (BBC, 2017). While Bahrain's Minister of Foreign Affairs stated that the coalition would be 'fine with it [Qatar] exiting the council' (Al Arabiya, 2017), in 2021, the blockade was eventually lifted despite the absence of substantive concessions by Qatar (Al-Eshaq & Rasheed, 2022; Umar & Ghurab, 2023). Qatar thus succeeded in its attempt to stabilise the applicatory scope of the norm defining GCC members' sovereign right to conduct an independent foreign policy, hence retaining the norm's strength.

Contesting the Applicatory Scope of Membership Duties (Quadrant 2)

SADC was founded in 1980 by several front-line states as the Southern African Development Coordination Conference to advance the liberation from white minority governments and reduce dependency on Apartheid South Africa. Today, SADC encompasses the whole Southern African region and focuses on a wide range of issue areas in the realms of economic development and regional security (SADC, 2022a, 2022b). In the context of Zimbabwe's 2008 general election, tensions between SADC and Zimbabwean long-term president Robert Mugabe emerged as the organisation pushed for more far-reaching democratic electoral standards (Aeby, 2017; Pallotti, 2013). In the run-up to the 2013 elections, SADC concerned about the elections' democratic credibility and recommended their postponement to implement electoral reforms (Deutsche Well, 2013). In this context, Mugabe's main competitor Morgan Tsvangirai approached Zimbabwe's constitutional court to seek the election's postponement. In response, Mugabe threatened to withdraw Zimbabwe from SADC during a speech at a rally: 'Let it be known that we are in SADC voluntarily; if SADC decides to do stupid things we can move out. No outsider is allowed to intervene in a situation where our courts have made a ruling' (Ndlovu, 2013).

Denying SADC's right to get involved in the matter, Mugabe questioned the applicatory scope of SADC's norms defining membership duties with regard to democracy and good governance. Instead, referring to the norm of sovereignty, Mugabe insisted on the membership right to not be challenged by SADC in this regard. SADC eventually backed down and Mugabe emerged victorious from elections that were considered free and peaceful but not fair (Aeby, 2017, p. 279). This result must be seen in the context of SADC's inability to clearly distinguish the membership duty to respect human rights from the more contested duty to pursue a—neoliberal—strategy of economic development, which enabled Mugabe to reject both (Pallotti, 2013, p. 18). As a result, Mugabe seemed to achieve a successful modification of the applicatory scope of norms defining membership duties in relation to democracy and good governance in SADC. However, over the following years, SADC conducted regular election observation missions in its member states, including in Angola, Eswatini, the Democratic Republic of Congo, Madagascar, the Seychelles, Zambia, and Zimbabwe (SADC, 2023). In 2023 'SADC set up an electoral observer mission that is supposed to see that before the [Zimbabwean general] election takes place, the conditions under which the election is going to be held are conducive, [so that] (…) every party or participant has equal opportunities' (Personal communication, 05 October 2023). Given SADC's continued engagement in election observation, it is thus questionable whether Mugabe's contestation attempts had lasting effects on norms defining democratic electoral standards within SADC. Instead, it appears that the applicatory scope of member states' good governance duties had been stabilised and the norm's strength remained unharmed.

Contesting the Substantive Content of Membership Rights (Quadrant 3)

The EAEU, initially set up as the Eurasian Economic Community in 2000, groups several former members of the Soviet Union. It has over time increased its economic policy competencies, eventually agreeing to establish an economic union in 2014 (Hancock & Libman, 2016; Kirkham, 2016; Libman & Vinokurov, 2012; Tarr, 2016). After this transformation, conflicts about the extent of desired political integration and the corresponding understanding of state sovereignty emerged within the EAEU. Whereas Russia preferred deep political integration to strengthen its position in the post-Soviet space, Kazakhstan proposed to 'build integration primarily on the basis of economic pragmatism…rather than abstract geopolitical ideas', with the EAEU thus being 'a union of states based on the principles of equality, non-interference…[and] respect for sovereignty' (Chernykh & Burnashev, 2021, p. 294; Satpayev, 2015). This struggle revolves around contestations of the substantive content of EAEU members' right to sovereignty. Expressing a popular sentiment among the Kazakh population (Malikbayeva & Gabdullin, 2023), President Nursultan Nazarbayev stated 'Kazakhstan has a right to withdraw from the Eurasian Economic Union…Our independence is our dearest treasure, which our grandfathers fought for…First of all, we will never surrender it to someone, and secondly, we will do our best to protect it' (BBC, 2014a; see also Brletich, 2015, p. 25).

In response, Russian President Vladimir Putin replied that 'Kazakhstan's history of independent statehood is scant' (BBC, 2014a) as '[t]he Kazakhs never had a state of their own' (Mostafa & Mahmood, 2018). In effect, in relation to Kazakhstan, Putin questioned the substance of the norm of sovereignty altogether. As Kazakhstan reaffirmed that threats to its statehood represented a red line Russia should not cross, Putin claimed that Nazarbayev 'has done a unique thing [by creating] a state on a territory that never had one' (BBC, 2014b). Yet, linking Kazakhstan's statehood to Nazarbayev personally, this statement still contests the substantive content of the norm of sovereignty concerning Kazakhstan. Putin's remarks thus 'prompted speculations on Russian social networks that [Kazakhstan's] statehood may draw to an end in Moscow's eyes after the Kazakh president is replaced by a successor' (BBC, 2014a). However, Russian Minister of Foreign Affairs, Sergey Lavrov, appeared to backtrack on this challenge, conceding that EAEU members 'share[d] a completely unanimous approach that the Customs Union is a union of sovereign states' (BBC, 2014b). In effect, the process of contestation did not harm the norm's strength but led to the stabilisation of a Westphalian understanding of the norm of sovereignty in relation to Kazakhstan.

Contesting the Substantive Content of Membership Duties (Quadrant 4)

The CoE, established in 1949, as of 2023, includes all internationally recognised states in Europe except Belarus and Russia and focuses on the protection of human rights, democracy, and the rule of law in its member states, as well as the promotion of European unity (Gawrich, 2015; Jordan, 2003; Kleinsorge, 2010; Stapel, 2022). Following Russia's aggression against Ukraine in 2014, the Russian delegation's voting rights in the Parliamentary Assembly of the CoE (PACE) were suspended. As a reaction, Russia stopped its participation in PACE, and, from 2017 onward, its financial contributions to the CoE. In 2018, the CoE's Secretary General warned that the organisation would expel Russia for non-payment of membership fees in 2019 (Dzehtsiarou & Coffey, 2019). In response, Russia threatened to withdraw from the CoE if its voting rights were not restored (TNS, 2018). On the surface, Russia contested the applicatory scope of its duty to pay its membership fees despite the suspension of its voting rights. More fundamentally, however, relating to Russia's initial suspension, the country substantially contested whether membership in the CoE involved certain membership duties, including respect for other states' sovereignty, and whether member states could be sanctioned for violating this duty. Russia thereby demanded that, in return for recommencing its financial contributions, the CoE should rescind its suspension provisions (TNS, 2018).

The outcome of this contestation remained ambiguous. While Russia recommenced its membership payments, the CoE, notwithstanding the threat by Ukraine to withdraw from PACE (Dpa, 2019) and fearful of the ripple effects of a potential 'Ruxit' (TNS, 2019), restored Russia's voting rights and adjusted the organisation's suspension provisions (BBC, 2019). Despite being attached to conditions, including respecting LGBTQI rights and investigating the downing of Flight MH17 (CoE, 2019), these conditions were disconnected from the original reasons for Russia's suspension. As Estonian President Kersti Kaljulaid stated, '[t]he reason for these sanctions was a blatant violation of international law by Russia. Not one of the reasons why Russia's voting rights were suspended in 2014 has changed' (INS, 2019). Thus, Russia's attempt to modify the duty to respect other member states' sovereignty was partially successful. However, following Russia's full-scale invasion of

Ukraine in February 2022, the CoE's swift decision to suspend Russia's voting rights in PACE before expelling it from the organisation altogether (AFP, 2022) represents a retroactive stabilisation of the membership norm. Therefore, in the longer run, the Russian contestation of the substance of membership duties did not decrease the norm's strength.

Conclusion

In this chapter, we analysed contestations of community norms in the context of withdrawal threats by RIO members. Differentiating among community norms defining membership rights and duties, as well as between the contestation of norms' applicatory scope and the validity of its substantive content, we distinguished four ideal-typical ways in which states can use exit threats to contest RIO community norms. Identifying 71 cases of threats to withdraw from RIOs connected to the contestation of community norms and conducting four qualitative case studies, we explored several patterns concerning the frequency of occurrence of different types of contestations and the effects in terms of norms' stabilisation, modification, or replacement. We show that contestations related to norms' applicatory scope occur more frequently than contestations of norms' substantive content. At the same time, the difference between the frequency of contestations of norms regulating membership rights and duties is less pronounced. Based on several qualitative case studies, and following our expectations, norm modification is rare, and norm replacement is completely absent. These conclusions raise interesting questions about norm withdrawal and appear to contrast with results from García Iommi (2025, Chap. 8).

Overall, contestations of RIOs' community norms in most cases result in the norms' stabilisation. This is the case both when states use exit threats to achieve the modification or replacement of a norm and when they seek to stabilise it. Moreover, concerning their effects on the norm strength, it does not appear to be the case that contestations of the applicatory scope differ systematically from contestations of a norm's substantive content or that contestations of membership duties have different effects than contestations of membership rights. Thus, RIOs' clusters of community norms—at least in the medium term—appear to be rather resilient and hardly changed by individual instances of member states threatening to withdraw from an RIO. This might suggest that in the case of RIOs' community norms, mutual reinforcements within norm clusters are more prevalent than norm collisions and spillover effects, thereby pointing towards the greater resiliency of norm clusters (Lantis, 2025, Chap. 2). Even in cases where member states succeeded in modifying specific community norms—as did Russia in the CoE—these changes are not necessarily permanent and can be potentially reversed. Incorporating research on norm contestation as well as on—regional—IOs, these findings contribute to our understanding of both.

This study also identifies several avenues for further research. First, scholars and practitioners need a more systematic understanding of the factors influencing the occurrence, type, and success of contestations of RIO community norms. Besides institutional characteristics of RIOs and different types of contested norms, this requires a better understanding of the influence of state-based factors. In this regard, research would benefit from conceptualising the contesting state's power—including its normative power in terms of its moral credibility—in the context of norm contestations (Bettiza & Lewis, 2020), thereby shifting 'attention to power dynamics inherent in processes of norm contestation and norm entrepreneurship' (Wunderlich, 2022, p. 365). Grasping the contesting state's relative position of moral authority within the RIO, for example, from a Bourdieuan perspective (Oskanian, 2023), would significantly contribute to our understanding of the state's angle with regard to exit threats. This will enable us to answer questions concerning the types of states engaging in the contestation of RIO community norms, their use of different strategies of contestation—including exit threats—as well as their chance of success.

Second, further research should examine the relationship between exit threats related to norm contestation and actual exits (Panke et al., 2025). On the one hand, we would expect that exit threats are realised if they fail to achieve their goals, and our analysis indicates that the type of contestation affects the chance of exit threats to accomplish those goals. Existing research shows that exits become more likely depending on states' voice opportunities within and loyalty towards an RIO (Hirschmann, 1970; Panke et al., 2023). In this respect, analysing the interplay between the institutional factors—e.g., the extent of delegation and pooling of authority in the organisation—affecting states' ability to achieve desired adjustments within the RIO and the type and direction of their contestation attempts represents a promising pathway for further research (Hooghe & Marks, 2015). This can contribute to a better understanding of both the factors impacting states' decisions to withdraw from—regional—IOs as well as the processes of norm contestation unfolding in these contexts. On the other hand, as many states re-join RIOs after having withdrawn from them,[7] and as states cannot physically leave their region, exits do not represent the end of the interaction between an RIO and the exiting state. The contestation of norms regulating their interaction is therefore likely to continue. The effect on RIOs' community norms thus depends on the characteristics of the norm cluster, the exiting state's relative power position, as well as its further relationship with the RIO (e.g. Jurado et al., 2021; Panke & Grundsfeld, 2024). Analysing exits not as one-off events, but continuous processes thereby contribute

[7] Re-entries after exits are a relatively frequent phenomenon. Most recently, Kiribati, which left the Pacific Island Forum in 2022 re-joined the organisation in 2023. Other states that withdrew from RIOs and later re-joined include: Eritrea (Intergovernmental Authority on Development, 2007–2011), Greece (CoE, 1968–1973), Morocco (African Union, 1984–2017), Rwanda (Economic Community of Central African States, 2007–2015), Seychelles (SADC, 2004–2007), UK (Pacific Community, 1996–1998 and 2005–2021), and Uzbekistan (Collective Security Treaty Organization, 2000–2005).

to a more nuanced and processual understanding of the relationship between regional disintegration and norm contestation.

Third, suspensions provide another beneficial opportunity to connect research on norm contestation and organisational practices. While exit threats represent instruments for states to contest community norms, suspensions of transgressive member states constitute an instrument for RIOs to react to contestations and violations of their organisational norms by member states (Grundsfeld, 2023: von Borzyskowski & Vabulas, 2019). Examining the suspensions of member states allows us to identify the forms of contestation relating to their community norms that RIOs perceive as especially threatening. Further, tracing contestation processes in the context of the onset and eventual revocation of suspensions would enhance our understanding concerning the ability of transgressive states and RIOs to achieve their respective goals in terms of the stabilisation, modification, or replacement of community norms.

References

Acharya, A. (2018). *Constructing global order: Agency and change in world politics*. Cambridge University Press. https://doi.org/10.1017/9781316756768

Aeby, M. (2017). Stability and sovereignty at the expense of democracy? The SADC mediation mandate for Zimbabwe, 2007–2013. *African Security, 10*(3–4), 272–291. https://doi.org/10.1080/19392206.2017.1348116

AFP. (2007, May 5). *Venezuela to quit IMF*, World Bank. Retrieved April 15, 2025, from https://advance.lexis.com/api/document?collection=news&id=urn:contentItem:4NMJ-KTM0-TWMD-62D3-00000-00&context=1516831

AFP. (2022, February 25). *Council of Europe suspends Russia over Ukraine invasion*. Retrieved April 15, 2025, from https://advance.lexis.com/api/document?collection=news&id=urn:contentItem:64VX-SHK1-JBV1-X4D4-00000-00&context=1516831

Al Arabiya. (2017, October 10). *Bahrain FM: Qatar aims to weaken, undermine GCC*. Retrieved April 15, 2025, from https://advance.lexis.com/api/document?collection=news&id=urn:contentItem:5PVK-4W21-F11P-X35B-00000-00&context=1516831

Al-Khodiry, A. (2012). The economic and monetary union of the Gulf Cooperation Council. *Journal of World Trade, 46*(1), 121–154. https://doi.org/10.54648/trad2012005

Al-Eshaq, S., & Rasheed, A. (2022). The 'David' in a divided gulf: Qatar's foreign policy and the 2017 Gulf crisis. *Middle East Policy, 29*(2), 30–45. https://doi.org/10.1111/mepo.12623

BBC. (2014a, September 2). *Moscow paper views reaction to Putin's comments on Kazakhstan's statehood*. Retrieved April 15, 2025, from https://advance.lexis.com/api/document?collection=news&id=urn:contentItem:5D23-7V11-JC8S-C0TV-00000-00&context=1516831

BBC. (2014b, September 1). *Russia's Lavrov praises Kazakhstan's role in customs union*. Retrieved April 15, 2025, from https://advance.lexis.com/api/document?collection=news&id=urn:contentItem:5D1X-3P51-JC8S-C4VP-00000-00&context=1516831

BBC. (2017, September 29). *Qatar refuses to extradite Islamist cleric to Egypt*. Retrieved April 15, 2025, from https://advance.lexis.com/api/document?collection=news&id=urn:contentItem:5PKK-B2Y1-DYRV-327J-00000-00&context=1516831

BBC. (2019, June 25). *Russia cleared to return to Europe's top rights body*. Retrieved April 15, 2025, from https://advance.lexis.com/api/document?collection=news&id=urn:contentItem:5WDS-VJ21-DYRV-34CN-00000-00&context=1516831

Beck, M. (2015). The end of regional Middle Eastern exceptionalism? The Arab league and the Gulf Cooperation Council after the Arab uprisings. *Democracy and Security, 11*(2), 190–207. https://doi.org/10.1080/17419166.2015.1037390

Bettiza, G., & Lewis, D. (2020). Authoritarian powers and norm contestation in the liberal international order: Theorizing the power politics of ideas and identity. *Journal of Global Security Studies, 5*(4), 559–577. https://doi.org/10.1093/jogss/ogz075

Bloomfield, A. (2015). Norm antipreneurs and theorising resistance to normative change. *Review of International Studies, 42*(2), 310–333. https://doi.org/10.1017/S026021051500025X

Brletich, S. (2015). The Crimea model: Will Russia annex the northern region of Kazakhstan? *Geopolitics, History, and International Relations, 7*(1), 11–29.

Chernykh, I. A., & Burnashev, R. R. (2021). Integration processes within the Eurasian Economic Union: Kazakhstan's narratives. *Kutafin Law Review, 8*(2), 289–313. https://doi.org/10.17803/2313-5395.2021.2.16.289-313

CoE. (2019). *PACE ratifies Russian delegation's credentials*. Retrieved April 15, 2025, from https://www.coe.int/en/web/portal/-/pace-ratifies-russian-delegation-s-credentials

Deitelhoff, N., & Zimmermann, L. (2020). Things we lost in the fire: How different types of contestation affect the robustness of international norms. *International Studies Review, 22*(1), 51–76. https://doi.org/10.1093/isr/viy080

Deutsch, K. W., Burrell, S. A., Kann, R. A., Lee, M., Jr., Lichterman, M., Lindgren, R., Lorwenheim, F. L., & Van Wagenen, R. W. (1957). *Political community and the North Atlantic area: International organization in the light of historical experience*. Princeton University Press.

Deutsche Well. (2013, July 5). President Robert Mugabe threatens to pull out of SADC. *Deutsche Welle*. Retrieved 15 April 2025 from https://www.dw.com/en/mugabe-threatens-to-pull-zimbabwe-out-of-regional-bloc/a-16932426

Dpa. (2019, June 25). *Ukraine threatens to exit Council of Europe body as Russia reinstated*. Retrieved April 15, 2025, from https://advance.lexis.com/api/document?collection=news&id=urn:contentItem:5WDV-6PR1-J9XT-N2T1-00000-00&context=1516831

Dzehtsiarou, K., & Coffey, D. K. (2019). Suspension and expulsion of members of the Council of Europe: Difficult decisions in troubled times. *International and Comparative Law Quarterly, 68*(2), 443–476. https://doi.org/10.1017/s0020589319000101

Financial Times. (2017, June 24). *Qatar casts aside list of demands by Arab states*. Retrieved April 15, 2025, from https://advance.lexis.com/api/document?collection=news&id=urn:contentItem:5NW2-FC91-JCM7-G283-00000-00&context=1516831

Finnemore, M., & Sikkink, K. (1998). International norm dynamics and political change. *International Organization, 52*(4), 887–917.

Gawrich, A. (2015). Too little, too late? Governance transfer and the Eastern European enlargement of the Council of Europe. In T. Börzel & V. van Hüllen (Eds.), *Governance transfer by regional organizations* (pp. 211–226). Palgrave.

García Iommi, L. (2025). Exceptions as contestation: Understanding norm withdrawal. In F. Lucenti, C. Ducci, C. Wunderlich, & J. S. Lantis (Eds.), *Contestation in prism: The evolution of norms and norm clusters in contemporary global politics* (pp. 143–161). Springer.

Goltermann, L., Lohaus, M., Spielau, A., & Striebinger, K. (2012). Roads to regionalism: Concepts, issues, and cases. In T. A. Börzel, L. Goltermann, M. Lohaus, & K. Striebinger (Eds.), *Roads to regionalism. Genesis, design and effects of regional organizations* (pp. 3–21). Ashgate.

Grundsfeld, L. (2023). Reacting to internal contestation: Regional international organizations and suspensions of member states. Paper presented at the *16th Pan European Conference on International Relations of the European International Studies Association*, Potsdam.

Hancock, K. J., & Libman, A. (2016). Eurasia. In T. Börzel & T. Risse (Eds.), *The Oxford handbook of comparative regionalism* (pp. 202–224). Oxford University Press.

Hirschmann, A. O. (1970). *Exit, voice, and loyalty: Responses to decline in firms, organizations, and states*. Harvard University Press.

Hooghe, L., & Marks, G. (2015). Delegation and pooling in international organizations. *The Review of International Organizations, 10*(3), 305–328. https://doi.org/10.1007/s11558-014-9194-4

INS. (2019, June 25). *Estonian PACE representatives vote against restoring Russia voting rights*. Retrieved April, 15 2025 from https://advance.lexis.com/api/document?collection=news&id=urn:contentItem:5WF5-NRK1-JDG9-Y230-00000-00&context=1516831

Jordan, P. A. (2003). Does membership have its privileges?: Entrance into the Council of Europe and compliance with human rights norms. *Human Rights Quarterly, 25*(3), 660–688. https://doi.org/10.1353/hrq.2003.0033

Jurado, I., Léon, S., & Walter, S. (2021). Brexit dilemmas: Shaping postwithdrawal relations with a leaving state. *International Organization, 76*(2), 273–304. https://doi.org/10.1353/hrq.2003.0033

Keating, V. C., & Abbott, L. M. (2021). Entrusted norms: Security, trust, and betrayal in the Gulf Cooperation Council crisis. *European Journal of International Relations, 27*(4), 1090–1113. https://doi.org/10.1177/13540661211044197

Keohane, R. O. (1988). International organizations: Two approaches. *International Studies Quarterly, 32*(3), 379–396. https://doi.org/10.2307/2600589

Kirkham, K. (2016). The formation of the Eurasian Economic Union: How successful is the Russian regional hegemony? *Journal of Eurasian Studies, 7*(2), 111–128. https://doi.org/10.1016/j.euras.2015.06.002

Kleinsorge, T. E. J. (2010). *Council of Europe*. Kluwer Law International.

Lantis, J. S., & Wunderlich, C. (2018). Resiliency dynamics of norm clusters: Norm contestation and international cooperation. *Review of International Studies, 44*(3), 570–593. https://doi.org/10.1017/s0260210517000626

Lantis, J. S., & Wunderlich, C. (2022). Reevaluating constructivist norm theory: A three-dimensional norms research program. *International Studies Review, 24*(1). https://doi.org/10.1093/isr/viab059

Lantis, J. S. (2025). Norm cluster resiliency in the face of contestation: Nuclear threats and international resolve. In F. Lucenti, C. Ducci, C. Wunderlich, & J. S. Lantis (Eds.), *Contestation in prism: The evolution of norms and norm clusters in contemporary global politics* (pp. 23–43). Springer.

Libman, A., & Vinokurov, E. (2012). Regional integration and economic convergence in the post-soviet space: Experience of the decade of growth. *Journal of Common Market Studies, 50*(1), 112–128. https://doi.org/10.1111/j.1468-5965.2011.02209.x

Linsenmaier, T. (2015). The interplay between regional international societies. *Global Discourse, 5*(3), 452–466.

Linsenmaier, T., Schmidt, D. R., & Spandler, K. (2021). On the meaning(s) of norms: Ambiguity and global governance in a post-hegemonic world. *Review of International Studies, 47*(4), 508–527.

Ndlovu, R. (2013, July 12). Zimbabwe can't leave SADC just yet. *Mail & Guardian*. Retrieved 15 April, 2025, from https://mg.co.za/article/2013-07-12-00-zimbabwe-cant-leave-sadc-just-yet/

Malikbayeva, S., & Gabdullin, G. (2023). The rise of anti-European sentiment in Kazakhstan. In A. Mihr, P. Sorbello, & B. Weiffen (Eds.), *Securitization and democracy in Eurasia—Transformation and development in the OSCE region* (pp. 63–76). Springer. https://doi.org/10.1007/978-3-031-16659-4_4

Milewicz, K. M. (2020). *Constitutionalizing world politics: The logic of democratic power and the unintended consequences of international treaty making*. Cambridge University Press.

Mostafa, G., & Mahmood, M. (2018). Eurasian Economic Union: Evolution, challenges and possible future directions. *Journal of Eurasian Studies, 9*(2), 163–172. https://doi.org/10.1016/j.euras.2018.05.001

Negri, A. (2018). Gulf regional crisis: Qatar-Saudi Arabia rivalry, tensions within the Gulf Cooperation Council. Italian Institute for International Political Studies. https://www.iemed.org/publication/gulf-regional-crisis-qatar-saudi-arabia-rivalry-tensions-within-the-gulf-cooperation-council/

Oskanian, K. (2023). Beyond state and hegemony: International orders as anarchic meta-fields. *International Studies Quarterly, 67*(2). https://doi.org/10.1093/isq/sqad034

Pallotti, A. (2013). Human rights and regional cooperation in Africa: SADC and the crisis in Zimbabwe. *Strategic Review for Southern Africa, 35*(1), 17–40. https://doi.org/10.35293/srsa.v35i1.97

Panke, D., & Grundsfeld, L. (2024). Epilogue – Responses to Brexit: Insights from small EU member states and lessons for exits from other regional organizations. In L. C. Ferreira-Pereira (Ed.), *Small States of the European Union and Brexit* (pp. 107–111). Routledge.

Panke, D., & Petersohn, U. (2012). Why international norms disappear sometimes. *European Journal of International Relations, 18*(4), 719–742. https://doi.org/10.1177/1354066111407690

Panke, D., & Petersohn, U. (2016). Norm challenges and norm death: The inexplicable? *Cooperation and Conflict, 21*(1), 3–19. https://doi.org/10.1177/0010836715597948

Panke, D., Grundsfeld, L., & Tverskoi, P. (2023). Ending cooperation: A comparative analysis of state exits from regional international organizations. Paper presented at the *64th Annual Conference of the International Studies Association*, Montréal.

Panke, D., Grundsfeld, L., & Tverskoi, P. (2025). Exit from regime complexity? Regional international organizations under scrutiny. *Global Studies Quarterly*.

Panke, D., Stapel, S., & Starkmann, A. (2020). *Comparing regional organizations. Global dynamics and regional particularities*. Bristol University Press.

Percy, S. V., & Sandholtz, W. (2022). Why norms rarely die. *European Journal of International Relations, 28*(4), 934–954. https://doi.org/10.1177/13540661221126018

Ramazani, R. K. (1988). *The Gulf Cooperation Council: Record and analysis*. University of Virginia Press.

Reus-Smit, C. (1999). *The moral purpose of the state*. Princeton University Press.

Reus-Smit, C. (2017). Cultural diversity and international order. *International Organization, 71*(4), 851–885. https://doi.org/10.1017/S0020818317000261

Reus-Smit, C. (2018). *On cultural diversity: International theory in a world of difference*. Cambridge University Press.

SADC. (2022a). *History and treaty*. Retrieved April 15, 2025, from https://www.sadc.int/pages/history-and-treaty

SADC. (2022b). *Integration milestones*. Retrieved April 15, 2025, from https://www.sadc.int/integration-milestones

SADC. (2023). *Election observation missions*. Retrieved April 15, 2025, from https://www.sadc.int/latest-news?title=election%20observation&items_per_page=16&page=0

Sandholtz, W. (2008). Dynamics of international norm change: Rules against wartime plunder. *European Journal of International Relations, 14*(1), 101–131. https://doi.org/10.1177/1354066107087766

Sandholtz, W. (2019). Norm contestation, robustness, and replacement. *Journal of Global Security Studies, 4*(1), 139–146. https://doi.org/10.1093/jogss/ogy042

Sandholtz, W., & Stiles, K. W. (2009). *International norms and cycles of change*. Oxford University Press.

Satpayev, D. (2015). Kazakhstan: Economic integration without relinquishing sovereignty. In F. Hett & S. Szkola (Eds.), *The Eurasian economic union: Analyses and perspectives from Belarus, Kazakhstan, and Russia* (pp. 11–15). Friedrich-Ebert Stiftung.

Schneiker, A. (2021). Norm sabotage: Conceptual reflection on a phenomenon that challenges well-established norms. *International Studies Perspectives, 22*(1), 106–123. https://doi.org/10.1093/isp/ekaa003

Searle, J. R. (1995). *The construction of social reality*. Penguin.

Slocum, N., & van Langenhove, L. (2005). Identity and regional integration. In M. Farrell, B. Hettne, & L. van Langenhove (Eds.), *Global politics of regionalism: Theory and practice* (pp. 137–151). Pluto.

Spandler, K. (2018). Regional standards of membership and enlargement in the EU and ASEAN. *Asia Europe Journal, 16*(2), 183–198. https://doi.org/10.1007/s10308-018-0506-9

Stapel, S. (2022). *Regional organizations and democracy, human rights, and the rule of law: The African Union, Organization of American States, and the diffusion of institutions*. Palgrave.

Tarr, D. G. (2016). The Eurasian economic Union of Russia, Belarus, Kazakhstan, Armenia, and the Kyrgyz Republic: Can it succeed where its predecessor failed? *Eastern European Economics, 54*(1), 1–22. https://doi.org/10.1080/00128775.2015.1105672

Thomas, D. C. (2017). Beyond identity: Membership norms and regional organization. *European Journal of International Relations, 23*(1), 217–240. https://doi.org/10.1177/1354066116634175

TNS. (2017, July 14). *Qatar says withdrawal from PGCC on table*. Retrieved April 15, 2025, from https://advance.lexis.com/api/document?collection=news&id=urn:contentItem:5P0Y-KH91-DXMS-83MX-00000-00&context=1516831

TNS. (2018, December 20). *Russia: Lower house speaker says no reason for Russia to resume PACE Financing*. Retrieved April 15, 2025, from https://advance.lexis.com/api/document?collection=news&id=urn:contentItem:5V0P-XMY1-DXMS-840C-00000-00&context=1516831

TNS. (2019, January 25). *World: Possible 'Ruxit' seen as disaster among Council of Europe Leadership*. Retrieved April 15, 2025, from https://advance.lexis.com/api/document?collection=news&id=urn:contentItem:5V8C-SSV1-JB5P-J041-00000-00&context=1516831

Trenta, L. (2021). Death by reinterpretation: Dynamics of norm contestation and the US ban on assassination in the Reagan years. *Journal of Global Security Studies, 6*(4). https://doi.org/10.1093/jogss/ogab012

Umar, S., & Ghurab, S. (2023). The 2017 gulf crisis and changes in Qatar's economic landscape. In M. M. Rahman & A. Al-Azm (Eds.), *Social change in the gulf region: Multidisciplinary perspectives* (pp. 457–473). Springer.

van Kersbergen, K., & Verbeek, B. (2007). The politics of international norms: Subsidiarity and the imperfect competence regime of the European Union. *European Journal of International Relations, 13*(2), 217–238. https://doi.org/10.1177/1354066107076955

von Borzyskowski, I., & Vabulas, F. (2019). Credible commitments? Explaining IGO suspensions to sanction political backsliding. *International Studies Quarterly, 63*(1), 139–152. https://doi.org/10.1093/isq/sqy051

von Borzyskowski, I., & Vabulas, F. (2023). When do withdrawal threats achieve reform in international organizations? *Global Perspectives, 4*(1), 1–18. https://doi.org/10.1525/gp.2023.67826

Wiener, A. (2008). *The invisible constitution of politics: Contested norms and international encounters*. Cambridge University Press.

Wiener, A. (2014). *A theory of contestation*. Springer.

Wiener, A. (2017). A theory of contestation – concise summary of its argument and concepts. *Polity, 49*(1), 109–125. https://doi.org/10.1086/690100

Wiener, A. (2018). *Contestation and constitution of norms in global international relations*. Cambridge University Press.

Winston, C. (2018). Norm structure, diffusion, and evolution: A conceptual approach. *European Journal of International Relations, 24*(3), 638–661. https://doi.org/10.1177/1354066117720794

Wunderlich, C. (2020). *Rogue states as norm entrepreneurs: Black sheep or sheep in wolves' clothing?* Springer.

Wunderlich, C. (2022). Blinded by delight? *European Review of International Studies, 9*(3), 363–388. https://doi.org/10.1163/21967415-09030002

Zimmermann, L. (2017). *Global norms with a local face: Rule-of-law promotion and norm translation*. Cambridge University Press.

Chapter 4
'Soft Contestation' of the Responsibility to Protect? Assessing Canada and Sweden's Norm Diplomacy

Andrea Knapp and Jonas Fritzler

R2P: A Contested Norm

The formal endorsement of the Responsibility to Protect (R2P) by the United Nations (UN) General Assembly at the 2005 World Summit represented a substantial commitment aimed at refining the organisation's response to mass atrocities: genocide, crimes against humanity, war crimes and ethnic cleansing (Thakur, 2016). Based on its three-pillar structure, R2P locates the primary responsibility for the safety of populations in the realm of states—Pillar I. But whenever local authorities manifestly fail to manage a crisis, this duty is transferred to the international community: either by assisting the struggling state—Pillar II—or, under Pillar III, by directly taking over this protection role (Ban, 2009).

Despite the R2P's prominence in UN discourse, opposition voiced by critical states like China or Russia has turned the norm into a prominent example of norm contestation in the constructivist literature (Deitelhoff & Zimmermann, 2020; Hofmann & Zimmermann, 2019). But contestation, understood as instances when actors challenge a norm's 'meaning-in-use' (Wiener, 2014), is not performed by 'rogue states' alone (Wunderlich, 2020, p. 3). Instead, also more subtle contestation practices by actors within the Liberal International Order (LIO) must be assessed (Dian & Dugar, 2022). This chapter seeks to complement existing research by identifying patterns of 'soft contestation' in the attitudes of two states that have traditionally supported liberal humanitarian norms, namely Canada and Sweden. While the advocacy of both states had been decisive in pushing R2P onto the international

A. Knapp (✉)
University of Bologna, Bologna, Italy
e-mail: andrea.knapp2@unibo.it

J. Fritzler
University of Amsterdam, Amsterdam, The Netherlands
e-mail: j.fritzler@uva.nl

F. Lucenti et al. (eds.), *Contestation in Prism*, Norm Research in International Relations, https://doi.org/10.1007/978-3-031-83639-8_4

agenda in the early 2000s (Amnéus, 2006; Björkdahl, 2013; Stefan, 2021; Weiss, 2013), their norm engagement has decreased in the latest years (Nossal, 2013; O'Malley & den Dunnen, 2019; Rhoads & Welsh, 2019). How has the commitment of these former norm champions evolved over time and how does their shifting diplomacy affect the robustness of R2P?

This contribution models the temporal trajectories of these early norm advocates through the lens of agentic constructivism (Lantis, 2016; Sikkink, 2011). Analysing practices of applicatory contestation based on Deitelhoff and Zimmermann's (2020) framework, it finds that the binary role descriptions of 'norm entrepreneurship' versus 'norm antipreneurship' do not fully capture the complexity of the Canadian and Swedish positions (see also Lantis, 2025, Chap. 2). Instead, we combine Bloomfield's (2016) typology of norm actors with recent contributions on norm contestation and showcase how their increasingly multifaceted engagement lies on the spectrum between these two extremes. On the one hand, Canada and Sweden continue to pay lip service to their early norm-setting role, as evidenced by their membership in relevant R2P networks or the affirmative votes on draft resolutions referring to the norm. On the other hand, they have evolved into 'competitor entrepreneurs' that engage in 'soft contestation'. Despite general support, both habitually avoid R2P mentions and substitute its reference with other norms from the broader protection cluster—e.g., accountability or Women, Peace, and Security (WPS).

While recent literature has highlighted that pragmatism facilitates short-term implementation by sidestepping political baggage (Mennecke, 2019; Ralph, 2017), such a repositioning can also be understood as a form of applicatory contestation. This practice is characterised by the decision of *not* prioritising or facilitating the implementation of the norm in question, while at the same time referring to its conceptual underpinnings instead of its concrete execution (Stimmer & Wisken, 2019; True & Wiener, 2019). Our analysis suggests that the Swedish and Canadian repositioning can ultimately undermine the norm in the long term, as it diverts attention from the distinct connotation that only exists for R2P in the wider protection cluster: the subsidiary international responsibility to prevent or respond to mass atrocities. This critical constructivist framework allows for a focus on the actors' influence on norms, even in situations where their engagement is more subtle and does not explicitly challenge its meaning.

The chapter is structured as follows. First, we situate the analysis within the scholarship on agentic constructivism and norm contestation. Second, the empirical section traces the Swedish and Canadian positions vis-à-vis the R2P norm cluster. While existing studies have mainly focused on their agency during the norm's emergence, we cover the extended period between 2000 and 2022 to account for temporal shifts alongside the norm's development. Finally, the consequences of this strategic repositioning are assessed together with the implications of these findings in the concluding section.

Contestation by Whom: Entrepreneurs, Antipreneurs, and In-Between

Theories of norm contestation have gained increasing traction in the constructivist literature over the past decade (see Orchard & Wiener, 2024; Wunderlich et al., 2025, Chap. 1). Challenging positivist assumptions of unidirectional and progressive norm development from first-wave scholarship, this research strand spotlights the processes and outcomes of contestation on international norms (Orchard & Wiener, 2024; Sandholtz & Stiles, 2009; Wiener, 2009, 2014). We draw on Deitelhoff and Zimmermann's (2020) distinction between applicatory contestation, which challenges a norm's appropriateness in a specific case, and validity contestation, which challenges its legitimacy. These conceptions allow us to reckon with the dual effect of these practices. Most scholars argue that while going against a norm's validity always weakens its robustness, challenging a norm's application can interactively stabilise its meaning and scope (Badescu & Weiss, 2010; Deitelhoff, 2019; Deitelhoff & Zimmermann, 2020; Wiener & Puetter, 2009). A parallel consensus also exists regarding the functioning of 'norm clusters', as defined by Lantis and Wunderlich (2018, p. 570). Embeddedness in these structures is believed to benefit a norm's resiliency against contestation (Wiener, 2014, p. 18; Winston, 2018). In line with the scope of this volume, this chapter calls into question the consistently positive effect of applicatory contestation particularly in norm clusters. Specifically, it probes whether disagreement over a norm's implementation undermines the robustness of both the individual norm and the entire cluster when this contestation emanates from key stakeholders in the respective normative order: its earliest supporters.

Shifting the focus from the contestation practice to the contesting agent, our analysis draws on the two ideal actor roles advanced by agentic constructivism (Lantis, 2016; Sikkink, 2011). On the one hand, the term 'norm entrepreneurs' is used to characterise actors that seek to advance normative change or implementation (Finnemore & Sikkink, 1998). These norm-makers (Checkel, 1999) or norm-shapers (Badescu & Weiss, 2010; Prantl & Nakano, 2011) pin topics on the international agenda, commit themselves to a norm's development, identify institutional homes, and solicit peer support (Björkdahl, 2002, 2008; Elgström, 2000; Finnemore & Sikkink, 1998). By modelling behaviour, entrepreneurs also play decisive roles in creating expectations about appropriate implementation behaviour or linking norm language to concrete cases. On the other hand, actors who openly obstruct the establishment, advancement, or implementation of norms through resistance (Carpenter, 2014) or sabotage (Prantl & Nakano, 2011; Schneiker, 2021) are labelled as 'norm antipreneurs'.[1] These actors are typically portrayed as primary agents of contestation (Payne, 2001; Wiener, 2009, 2014). Despite the clarity offered

[1] Although some scholars distinguish norm antipreneurs from saboteurs based on the stages of the norm life cycle, we do not make this distinction for the purposes of this chapter. Both actor roles are categorised as strong norm opponents. Norm antipreneurs resist norm change at emergence

by the 'entrepreneur-antipreneur dichotomy', this characterisation suffers from three limitations that obfuscate the empirical operationalisation of the model. First, Bloomfield (2016, p. 331) criticises this dichotomy, arguing that 'entrepreneurs treated as 'pure changers' and antipreneurs characterised as 'implacable resisters' should be seen as ideal types' that hardly materialise empirically. Second, the theory suggests that role assignment is fixed. This tends to discourage research on how actors may shift their position and adjust their norm engagement over time. Third, the impact of varying degrees of contestation on norm robustness is not comprehensively theorised within this actorness framework. Summing up, agentic constructivism suffers from a 'lack of theoretically founded and systematic comparison of alleged norm antipreneurs and norm entrepreneurs' that has ultimately hampered its application in research on norm contestation (Wunderlich, 2020, p. 76).

Soft Contestation on a Continuum

To meaningfully advance the current understanding of R2P, the analytical framework of this chapter complements the agentic constructivist framework with contributions on norm contestation. Importantly, it challenges the absoluteness of the dichotomous actorness distribution and borrows two intermediate roles from Bloomfield (2016, pp. 330–331): competitor entrepreneurs, which sit close to entrepreneurs and 'agree on the need for change but differ on the exact scope and content', and 'creative resisters', which resemble antipreneurs but 'are forced by circumstance or because they have been partially persuaded [...] that some minimal change is acceptable'. This structural adjustment breaks the binary logics of traditional agentic constructivism but has to date not been explicitly linked to the literature concerning the scope and constancy of contestation. We aim to close this gap, building on an original conceptual framework based on the actor roles advanced by Bloomfield (2016), which we specify in Table 4.1. These intermediate roles are flexible over time, as well as account for pragmatic attitudes combined with subtle degrees of contestation and exploitation of norm ambiguity. This perspective offers an innovative lens to link the agents of applicatory contestation to research on norm robustness. As we show in our empirical analysis, the focus on 'soft applicatory contestation' offers a more realistic description of the complexity of actors' roles and the consequences of their actions compared to dichotomous role descriptions.

This visualisation suggests that while 'competitor entrepreneurs'—rather positive—and 'creative resisters'—rather negative—clearly differ in the direction of their norm commitment, they engage in remarkably similar forms of diplomacy in practice. We contend that this nuanced description of norm engagement is

stage. Contrarily, norm saboteurs oppose norms in later phases, when they are already widely accepted, by undermining their implementation (see Bloomfield, 2016; Schneiker, 2021).

Table 4.1 Analytical framework

Role	Norm attitude	Contestation degree	Norm ambiguity
Norm entrepreneur	Positive	No contestation	No ambiguity
Competitor entrepreneur	Pragmatic positive	Soft applicatory contestation aimed at consensus-building, but no validity contestation	Exploit ambiguity
Creative resisters	Pragmatic negative	Soft applicatory contestation based on a more critical stance, but support for validity	Exploit ambiguity
Norm antipreneur/ norm saboteurs	Negative	Hard contestation of validity and application	No ambiguity

particularly relevant when norms contain vague policy prescriptions and are embedded in a norm cluster.

Which exact norms are understood to make up a said cluster depends on the actors' framing (Staunton & Ralph, 2020, p. 663) and is socially constructed through discourse. In the case of R2P, two prevailing logics exist. An internal R2P cluster is commonly represented by the norm's three pillars that incrementally scale existing responsibilities in the face of mass atrocities (Sandholtz, 2019; Winston, 2018). More broadly, R2P can be understood as embedded in a cluster of protection norms that includes agendas such as accountability, the Protection of Civilians (PoC) and WPS.[2] When studying how actors engage with this complex R2P norm cluster, the multifaceted norm engagement of competitor entrepreneurs and creative resisters manifests on three dimensions that differ from the two traditional actor roles.

First, there is a divergence in actors' attitudes towards norms. Both competitor entrepreneurs and creative resisters do not engage in norm development with the same consistency or intensity as norm entrepreneurs—only positive—and antipreneurs—only negative. Instead, these actors rely on pragmatism to prioritise the practical aspects of a norm and secure its implementation through utilitarian compromises that focus only on those aspects that best serve their cause. As a result of this hands-on normative engagement, their positions tend to fluctuate more. Both types of actors support norm development when it benefits their cause. Accordingly, this framework defies traditional logics of stability in role allocation. Just as norms are constantly reshaped through 'meaning-in-use' (Wiener, 2009, p. 176), actor roles are not necessarily embodied consistently throughout the norm life cycle and

[2] See also Lucenti et al. (2025, Chap. 5). In line with Fehl's (2018) and Mills' (2015, p. 14, pp. 23–24) definition, we situate R2P within what we define as a 'humanitarian cluster'. This consists of norms that are linked by their orientation and scope to the idea that the sovereignty of the state is dependent on its responsibility. In addition to R2P, it includes the Responsibility to Prosecute, the Protection of Civilians, Women, Peace and Security, and the prohibition of genocide, war crimes and crimes against humanity. See also Huelss (2025, Chap. 6), who refers to the 'protection of civilians legal norm cluster', which also comprises International Humanitarian Law and International Human Rights Law.

may shift over time. This calls for the adoption of a longitudinal and dynamic perspective that combines agentic constructivism with studies on norm contestation to account for actors' positional changes.

Second, the intermediate roles can be distinguished based on the degree of contestation that they exercise. In fact, their commitment vis-à-vis a norm takes on more elusive forms compared to players located on the extremities of the scale. Both competitor entrepreneurs and creative resisters are believed to execute what recent literature terms 'soft contestation' (Johansson-Nogués et al., 2020, p. 10). Instead of explicitly sustaining—like entrepreneurs—or opposing—like antipreneurs—norm development, they advocate for more subtle forms of contestation that mainly involve the applicatory dimension. Actors may support a norm in general terms and refer to its conceptual underpinning, while at the same time not prioritising its advancement and implementation in concrete terms. For instance, competitor entrepreneurs may substitute norms with references to less contentious adjacent agendas—e.g., substituting R2P with accountability. Conversely, creative resisters may proactively reformulate norm alternatives that align more closely with their preferences—e.g., Brazil's introduction of the 'Responsibility While Protecting' (Kenkel & Stefan, 2016). The implications of these softer forms of contestation on norm robustness have to date remained under-theorised. Existing scholarship has analysed the consequences of the diplomatic actions of the strongest norm proponents and opponents, while overlooking these intermediate roles.

Third, both intermediate actors exploit a norm's ambiguity as a subtle form of engagement to facilitate cooperation (Bode & Karlsrud, 2019; Hansen, 2016; Sandholtz, 2019) but simultaneously hamper normative development (Widmaier & Glanville, 2015). Actors cherry-pick distinct elements from the narrower R2P cluster and the broader protection cluster it is embedded in, while at the same time neglecting or substituting incovenient norm elements (Wiener, 2014, p. 49). Competitor entrepreneurs may thus concentrate on widely accepted elements to foster consensus—e.g., around Pillar I of R2P—while creative resisters may primarily emphasise the contentious aspects of a norm as a justification to avoid compliance—e.g., concerning Pillar III.

Whereas some scholars have emphasised the positive effects of such pragmatic strategies, which help to sidestep political obstacles and ensure practical implementation (Mennecke, 2019; Ralph, 2017), this chapter centres also on negative consequences of such strategies. Pragmatic implementation does not necessarily occur on the terms and to the extent envisioned by norm entrepreneurs, which influences the norm's scope and long-term robustness. Forms of soft contestation do not automatically signal concern about a norm's future viability (Percy & Sandholtz, 2022), but international norms are shaped through repeated enactment (Gifkins, 2016; Krook & True, 2012; Welsh, 2019; Wiener, 2014). In light of these observations, the difference between discursive and behavioural contestation is analytically useful. Whereas hard contestation consists of open norm resistance, consistent with Stimmer and Wisken's (2019, p. 533) observations on behavioural contestation, namely, concerning actions that undermine a norm's implementation, we expect strategies of soft contestation in applicatory discourses to be 'self-reinforcing and damaging [to] the norm'. The continual avoidance or redefinition of the norm terminology can undermine its long-term viability, eroding its overall acceptance and legitimacy (Clark et al., 2018; Krook & True, 2012). We consider these processes to be particularly consequential for norm robustness when former norm entrepreneurs from within the LIO contest a norm's application (Zimmermann et al., 2024, p. 258). Norm life cycles hence need to be analysed in conjunction with the shifting commitments of their key stakeholders.

A Multi-source Methodological Approach

In our analysis, we identify patterns in Canada and Sweden's commitment to R2P since 2000 both in quantitative—i.e., the frequency of mentions when debating mass atrocity cases—and qualitative terms—i.e., the sentiment and contexts in which R2P is used. We therefore recognise instances of contestation when actors 'discursively express disapproval of norms' or their individual segments (Wiener, 2014, p. 1). These strategies can take both explicit and implicit forms, which are identified by evaluating a state's position over time or comparing its stance to other peers from within the LIO. Beyond mere rhetorical commitment, using the R2P labels is significant as '[t]he negotiated wording of resolutions shapes future deliberations' (Gifkins, 2016, pp. 150–151). Subtle acts of neglect or substitution 'can express important information on how a norm is […] contested' (Gilgan, 2021, p. 1463). In doing so, we use a comprehensive set of data sources to assess the evolving roles of Sweden and Canada in relation to the R2P norm. We draw on a pool of 35 semi-structured expert interviews conducted between 2021 and 2022. Combining both purposive and snowball sampling (Tansey, 2007, p. 770), interviewees included diplomats from permanent missions to the UN, personnel from Non-Governmental Organisations (NGOs) and officials from foreign ministries. Personal information was anonymised to maintain confidentiality. In addition, we triangulate our findings with data from the websites of the Dag Hammarskjöld Library and the Global Centre for the Responsibility to Protect (GCR2P). This includes resolutions, speeches, and reports from various UN fora as well as voting patterns and attendance records from thematic events. We believe that different types of data contain distinct nuances of insight. For instance, high-level speeches reveal the states' policy priorities (Baturo et al., 2017; Kentikelenis & Voeten, 2021), while interviews (see Table 4.2) provide insight into the diplomats' commitment to R2P initiatives (Tansey, 2007).

Furthermore, we assess the consequence of the Canadian and Swedish repositioning on the R2P's robustness, terms of acceptance, and compliance (Deitelhoff & Zimmermann, 2020, p. 53). We argue that the two states' partial disregard of R2P negatively affected its robustness if (1) it caused a detrimental shift in the norm's narrative, (2) it resulted in lower levels of international support, (3) it weakened the norm's influence on shaping policies and practices, or (4) the failure to invoke the R2P label ultimately hindered civilian protection on the ground. This effect is

Table 4.2 List of interviews cited in this chapter

#	Position	Date
1.	Diplomat/bureaucrat	19/10/2021
2.	NGO/think tank practitioner	10/3/2022
3.	Diplomat/bureaucrat	26/4/2022
4.	Diplomat/bureaucrat	9/5/2022
5.	Diplomat/bureaucrat	13/5/2022
6.	Diplomat/bureaucrat	2/6/2022
7.	Diplomat/bureaucrat	14/6/2022
8.	NGO/think tank practitioner	29/11/2022

investigated both for the individual norm and the wider protection cluster. At the same time, the role of norm entrepreneurs should not be overestimated. The withdrawal of two actors alone may have very limited immediate and measurable effects on the international arena. We argue rather that practices of subtle neglect by former key proponents may result in long-term substitution. In the following sections, after outlining the background of Canada and Sweden as soft contesters, we examine their engagement with the R2P norm individually and then look for common trends. As the early years of R2P norm entrepreneurship have been extensively studied, our focus is on the later stages of repositioning.

Background: Canada and Sweden as Soft Contesters

While R2P has been referenced by many different actors in relation to more than a dozen humanitarian crises in Security Council (UNSC) and General Assembly (UNGA) resolutions, its implementation remains a highly contentious issue in UN diplomacy. The norm's appropriateness has been extensively challenged not only by Russian and Chinese delegates (Burai, 2016; Evans, 2009; Welsh, 2021), but also by 'rogue states' (Wunderlich, 2020, p. 3) from the Global South, like Venezuela, North Korea, and Sudan. As a result, existing research on R2P contestation has focused on these states based on a two-fold rationale. On the one hand, because China and Russia's permanent Council seats come with veto power, they wield decisive weight in shaping the international agenda and thereby influencing the R2P development. On the other hand, contestation by 'rogue states' clearly exceeds the intensity of criticism voiced by Western representatives. Instead, states from within the LIO enjoy the reputation of being 'honest brokers', which gives them little incentive to contest liberal norms (Garris, 1973, p. 201, cited in Wunderlich, 2020).

By focusing on the trajectories of Canada and Sweden's R2P soft contestation, we critically assess this narrative. Regarding the former argument, a burgeoning literature showcases how elected Council members (Gifkins, 2021; Oksamytna, 2023) and small states/middle powers engaged in 'niche diplomacy' (Björkdahl, 2013; Fritzler, 2023; Shawki, 2008; Taulbee, 2017) can mould UN decisions.

Regarding the latter point, the Canadian and Swedish implicit forms of criticism of R2P undoubtedly do not reach the blunt levels voiced by states from outside the LIO. But while they may not refute the norm altogether and thus do not become antipreneurs, subtle practices of contestation and shifting (dis)engagement of former norm supporters can nonetheless affect the norm's robustness.

Canada and Sweden serve as compelling cases due to their longstanding advocacy for human rights norms in the international arena (Petrasek, 2019). Both belong to a group of nations that are 'fairly small, fairly wealthy, democratic and all eager to spread their moral capital' (de Carvalho & Neumann, 2014, p. 13). The significant role of the two states in shaping the R2P development through their commission diplomacy (Evans, 2013; Evans & Sahnoun, 2001) and personal investment of high-level politicians (Bergman-Rosamond, 2012, p. 65; Björkdahl, 2013; Chapnick, 2020; Smith & Ajadi, 2020) is extensively theorised in the literature. Nevertheless, the complex evolution of their commitment to R2P after 2005 is only partially acknowledged. Existing studies provide some episodic evidence of change, for instance by focusing on the Canadian government's disregard of R2P in the Libya intervention (Nossal, 2013; Stefan, 2021) and Sweden's prioritisation of WPS (Ekengren & Möller, 2021; O'Malley & den Dunnen, 2019). But the long-term trajectories and implications of this partial disregard for R2P as well as the effect on the broader norm cluster have been overlooked.

Analysis and Results: Canada and Sweden's Changing Role

Canada: Sudden Shift from Entrepreneur to Competitor Entrepreneur

As Evans (2016, p. 5) notes, '[i]f it was not for Canada, we would not have the Responsibility to Protect'. The country's active engagement in building R2P can be seen as a paradigmatic example of norm entrepreneurship, which ultimately paved the way for the norm's adoption by the UNGA in 2005 (Stefan, 2021). The human security agenda had already been a cornerstone during Canada's campaign for an elected Council seat in 1999–2000 (Oksamytna, 2023), but these commitments became even more concrete when Ottawa answered the request of the then-UN Secretary-General Kofi Annan to develop strategies to reconcile national sovereignty with the duty to protect populations from risks of atrocity crimes. As a direct response, the Canadian government established and financed the International Commission on Intervention and State Sovereignty (ICISS) in 2000. The commissioner's report in 2001 marked a significant shift in the international narrative from a *right* to a *responsibility* to protect populations, while also offering criteria for just intervention and proposing a prevention toolkit against atrocity crimes (ICISS, 2001).

Beyond commission diplomacy, Canada's explicit focus on R2P during this early phase was routinely reiterated in speeches delivered at the General Assembly

(Chrétien in UNGA, 2003a; Graham in UNGA, 2002; Harper in UNGA, 2006a; Martin in UNGA, 2004b, 2005; Pettigrew in UNGA, 2006b). In advancing the normative agenda, Canadian diplomats strategically avoided direct links between human protection and military intervention. Instead, they built on established formulas of civilian immunity that were more conducive to consensus building (Oksamytna, 2023). In their high-level speeches, it was particularly the inferences drawn to country cases that critically reinforced the norm. For instance, Canadian delegates were among the first to denounce mass atrocities in Darfur (Martin in UNGA, 2004b, 2005). Combined with habitual norm repetition, this norm application was central to maintaining the R2P's momentum and fulfilling Canada's entrepreneurial role in promoting implementation (Gifkins, 2016; Neumann, 2007). Canada's pride in its early norm leadership is evident in the words of former Prime Minister Paul Martin, who stated: 'We are proud that R2P has Canadian lineage' (Martin in UNGA, 2005).

Despite this initial enthusiasm, Canada's engagement with R2P experienced a notable shift after 2006. The driving force behind this break can be primarily found in the country's domestic political developments. Following the Liberal Party's defeat in the 2006 national election, the Conservative government redirected much of its diplomatic resources away from international human rights promotion (Fisher & Stefan, 2018). As one interviewee pointed out, '[t]he conservative government had [...] different foreign policy priorities and objectives. And those [...] liberally promoted ideas weren't among those priorities' (Interview 1, Table 4.2). This shift is most evident at the discursive level, as Canadian representatives ceased explicitly referring to R2P in high-level General Debate speeches after 2006. Departing from the language originally championed by the Liberal Party (Duncan in Adams, 2015), 'shortly after the change of government [...], Canadian ambassadors received instructions from Ottawa to no longer use the terms "international responsibility to protect", "human security" and "good governance" publicly' (Beck, 2015). This backlash peaked when Ottawa refrained from invoking R2P in the context of the 2011 NATO-led intervention in Libya, which had been internationally framed as an R2P scenario (Nossal, 2013; Rhoads & Welsh, 2019). Instead, the Canadian foreign minister justified the enforcement of the no-fly zone with the concept of 'enlightened sovereignty' (Baird in UNGA, 2011b). This narrative sharply contrasts with the R2P framing of other norm-supporting peers, like Sweden (Reinfeld in UNGA, 2011a), and can be classified as a clear instance of applicatory contestation.

At the same time, Canada's commitment to the norm has remained more congruous in behavioural terms. For example, military contributions to the Libyan mission amounted to a deployment of 655 personnel at its peak (Government of Canada, 2014). Additionally, Ottawa played a central role in establishing the Group of Friends of the R2P—a network that supports the norm at the UN—and the GCR2P in 2008 (Interview 1, Table 4.2). This means that while Canada has moved away from its entrepreneurship, these actions do not represent a case of open contestation. A discrepancy emerges between the R2P neglect in public statements and implicit government action in support of associated initiatives. Contrary to the applicatory dimension, the validity of R2P has indeed remained undisputed. This represents a diplomatic strategy of soft applicatory contestation exercised by competitor entrepreneurs. Canada's position became pragmatic and ambiguous: the government did not openly question R2P narratives but neglected them, while at the same time some of its behaviour still aligned with the norm.

Canada's mixed record persisted even after the election victory of the Liberal Party in 2015. With Justin Trudeau as prime minister, Canada remained generally supportive of norm-related initiatives. This is illustrated by the uniformly affirmative votes on R2P resolutions at the UNGA, but also by the continued membership in the Group of Friends and the Atrocity Prevention Network. Additionally, Ottawa joined the capital-based R2P Focal Points network in 2017 after years of conspicuous absence (GCR2P, 2020). Yet, Canada never picked up its leadership position again and its support faded from the international spotlight. As one interviewee put: 'just because [Canada] helped establish something, does that mean [they] need to continue leading on it?' (Interview 1, Table 4.2). In this regard, the country's absence from the core group of states advocating for the norm's application across countries has been striking (Interviews 1, 6, 7, Table 4.2).

In the discursive realm, the Canadian delegates' avoidance of the R2P label in their high-level foreign policy discourses is indicative of this deliberate shift. With a few striking exceptions, such as Trudeau's framing of Syria as an R2P case in 2016 (Office of the Canadian Prime Minister, 2016), references to R2P have mainly been replaced by adjacent norms from the wider protection cluster. Specifically, discussions on atrocity crimes are often embedded in the language of accountability. This can be observed in the condemnation of violence against the Rohingya in Myanmar (Joly in UNGA, 2022) or when 'naming and shaming' human rights violations in China (Interview 8, Table 4.2). Canada has also partnered with the Dutch government to hold the Syrian government accountable for its atrocity crimes without explicitly framing the proceeding under R2P (Government of Canada, 2021). This substitution seems to represent a favourable diplomatic strategy in highly politicised contexts. According to one interviewee 'co-sponsor[ing] an event […] on R2P and the Uighurs' is regarded as 'politically indigestible', whereas organising thematic events on the norm is perceived as less salient (Interview 7, Table 4.2). Simultaneously, Ottawa's commitment to WPS has intensified and is now identified as the top foreign policy priority in a recent foreign minister mandate letter (Office of the Prime Minister of Canada, 2021). No equivalent level of commitment exists for R2P. The reference to other norms appears to fit our description of a pragmatic stance to 'getting mass atrocity prevention done' without a fixation on the R2P label, despite continuing to support the broader protection cluster. Thus, we observe a continuation of ambivalence vis-à-vis R2P, neglecting formerly prioritised R2P language combined with some pragmatic discursive engagement and behaviour in support of the norm.

Sweden: A Gradual Process Towards Competitor Entrepreneurship

Although not as prominent as Canada, Sweden has also played a critical role in bringing R2P to the forefront of the international agenda (Amnéus, 2006; Björkdahl, 2013). Sweden's government-sponsored report on lessons learned from Kosovo contributed to a discursive shift towards the concept of human security (Evans & Sahnoun, 2001). To help implement this new conception of security, the state made important contributions to intergovernmental discussions on combating mass atrocities through the organisation of the Stockholm International Forum on the Prevention of Genocide in 2004 (Amnéus, 2006). In line with its entrepreneurial role, Stockholm consistently expressed support in General Debate speeches during the emergence phase of R2P. Notably, delegates referred to the R2P norm every year between 2003 and 2011 (for instance, Lindh in UNGA, 2000; Karlsson in UNGA, 2003b; Persson in UNGA, 2004a; Lidén in UNGA, 2008; Grunditz in UNGA, 2010). Sweden was at the forefront when it came to supporting the implementation of R2P in concrete cases of mass atrocities, although such a direct link was seen as more controversial than general expressions of support in (in)formal settings. It is therefore easier to agree on general R2P statements than to condemn specific country situations using R2P language (Interview 3, Table 4.2). For example, the Swedish representative stressed the need to implement R2P during a General Assembly debate on Darfur in 2006 by saying:

> We need to live up to [...] the responsibility to protect [...]. The Security Council must show the will to act when civilian populations are threatened by the most serious crimes (Lidén in UNGA, 2006c).

Sweden's engagement with R2P underwent a shift with the Libyan civil war, marking a more ambiguous stance that moved away from norm entrepreneurship. Although the government had actively endorsed the 2011 NATO-led intervention, which had received vast support from the national parliament (Doeser, 2014), Sweden's commitment to R2P became less explicit following the mission's termination. This mixed diplomatic track record aligns with the role description of competitor entrepreneurs and their practices of soft contestation. On the one hand, Sweden continued to support the norm through joint—e.g., on behalf of the Nordic countries or the European Union—or individual statements, while also backing R2P resolutions with affirmative votes at the Assembly. During Sweden's Council term (2017–2018), 22 resolutions were adopted with an explicit reference to R2P, and Sweden voted in favour of all of them. Furthermore, as a co-penholder of several resolutions (e.g., UNSC, 2018a, 2018b, 2018d), Sweden demonstrated comfort with including the associated terminology in official documents.

On the other hand, high-level commitment to R2P became less explicit. As one interviewee noted, Stockholm has generally 'been supportive of [R2P]' but no longer sees it as its top priority (Interview 5, Table 4.2). Delegates have instead focused on other policy areas during the most recent Council term, particularly its feminist foreign policy framework (Ekengren & Möller, 2021; Olsson et al., 2021). Moreover, R2P has gradually lost its salience in speeches. When dealing with country cases involving mass atrocity risks, 'accountability is [Sweden's] guiding star' (Interview 5, Table 4.2). Violence in Syria, Myanmar, or South Sudan has been condemned by emphasising the importance of juridical accountability to end impunity (Bildt in UNGA, 2012; Reinfeld in UNGA, 2013; Skoog in UNGA, 2018; Skoog in UNSC, 2018c). This frame aids Sweden to circumvent the political disagreement associated with R2P's Pillar III, while still successfully drawing international attention to critical humanitarian environments. A similar diplomatic approach is reflected also in Sweden's recent commitment to establishing two Fact-Finding Missions to Syria and Myanmar as well as the attempted referral of the Bashir Al-Assad regime to the International Criminal Court (Interview 5, Table 4.2). While these initiatives actively contribute to the prevention and mitigation of mass atrocities, clearly falling into the applicatory scope of the agenda, they are 'just [...] not always labelled as R2P' (Interview 5. See also Interview 2, Table 4.2).

The Effects of Soft Contestation by Canada and Sweden

Our findings reveal a common trend in Canada and Sweden's R2P commitment, albeit at different times: despite their initial involvement in norm-making and norm-shaping, both countries have progressively moved away from their entrepreneurial leadership in recent years. This mixed stance qualifies them as competitor entrepreneurs. Although general support on the behavioural level, including affirmative votes or participation in R2P-related events, remains strong, both states have become increasingly reluctant to employ R2P language in high-level discourses. This is particularly prominent on the applicatory dimension, where the mention of the contested agenda hinders implementation of concrete measures for mass atrocity prevention. By exploiting the ambiguity surrounding R2P, both countries prioritise pragmatic implementation and cherry-pick elements from the norm cluster that have a high potential of avoiding political disagreements at the UN. As a result, they opt for adjoining norms such as accountability or WPS to frame conflicts involving mass atrocities. We term this a form of 'soft contestation'. The Canadian and Swedish diplomatic repositioning is particularly interesting given their significant status in the R2P development due to the earlier entrepreneurship. The activities of norm proponents play a crucial role in shaping the future trajectories of support, as these norm champions are expected to continuously reiterate its principles and identify cases of appropriate application (Gifkins, 2016; Jacob, 2021; Neumann, 2007). Both Canada and Sweden have failed to satisfy this expectation. But how has soft contestation influenced the robustness of the R2P and the wider protection cluster?

On the one hand, it can reasonably be argued that this partial retreat had a positive effect on the development of R2P. Importantly, the entrepreneurial void in the international arena has been filled by other states such as Denmark, Croatia, Ghana, and Australia. This has geographically widened the related leadership. Furthermore, references to R2P in official UNSC or UNGA resolutions have not significantly decreased in their frequency (GCR2P, 2023). In line with a critical constructivist understanding (Percy & Sandholtz, 2022), this suggests that R2P has not withered away in response to the withdrawal of these two entrepreneurs. Instead, the norm keeps evolving. Despite the shifts in their language, moreover, mass atrocity prevention and mitigation continue to be prioritised by both Canada and Sweden on a more behavioural level. This means that the robustness of the wider protection norm cluster does not seem to have suffered from this diplomatic repositioning. As the empirical section has showed, references to norms like WPS and accountability as a substitution strategy are flourishing.

Paradoxically, this approach may wield pragmatic benefits because ‘sometimes a less explicit approach to R2P may result in more R2P’ (Mennecke, 2019, p. 44). As the language of R2P remains politically charged and difficult to label at multilateral fora, insisting on the inclusion of the norm’s terminology in a mandate may actually hinder the effective protection of populations from mass atrocities on the ground. To circumvent such difficulties, convenient ‘[o]missions and modulations occur’ (Bellamy & Dunne, 2016, p. 12). Norms within the same cluster are straightforward venues for such tendency. By emphasising consensus-building elements such as the vulnerable position of women, states can concretely advance R2P objectives without any direct norm mention. Drawing on this pragmatic perspective, we agree that the practical implementation of protection measures enhancing the safety of people must be prioritised regardless of their specific terminology. How these measures are framed, contrarily, should only be a secondary concern. This perspective is echoed by one interviewee:

> [T]hese R2P champions [...] are very much at the forefront and would support every action at the UN taken aimed at preventing [mass atrocities]. Only focusing on R2P and their references, so supporting only the narrow view of R2P, would miss out a lot on what they are doing (Interview 8, Table 4.2).

On the other hand, the critical constructivist perspective adopted in this chapter evinces the potential negative consequences of a sustained soft contestation. The continual omission of references to R2P in resolutions and speeches may lead to a questioning of its relevance and potentially narrow ‘applicatory scope’ (Panke & Petersohn, 2016; Pattison, 2021). As entrepreneurs are expected to be the most vocal and decisive supporters, R2P risks eventually being permanently marginalised or perceived as too politicised if even generally supportive states from within the LIO have stopped their explicit referrals. We have not found any indications of such a tendency at present, but the risk remains relevant for the future. Moreover, replacing R2P with adjacent norms risks omitting contextual details that signal the gravity of a conflict. As one interviewee summarises:

> Actions that [align] with R2P but are not labelled as such represent a missed opportunity. References to R2P set the tone [and] shows that mass atrocities are taking place (Interview 4, Table 4.2).

Although both accountability and WPS belong to the same norm cluster aimed at protecting individuals in conflict situations, the substitution of R2P with these latter references should not be interpreted as simple 'borrowing and sharing' from related agendas traditionally pursued by norm entrepreneurs (Hofmann & Suthanthiraraj, 2019). Other agendas fail to capture two of the most politicised yet innovative aspects of R2P: the recognition that mass atrocities occur in a specific context and the responsibility of the international community to take action in the event of domestic failures to protect populations from atrocity risks (Pillar III). Other norms within the cluster do therefore not fully cover the scope of R2P, which risks hollowing out if references continue to be avoided for pragmatic reasons. As a result, decision-making on civilian protection significantly varies according to the norm chosen for its framing.

Conclusion

This chapter has examined Canada and Sweden's evolving commitment to the Responsibility to Protect since 2000. In both cases, there is evidence of a shift from norm entrepreneurship towards competitor entrepreneurship, which involves an increased reliance on practices of soft contestation through neglect and substitution over time. This pragmatic approach can be conducive to policy implementation in a short-term perspective, and in some situations, it may strengthen the norms that are referenced as substitutes to R2P, such as WPS or PoC. However, this practice also undermines critical parts of the norm cluster and contributes to applicatory contestation by changing the meaning-in-use of R2P. As a result, it is critically associated with the norm's robustness and scope. Considering Canada and Sweden as agents contributing to the reframing or—partial—substitution of R2P with other norms from the protection cluster enriches our understanding of the diverse effects of these forms of diplomacy executed by the former norm entrepreneurs. We do not observe a negative effect on the entire protection cluster, but only on the R2P norm within it.

More generally, we make three theoretical contributions to broader norm research. First, zooming into Canada and Sweden's engagement with R2P highlights a type of contestation that is of a different quality than other forms analysed in the related literature: a subtle type of contestation from within the LIO that takes on a pragmatic stance, which is primarily expressed through substitution and neglect rather than open criticism. This also diverges from research on proactive norm engagement, for instance through Brazil's Responsibility While Protecting initiative (Kenkel & Stefan, 2016), as no alternative norm proposals are elaborated in this process. As this form of contestation is overlooked, more research on this subtle form of contestation is needed to explicate its effect on norm robustness comprehensively. Second, the shifting R2P engagement of Canada and Sweden illustrates the existing flexibility of the norm actor role assignment. Actors can move along the spectrum between entrepreneurship and antipreneurship, which means that they can critically reassess their past engagement and actively seek different paths. Our findings contribute to a better empirical understanding of Bloomfield's (2016) typology of actorness and add tangible criteria for role membership. As both Canada and

Sweden have continued to pay lip service to their earlier norm commitment, although at a more implicit level, this research hints that actors are unlikely to move far from their initial role. While entrepreneurs may move towards competitor entrepreneurship over time, we argue that these actors could eventually become norm antipreneurs only in exceptional cases of significant changes in domestic politics. Finally, by analysing these forms of soft contestation executed by former norm entrepreneurs, we also contribute to this volume's overall objective of calling into question the positive effects of norm contestation. Although unfolding slowly and only in the long term, these subtle processes of substitution and neglect nonetheless affect the applicatory scope and robustness of R2P. This calls for further research on the changing trajectories of soft contestation within the LIO and on norm substitution within a cluster. More broadly, our findings offer valuable insight for practitioners, especially concerning the long-term effects of diplomacy.

References

Adams, S. (2015, May 8). *The Responsibility to Protect: 10 years on*. Retrieved June 5, 2024, from https://opencanada.org/the-responsibility-to-protect-10-years-on/

Amnéus, D. (2006). Swedish state practice 2004–5: The responsibility to protect. *Nordic Journal of International Law, 75*(2), 311–315. https://doi.org/10.1163/157181006778666597

Badescu, C. G., & Weiss, T. G. (2010). Misrepresenting R2P and advancing norms: An alternative spiral? *International Studies Perspectives, 11*(4), 354–374. https://doi.org/10.1111/j.1528-3585.2010.00412.x

Ban, K. (2009). *Implementing the responsibility to protect*. Report of the Secretary-General (A/63/677).

Baturo, A., Dasandi, N., & Mikhaylov, S. J. (2017). Understanding state preferences with text as data: Introducing the UN general debate corpus. *Research & Politics, 4*(2), 1–9. https://doi.org/10.1177/2053168017712821

Beck, C. (2015, October 5). *From Founding father to backslider: Canada and the R2P*. Retrieved June 5, 2024, from https://us.boell.org/en/2015/10/05/founding-father-backslider-canada-and-r2p

Bellamy, A. J., & Dunne, T. (Eds.). (2016). *The Oxford handbook of the responsibility to protect*. Oxford University Press.

Bergman-Rosamond, A. (2012). The cosmopolitan—Communitarian divide and the Swedish military. In A. Bergman-Rosamond & M. Phythian (Eds.), *War, ethics and justice* (pp. 55–75). Routledge.

Björkdahl, A. (2002). Norms in international relations: Some conceptual and methodological reflections. *Cambridge Review of International Affairs, 15*(1), 9–23. https://doi.org/10.1080/09557570220126216

Björkdahl, A. (2008). Norm advocacy: A small state strategy to influence the EU. *Journal of European Public Policy, 15*(1), 135–154. https://doi.org/10.1080/13501760701702272

Björkdahl, A. (2013). Ideas and norms in Swedish peace policy. *Swiss Political Science Review, 19*(3), 322–337. https://doi.org/10.1111/spsr.12046

Bloomfield, A. (2016). Norm antipreneurs and theorising resistance to normative change. *Review of International Studies, 42*(2), 310–333. https://doi.org/10.1017/S026021051500025X

Bode, I., & Karlsrud, J. (2019). Implementation in practice: The use of force to protect civilians in United Nations peacekeeping. *European Journal of International Relations, 25*(2), 458–485. https://doi.org/10.1177/1354066118796540

Burai, E. (2016). Parody as norm contestation: Russian normative justifications in Georgia and Ukraine and their implications for global norms. *Global Society, 30*(1), 67–77. https://doi.org/10.1080/13600826.2015.1092424

Carpenter, C. (2014). *"Lost" causes: Agenda vetting in global issue networks and the shaping of human security*. Cornell University Press.

Chapnick, A. (2020). *Canada's campaign for a seat on the United Nations Security Council: The Historical Context.* Retrieved June 5, 2024, https://www.cgai.ca/canadas_campaign_for_a_seat_on_the_united_nations_security_council_the_historical_context

Checkel, J. (1999). Norms, institutions and national identity in contemporary Europe. *International Studies Quarterly, 41*(1), 83–114. https://doi.org/10.1111/0020-8833.00112

Clark, I., Kaempf, S., Reus-Smit, C., & Tannock, E. (2018). Crisis in the laws of war? Beyond compliance and effectiveness. *European Journal of International Relations, 24*(2), 319–343. https://doi.org/10.1177/1354066117714528

de Carvalho, B., & Neumann, I. B. (2014). Small states and status. In B. de Carvalho & I. B. Neumann (Eds.), *Small state status seeking: Norway's quest for international standing* (pp. 1–21). Routledge.

Deitelhoff, N. (2019). Is the R2P failing? The controversy about norm justification and norm application of the responsibility to protect. *Global Responsibility to Protect, 11*(2), 149–171. https://doi.org/10.1163/1875984X-01102003

Deitelhoff, N., & Zimmermann, L. (2020). Things we lost in the fire: How different types of contestation affect the robustness of international norms. *International Studies Review, 22*(1), 51–76. https://doi.org/10.1093/isr/viy080

Dian, M., & Dugar, G. (2022). A post-western world in the making. The conceptual framework. *Interdisciplinary. Political Studies, 8*(2), 233–245. https://doi.org/10.1285/i20398573v8n2p233

Doeser, F. (2014). Sweden's Libya decision: A case of humanitarian intervention. *International Politics, 51*(2), 196–213. https://doi.org/10.1057/ip.2014.3

Ekengren, A. M., & Möller, U. (2021). Campaigning for the prize: The quests by Sweden and the Kingdom of the Netherlands for security council membership, 2017–2018. *The Hague Journal of Diplomacy, 56*(3), 1–26. https://doi.org/10.1163/1871191X-BJA10055

Elgström, O. (2000). Norm negotiations. The construction of new norms regarding gender and development in EU foreign aid policy. *Journal of European Public Policy, 7*(3), 457–476. https://doi.org/10.1080/135017600500086125

Evans, G. (2009). *The responsibility to protect: Ending mass atrocity crimes once and for all.* Brookings Institution Press.

Evans, G. (2013). Commission diplomacy. In A. Cooper, J. Heine, & R. Thakur (Eds.), *The Oxford handbook of modern diplomacy* (pp. 278–302). https://doi.org/10.1093/oxfordhb/9780199588862.013.0043.

Evans, G. (2016). *Responsibility to protect (R2P): The ICISS commission fifteen years on.* Simons papers in security and development, (54/2016).

Evans, G., & Sahnoun, M. (2001). Intervention and state sovereignty: Breaking new ground. *Global Governance, 7*(2), 119–125. https://www.jstor.org/stable/27800292

Fehl, C. (2018). *Navigating norm complexity: A shared research agenda for diverse constructivist perspectives.* PRIF Working Papers, 41. Frankfurt am Main: Hessische Stiftung Friedens- und Konfliktforschung. Retrieved July 15, 2024, from https://www.ssoar.info/ssoar/handle/document/59468

Finnemore, M., & Sikkink, K. (1998). International norm dynamics and political change. *International Organization, 52*(4), 887–917. https://doi.org/10.1162/002081898550789

Fisher, K. J., & Stefan, C. G. (2018). The ICC, R2P, and Canada's "return": Opportunity and moral duty in an anti-cosmopolitan global climate. In J. Packer, D. Yeo, J. Velloso, &, K. Fisher, Canadian yearbook of human rights, (Vol 2, pp. 3–19). University of Ottawa Press.

Fritzler, J. (2023). R2P niche diplomacy and norm development in times of politicization: A look at Denmark, The Netherlands, and Sweden. *Nordic Journal of Human Rights, 42(4)*, 504–523. https://doi.org/10.1080/18918131.2023.2284490

Garris, J. (1973). Sweden's debate on the proliferation of nuclear weapons. *Cooperation and Conflict, 8*(3–4), 189–208. https://doi.org/10.1177/001083677300800305

Gifkins, J. (2016). R2P in the UN Security Council: Darfur, Libya and beyond. *Cooperation and Conflict, 51*(2), 148–165. https://doi.org/10.1177/0010836715613365

Gifkins, J. (2021). Beyond the veto: Roles in UN security council decision-making. *Global Governance, 27*(1), 1–24. https://doi.org/10.1163/19426720-02701003

Gilgan, C. M. (2021). Human rights localisation in liberal states: The UK's responsibility to protect as regime change and political transition in Syria. *International Journal of Human Rights, 25*(9), 1457–1488. https://doi.org/10.1080/13642987.2020.1845159

GCR2P. (2020, November 8). *Members of the global network of R2P focal point, signatory list.* Retrieved July 15, 2024, from https://www.globalr2p.org/resources/members-of-the-global-network-of-r2p-focal-points/

GCR2P. (2023, March 15). Resources. Security council and general assembly resolutions. Retrieved July 15, 2024, from https://www.globalr2p.org/resources/

Government of Canada. (2014, January 22). *Operation MOBILE.* Retrieved July 15, 2024, from https://www.canada.ca/en/department-national-defence/services/operations/military-operations/recently-completed/operation-mobile.html

Government of Canada. (2021, March 4). *Minister of foreign affairs takes action on Syria's human rights violations.* Retrieved July 15, 2024, from https://www.canada.ca/en/global-affairs/news/2021/03/minister-of-foreign-affairs-takes-action-on-syrias-human-rights-violations.html

Hansen, S. T. (2016). Taking ambiguity seriously: Explaining the indeterminacy of the European Union conventional arms export control regime. *European Journal of International Relations, 22*(1), 192–216. https://doi.org/10.1177/1354066115584086

Hofmann, G. P., & Suthanthiraraj, K. (2019). Norm contestation and norm adaptation: R2P's reframing over time. *Global Responsibility to Protect, 11*(2), 226–253. https://doi.org/10.1163/1875984X-01102006

Hofmann, G. P., & Zimmermann, L. (2019). Introduction: Norm contestation and its effects: Challenges to the responsibility to protect and the responsibility to prosecute. *Global Responsibility to Protect, 11*(2), 137–148. https://doi.org/10.1163/1875984X-01102002

Huelss, H. (2025). Contestation of normativity in military practices and the AI transformation. In F. Lucenti, C. Ducci, C. Wunderlich, & J. S. Lantis (Eds.), *Contestation in prism: The evolution of norms and norm clusters in contemporary global politics* (pp. 107–124). Springer.

ICISS. (2001). *The responsibility to protect. Report of the International Commission of Intervention and State Sovereignty.* International Development Research Centre. Retrieved July 15, 2024, from https://idl-bnc-idrc.dspacedirect.org/server/api/core/bitstreams/7321d402-4733-4e62-98f2-8fbed4db04c1/content

Jacob, C. (2021). Navigating between pragmatism and principle: Australia's foreign policy response to the 2017 Rohingya crisis. *Global Responsibility to Protect, 13*(2–3), 186–217. https://doi.org/10.1163/1875-984X-13020002

Johansson-Nogués, E., Vlaskamp, M., & Barbé, E. (2020). *European Union contested.* Springer.

Kenkel, K. M., & Stefan, C. G. (2016). Brazil and the responsibility while protecting initiative: Norms and the timing of diplomatic support. *Global Governance, 22*, 41–58. https://doi.org/10.1163/19426720-02201004

Kentikelenis, A., & Voeten, E. (2021). Legitimacy challenges to the liberal world order: Evidence from United Nations speeches, 1970–2018. *The Review of International Organizations, 16*, 721–754. https://doi.org/10.1007/s11558-020-09404-y

Krook, M. L., & True, J. (2012). Rethinking the life cycles of international norms: The United Nations and the global promotion of gender equality. *European Journal of International Relations, 18*(1), 103–127. https://doi.org/10.1177/1354066110380963

Lantis, J. S. (2016). Agentic constructivism and the proliferation security initiative: Modeling norm change. *Cooperation and Conflict, 51*(3), 384–400. https://doi.org/10.1177/0010836716640831

Lantis, J. S. (2025). Norm cluster resiliency in the face of contestation: Nuclear threats and international resolve. In F. Lucenti, C. Ducci, C. Wunderlich, & J. S. Lantis (Eds.), *Contestation in prism: The evolution of norms and norm clusters in contemporary global politics* (pp. 23–43). Springer.

Lantis, J. S., & Wunderlich, C. (2018). Resiliency dynamics of norm clusters: Norm contestation and international cooperation. *Review of International Studies, 44*(3), 570–593. https://doi.org/10.1017/S0260210517000626

Lucenti, F., Ducci, C., & Lee, P. K. (2025). Conceptualising the responsibility to prosecute norm as a cluster: Impunity for war crimes in Sri Lanka. In F. Lucenti, C. Ducci, C. Wunderlich, & J. S. Lantis, (Eds.), *Contestation in prism: The evolution of norms and norm clusters in contemporary global politics* (pp. 87–105). Springer.

Mennecke, M. (2019). Denmark and the implementation of R2P. In M. Mennecke & C. Jacob (Eds.), *Implementing the responsibility to protect: A future agenda* (pp. 37–60). Routledge.

Mills, K. (2015). *International responses to mass atrocities in Africa: Responsibility to protect, prosecute, and palliate*. University of Pennsylvania Press.

Neumann, I. B. (2007). 'A speech that the entire ministry may stand for' or: Why diplomats never produce anything new. *International Political Sociology, 1*(2), 183–200. https://doi.org/10.1111/j.1749-5687.2007.00012.x

Nossal, K. R. (2013). The use – and misuse – of R2P: The case of Canada. In A. Hehir & R. W. Murray (Eds.), *Libya, the responsibility to protect and the future of humanitarian intervention* (pp. 110–129). Palgrave.

Office of the Canadian Prime Minister. (2016, October 20). *Statement by the Prime Minister of Canada on UN General Assembly plenary meeting on Syria*. Retrieved July 15, 2024, from, from https://pm.gc.ca/en/news/statements/2016/10/20/statement-prime-minister-canada-general-assembly-plenary-meeting-syria

Office of the Canadian Prime Minister. (2021, December 16). *Minister of foreign affairs mandate letter*. Retrieved July 15, 2024, from https://pm.gc.ca/en/mandate-letters/2021/12/16/minister-foreign-affairs-mandate-letter

Oksamytna, K. (2023). *Advocacy and change in international organizations: Communication, protection and reconstruction in UN peacekeeping*. Oxford University Press.

Olsson, L., Muvumba Sellström A., Chang P., Tryggestad L.T., Wallensteen P., & Finnbakk I. (2021). Sweden as an elected member of the UN security council. *PRIO paper 2021*. Retrieved June 22, 2024, from https://www.prio.org/publications/12759

O'Malley, A., & den Dunnen, D. (2019). Stretching horizons and testing limits. The Netherlands and Sweden as norm entrepreneurs at the United Nations security council. *Journal of International Organizations Studies, 10*(2), 85–107.

Orchard, P., & Wiener, A. (Eds.). (2024). *Contesting the world: Norm research in theory and practice*. Cambridge University Press.

Panke, D., & Petersohn, U. (2016). Norm challenges and norm death: The inexplicable? *Cooperation and Conflict, 51*(1), 3–19. https://doi.org/10.1177/0010836715597948

Pattison, J. (2021). The international responsibility to protect in a post-liberal order. *International Studies Quarterly, 65*(4), 891–904. https://doi.org/10.1093/isq/sqab081

Payne, R. A. (2001). Persuasion, frames and norm construction. *European Journal of International Relations, 7*(1), 37–61. https://doi.org/10.1177/1354066101007001002

Percy, S., & Sandholtz, W. (2022). Why norms rarely die. *European Journal of International Relations, 28*(4), 934–954. https://doi.org/10.1177/13540661221126018

Petrasek, D. (2019). Not dead yet: Human rights in an illiberal world order. *International Journal, 74*(1), 103–118. https://doi.org/10.1177/0020702019827642

Prantl, J., & Nakano, R. (2011). Global norm diffusion in East Asia: How China and Japan implement the responsibility to protect. *International Relations, 25*(2), 204–223. https://doi.org/10.1177/0047117811404450

Ralph, J. (2017). The responsibility to protect and the rise of China: Lessons from Australia's role as a 'pragmatic' norm entrepreneur. *International Relations of the Asia-Pacific, 17*(1), 35–65. https://doi.org/10.1093/irasia/lcw002

Rhoads, E. P., & Welsh, J. M. (2019). Close cousins in protection: The evolution of two norms. *International Affairs, 95*(3), 597–617. https://doi.org/10.1093/ia/iiz054

Sandholtz, W. (2019). Norm contestation, robustness and replacement. *Journal of Global Security Studies, 4*(1), 139–146. https://doi.org/10.1093/jogss/ogy042
Sandholtz, W., & Stiles, K. W. (2009). *International norms and cycles of change*. Oxford University Press.
Schneiker, A. (2021). Norm sabotage: Conceptual reflection on a phenomenon that challenges well-established norms. *International Studies Perspectives, 22*(1), 106–123. https://doi.org/10.1093/isp/ekaa003
Shawki, N. (2008). Civil society, middle powers, and R2P: An analysis of Canada's response to the crisis in Darfur. *Peace Research, 40*(1), 24–54. http://www.jstor.org/stable/23607695
Sikkink, K. (2011). *The justice cascade: How human rights prosecutions are changing world politics*. WW Norton & Company.
Smith, H., & Ajadi, T. (2020). Canada's feminist foreign policy and human security compared. *International Journal, 75*(3), 367–382. https://doi.org/10.1177/0020702020954547
Staunton, E., & Ralph, J. (2020). The responsibility to protect norm cluster and the challenge of atrocity prevention: An analysis of the European Union's strategy in Myanmar. *European Journal of International Relations, 26*(3), 660–686. https://doi.org/10.1177/1354066119883001
Stefan, C. G. (2021). The responsibility to protect: Locating norm entrepreneurship. *Ethics & International Affairs, 35*(2), 197–211. https://doi.org/10.1017/S0892679421000216
Stimmer, A., & Wisken, L. (2019). The dynamics of dissent: When actions are louder than words. *International Affairs, 95*(3), 515–533. https://doi.org/10.1093/ia/iiz019
Tansey, O. (2007). Process tracing and elite interviewing: A case for non-probability sampling. *PS: Political Science and Politics, 40*(4), 765–772. https://doi.org/10.1017/S1049096507071211
Taulbee, K. (2017). Lesser states and niche diplomacy. In J. Taulbee, A. Kelleher, & P. Grosvenor (Eds.), *Norway's peace policy: Soft power in a turbulent world* (pp. 1–22). Palgrave.
Thakur, R. (2016). Rwanda, Kosovo and the international commission on intervention and state sovereignty. In A. J. Bellamy & T. Dunne (Eds.), *Oxford handbook of the responsibility to protect* (pp. 94–113). Oxford University Press. https://doi.org/10.1093/oxfordhb/9780198753841.013.6
True, J., & Wiener, A. (2019). Everyone wants (a) peace: The dynamics of rhetoric and practice on 'women peace and security'. *International Affairs, 95*(3), 533–574. https://doi.org/10.1093/ia/iiz027
UNGA. (2000, September 14). *Fifty-fifth session, 14th plenary meeting* (A55/PV.14).
UNGA. (2002, September 12). *Fifty-seventh session, 3rd plenary meeting* (A/57/PV.3).
UNGA. (2003a, September 23). *Fifty-eighth session, 8th plenary meeting* (A/58/PV.8).
UNGA. (2003b, September 25). *Fifty-eighth session, 11th plenary meeting* (A/58/PV.11).
UNGA. (2004a, September 21). *Fifty-ninth session, 4th plenary meeting* (A/59/PV.4).
UNGA. (2004b, September 22). *Fifty-ninth session, 5th plenary meeting* (A/59/PV.5).
UNGA. (2005, September 16). *Sixtieth session, 7th plenary meeting* (A/60/PV.7).
UNGA. (2006a, September 21). *Sixty-first session, 14th plenary meeting* (A/61/PV.14).
UNGA. (2006b, September 21). *Sixty-first session, 18th plenary meeting* (A/60/PV.18).
UNGA. (2006c, September 27). *Sixty-first session, 22nd plenary meeting* (A/61/PV.22).
UNGA. (2008, September 29). *Sixty-third session, 16th plenary meeting* (A/63/PV.16).
UNGA. (2010, September 28). *Sixty-fifth session, 22nd plenary meeting* (A/65/PV.22).
UNGA. (2011a, September 23). *Sixty-sixth session, 19th plenary meeting* (A/66/PV.19).
UNGA. (2011b, September 26). *Sixty-sixth session, 26th plenary meeting* (A/66/PV.26).
UNGA. (2012, September 28). *Sixty-seventh session, 17th plenary meeting* (A/67/PV.17).
UNGA. (2013, September 24). *Sixty-eighth session, 7th plenary meeting* (A/68/PV.7).
UNGA. (2018, October 1). *Seventy-third session, 16th plenary meeting* (A/73/PV.16).
UNGA. (2022, September 26). *Seventy-seventh session, 14th plenary meeting* (A/77/PV.14).
UNSC. (2018a, May 24). *Protection of civilians in armed conflict* (S/RES/2417).
UNSC. (2018b, June 6). *Maintenance of international peace and security* (S/RES/2419).
UNSC. (2018c, July 13). *Reports of the secretary-general on Sudan and South Sudan* (S/PV.8310).
UNSC. (2018d, December 2013). *The situation in the Middle East* (S/RES/2449).

Weiss, T. G. (2013). The responsibility to protect (R2P) and modern diplomacy. In A. Cooper, J. Heine, & R. Thakur (Eds.), *The Oxford handbook of modern diplomacy* (pp. 763–778). https://doi.org/10.1093/oxfordhb/9780199588862.013.0043.
Welsh, J. M. (2019). Norm robustness and the responsibility to protect. *Journal of Global Security Studies, 4*(1), 53–72. https://doi.org/10.1093/jogss/ogy045
Welsh, J. M. (2021). The Security Council's role in fulfilling the responsibility to protect. *Ethics & International Affairs, 35*(2), 227–243. https://doi.org/10.1017/S089267942100023X
Widmaier, W. W., & Glanville, L. (2015). The benefits of norm ambiguity: Constructing the responsibility to protect across Rwanda, Iraq and Libya. *Contemporary Politics, 21*(4), 367–383. https://doi.org/10.1080/13569775.2015.1014178
Wiener, A. (2009). Enacting meaning-in-use: Qualitative research on norms and international relations. *Review of International Studies, 35*(1), 175–193. https://doi.org/10.1017/S0260210509008377
Wiener, A. (2014). *A theory of contestation*. Springer.
Wiener, A., & Puetter, U. (2009). The quality of norms is what actors make of it. *Journal of International Law and International Relations, 5*(1), 1–16.
Winston, C. (2018). Norm structure, diffusion, and evolution: A conceptual approach. *European Journal of International Relations, 24*(3), 638–661. https://doi.org/10.1177/1354066117720794
Wunderlich, C. (2020). *Rogue States as norm entrepreneurs*. Springer.
Wunderlich, C., Lucenti, F., Ducci, C., & Lantis, J. S. (2025). Contestation in prism: An introduction. In F. Lucenti, C. Ducci, C. Wunderlich, & J. S. Lantis (Eds.), *Contestation in prism: The evolution of norms and norm clusters in contemporary global politics*. (pp. 1–21). Springer.
Zimmermann, L., Deitelhoff, N., Lesch, M., Arcudi, A., & Peez, A. (2024). *International norm disputes. The link between contestation and norm robustness*. Oxford University Press.

Chapter 5
Conceptualising the Responsibility to Prosecute Norm as a Cluster: Impunity for War Crimes in Sri Lanka

Flavia Lucenti, Cecilia Ducci, and Pak K. Lee

Norm Contestation and Robustness: The Responsibility to Prosecute and Sri Lanka

The norm of Responsibility to Prosecute, enshrined in the Rome Statute of the International Criminal Court (ICC), aims at ending impunity and facilitating prosecution for atrocity crimes, including genocide, crimes against humanity, war crimes, and the crime of aggression. Through the Rome Statute, the applicability of the Responsibility to Prosecute was strengthened to the extent that it and the Responsibility to Protect (R2P) have become a pair of 'twin' norms (Hofmann & Zimmermann, 2019, p. 139; Schroeder & Tiemessen, 2014). Akin to the R2P, the Responsibility to Prosecute presupposes that the primary responsibility for ensuring justice lies with the state and, only when it is unable or unwilling to do so, the international community can intervene, as the Rome Statute specifies. This is known as the principle of 'complementarity', which is a fundamental and recurring element in

We would like to thank Jeffrey Lantis and Carmen Wunderlich for their helpful comments, which enabled us to improve this work.

F. Lucenti
Department of Political Science, LUISS Guido Carli University, Rome, Italy
e-mail: flucenti@luiss.it

C. Ducci (✉)
Department of Political and Social Sciences, University of Bologna, Bologna, Italy
e-mail: cecilia.ducci2@unibo.it

P. K. Lee
Conflict Analysis Research Centre (CARC) and Global Europe Centre, School of Politics and International Relations, University of Kent, Canterbury, UK
e-mail: p.k.lee@kent.ac.uk

F. Lucenti et al. (eds.), *Contestation in Prism*, Norm Research in International Relations, https://doi.org/10.1007/978-3-031-83639-8_5

humanitarian norms. However, unlike its twin norm, the Responsibility to Prosecute further establishes an international legal duty for *all* state parties to the ICC, which embodies the principle of 'universal jurisdiction' over the aforementioned crimes (Ralph, 2016, p. 642). Despite its codification into an international treaty, the norm of Responsibility to Prosecute faces obstacles to its enforcement, as most evident in the ICC's failure to deter rulers from committing serious crimes nor to bring them to justice. Reasons are twofold. On the one hand, several major powers, notably China, India, Russia, and the US, have yet to sign and ratify the Rome Statute (Ducci & Lucenti, 2022; Hall & Jeffery, 2021; Mills, 2015, pp. 28–29). On the other hand, there are countries that, albeit being state parties to the ICC, openly flout and contest this norm, as in the case of Sri Lanka, which strives to guarantee impunity for the state officials allegedly involved in the country's civil war crimes (1983–2009).

Norm contestation has, therefore, made continuous impunity for war crimes possible. By conceptualising the Responsibility to Prosecute as a *cluster in itself* (e.g., Winston, 2018), this chapter explores whether and how the contestation practices of the post-2009 Sri Lankan government undermine the robustness of the norm at the international level by contrasting its underlying principles. To this end, and in line with the norm cluster literature and the conceptual framework outlined in this volume, we mention the various interpretations of the norm cluster concept and argue for the need to also consider a bipartite structure of the Responsibility to Prosecute. Furthermore, and more importantly, by observing the Responsibility to Prosecute as a norm cluster in itself, we claim that the clustering of two underlying principles makes the norm *per se* more susceptible to contestation, posing a risk to, rather than enhancing, its robustness. Indeed, contrary to conventional interpretations, our empirical case highlights that the practices of contestation between the juxtaposing underlying principles of the Responsibility to Prosecute norm ultimately affect the application of the norm adversely, instead of providing mechanisms for resiliency. We proceed then to investigate how the Sri Lankan government has mostly leveraged on the principle of complementarity to oppose that of universal jurisdiction, impinging on the application of the Responsibility to Prosecute. Given that this type of contestation occurs both discursively (Sandholtz, 2008, 2019; Sandholtz & Stiles, 2008; Wiener, 2014) and behaviourally (Stimmer & Wisken, 2019), we undertake a qualitative and interpretative analysis to identify the forms of contestation directed at the norm of the Responsibility to Prosecute.

We assess first the type of behavioural contestation, which is equally aimed at contrasting universal jurisdiction with the principle of complementarity. To do so, we take into account the domestic tribunals and the so-called 'home-grown mechanisms' of transitional justice, set up by successive Sri Lankan governments post-2009, regardless of political affiliation. Through these mechanisms the Sri Lankan government showcases its ability and willingness to pursue justice on its own, thus contrasting the principle of complementarity with that of universal jurisdiction, which it rejects. Nevertheless, we do not believe that they can be seen as an example of 'norm localisation' (Acharya, 2004), whereby an outside norm is reconstituted and reinterpreted at the local level. Instead, home-grown mechanisms have been essentially designed to protect the Sri Lankan governments from international criticism for failing to respect the norm of Responsibility to Prosecute. In other words, they were used as a *façade* to demonstrate that Sri Lanka was complying with the international norm of the Responsibility to Prosecute, while not actually abiding by it. The paper therefore argues that home-grown mechanisms are a subtle form of behavioural contestation.

Alongside the behavioural contestation, by distinguishing discourses concerning the applicability or validity of the norm (Deitelhoff & Zimmermann, 2020; Panke & Petersohn, 2012; Wiener, 2014), we examine the statements of various Sri Lankan leaders since 2009 to the present day. In detail, we look at those that contest the applicability of the principle of universal jurisdiction by arguing that the government of Colombo would be both able and willing to conduct investigations on its own in accordance with the principle of complementarity, but it refuses to do so. In total, we collected and analysed 21 speeches publicly available in the UN Digital Library, which account for the government's official position before the international community and reveal practices of contestation against the international norm of the Responsibility to Protect. We also consider the official documents reporting the position of Sri Lanka's leaders, with particular attention to the 2011 Lessons Learnt and Reconciliation Commission (LLRC) report. The LLRC report is significant because it represented the Mahinda Rajapaksa government's (2005–2015) most authoritative response to international accusations that it was unable or unwilling to investigate and prosecute war crimes allegedly committed during the civil war.

Responsibility to Prosecute as a Norm Cluster

The norm on the Responsibility to Prosecute emerged after World War II when the Allies established two military tribunals, namely the Nuremberg and Tokyo Tribunals, to prosecute mass atrocities and human rights violations (Schabas, 2017, pp. 5–8). Later, it evolved in the context of the post-Cold War focus on human security discourse that grew out of the threat of violent intrastate civil wars, in particular, in the former Yugoslavia (1991–2001), Rwanda (1994), and Sierra Leone (1991–2002), which led to the establishment of *ad hoc* international criminal tribunals (Schabas, 2017, pp. 11–14). The experiences contributed to the definition of the international norm of Responsibility to Prosecute (Mills, 2015, p. 24), according to which States should be responsible for protecting their populations from human rights abuses within their own territory (Birdsall, 2015, p. 54; Turan, 2016, p. 25). This norm officially came into force in July 2002, through an international treaty that codifies and enshrines the concept of 'responsibility': the Rome Statute. According to this, if States take the responsibility for prosecution (ICC, 2002, art. 12), impunity will no longer remain possible. This makes—or should make—non-impunity a logical consequence of the Responsibility to Prosecute, which is one of the most legalised humanitarian norms (Abbott et al., 2000; Schabas, 2009), being enshrined in an international treaty and binding on all States Parties that have ratified it.

Nevertheless, it is not obvious that legalised norms, which are considered to be highly precise norms (Zimmermann, 2017, p. 11), are the most effective normative means to tackle violations, especially when it comes to mass atrocity crimes. Norms can be contested at any point in their life cycle (Wiener, 2014, 2018), regardless of their degree of legalisation. And, when a norm in the name of the principle of responsibility necessitates a derogation of the cardinal principle of sovereignty (Teitt, 2017), as in the case of humanitarian norms, legalisation cannot be enough to guarantee their compliance. Thus, despite its institutionalisation and embeddedness in international law, the Responsibility to Prosecute, like other social norms, is a highly contested norm. This is especially the case in Asia, including Sri Lanka, but also Africa, and its implementation poses several challenges, with most countries even refusing to adhere to the ICC.[1]

Building on this awareness, we address the contestation of the Responsibility to Prosecute through the concept of norm cluster, in line with the scope of this volume. According to the literature on norm contestation, there are two ways of relating international norms to norm clusters. First, a norm can be assessed as part of a cluster of norms, consistent with Lantis and Wunderlich's (2018, 2022) theorisation. In this respect, the Responsibility to Prosecute norm fits into a cluster of norms that envision a strong link between state sovereignty and state responsibility, in particular, the obligation to protect one's own population from mass atrocity crimes (Birdsall, 2015, p. 51). This humanitarian cluster includes norms that share a similar orientation and pursue a similar scope, namely, the Responsibility to Protect, the Protection of Civilians, Women, Peace and Security, prohibition of genocide, war crimes, and crimes against humanity (Fehl, 2018; Mills, 2015, pp. 14, 23–24).[2] Second, the cluster can be seen as inherent to the norm, with reference to the intrinsic components, or principles, to which the norm is necessarily linked (Winston, 2018). These two conceptualisations allow clusters to be viewed in a multifaceted and dynamic way, considering them as existing both inside and outside the norm, also depending on the case we are observing.

In this chapter, we choose to focus on Winston's norm cluster approach, but also go beyond her original conceptualisation to analyse the Responsibility to Prosecute and capture the intrinsic contestedness of the norm *per se*. According to Winston (2018, p. 640), a norm cluster is made up of a problem, a value, and a—prescribed—behaviour, which are the principles that comprise the norm and are assessed when we think of the norm as a cluster in itself. Similarly, we unpack the norm by

---

[1] Among the major or populous states in Asia, only Australia, Bangladesh, Cambodia, Japan, New Zealand, and South Korea are State Parties to the Rome Statute while China, India, Pakistan, Sri Lanka, and many ASEAN member states have yet to be. Note that Australia and New Zealand are considered parts of 'Western European and Other States' while Cyprus a 'Asia-Pacific state' by the ICC. See 'The State Parties to the Rome Statute', International Criminal Court, https://asp.icc-cpi.int/states-parties, (accessed 4 April 2025).

[2] In contrast to this chapter, which situates R2P in what we define as a 'humanitarian cluster', Knapp and Fritzler (2025, Chap. 4) include R2P in what they refer to as a 'wider protection cluster' See also Huelss (2025, Chap. 6), who includes International Humanitarian Law the International Human Rights Law in what he terms the 'protection of civilians legal norm cluster'.

conducting an exploration on the clustering dynamics, but to observe how contesting its underlying principles can affect the robustness and resiliency of the norm. We suggest that the Responsibility to Prosecute treats impunity as undesirable. However, contestation over the Responsibility to Prosecute can be based on challenging its two fundamental components that prescribe measures to ensure a punitive response. While universal jurisdiction allows for the internationalisation of punishment, complementarity emphasises the primacy of the state, and it is the combination of the two that makes the common goal of non-impunity achievable. Hence, our contribution contends that the advocacy of the Responsibility to Prosecute norm as a cluster in itself has facilitated contestation on the part of its alleged violators, with negative implications for the norm's robustness and resiliency. In doing so, our work also recalls Mende's (2024, p. 21) contribution to norm decoupling 'as a distinct form of norm contestation, generating contradictory interpretations of shared norms'. However, instead of focusing on the distinction between norms and values (Mende, 2024, p. 6), we direct our attention to the principles inherent in the norm itself.

This, however, does not exclude the possibility that the contestation of the Responsibility to Prosecute norm may also have impacts on other norms that make up the cluster of humanitarian norms, but this is not the primary aspect of the contestation in the case study. In this chapter, in fact, the discussion mainly revolves around the internal contestation between universal jurisdiction and complementarity within the Responsibility to Prosecute norm in the pursuit of post-war accountability in Sri Lanka.

Universal Jurisdiction and Complementarity

Universal jurisdiction implies that all crimes that 'harm the entire international community' (Philippe, 2006, p. 378) can be prosecuted globally by international courts. Universal jurisdiction is 'criminal jurisdiction based *solely* on the nature of the crime, without regard to where the crime was committed, the nationality of the alleged or convicted perpetrator, the nationality of the victim, or any other connection to the state exercising such jurisdiction' (Mills, 2015, p. 27, emphasis added). According to this view, the crime has 'transcended nationality' and goes under the Princeton Principles on Universal Jurisdiction to ensure that national laws conform to international law (Mills, 2015, p. 27). However, controversy has always been raging over the application of universal jurisdiction, even at the time of the drafting of the Rome Statute. Major powers such as the US do not, in principle, oppose the prosecution of grave international crimes, but rather reject the idea that an international court could have jurisdiction over their own citizens (Ducci & Lucenti, 2022; Kersten, 2016, p. 6; Ralph, 2007, p. 125; Schabas, 2004). This led to the addition of Article 17 to the Rome Statute (ICC, 2002), which brings in the principle of complementarity to the norm of the Responsibility to Prosecute. This limits the authority of the ICC, at least in its initial formative phase, as it dictates that states, through their national courts, have the primary responsibility to ensure accountability for mass atrocities and humanitarian crimes committed on their territory. It follows that the ICC is 'a court of last resort, [which …] seeks to complement, not replace, national courts' (ICC, n.d.).

Complementarity is, nonetheless, not irreconcilable with universal jurisdiction. On the contrary, the two principles are compatible insofar as they synergistically guide the work of the ICC to ensure that whenever justice is not achieved at the national level, it will be attained at the international one. According to Article 13 of the Rome Statute, the ICC has jurisdiction over situations that have been referred to by the United Nations (UN) Security Council (UNSC) under Chapter VII of the UN Charter or by the Prosecutor acting *proprio motu* (ICC, 2002, arts. 13, 15). Moreover, Article 17 of the Rome Statute highlights the relationship between the principle of universal jurisdiction and that of complementary, which combine to constitute the norm of the Responsibility to Prosecute. To begin with, it establishes the boundaries of universal jurisdiction that the ICC must follow, dictating that a case is inadmissible before the ICC when it 'is being investigated or prosecuted by a State which has jurisdiction over it', 'the State [having jurisdiction] has decided not to prosecute the person concerned', '[t]he person concerned has already been tried for conduct which is the subject of the complaint', or '[t]he case is not of sufficient gravity to justify further action by the Court' (ICC, 2002, art. 17). Then, Article 17 specifies that whenever the state is unwilling or unable to carry out investigations and prosecute an individual who has committed such grave international crimes, the case is no longer considered inadmissible before the ICC (ICC, 2002, art.17). Accordingly, this article embodies the limits of the principle of universal jurisdiction, while establishing the ICC as complementary to national justice. As outlined in the Rome Statute, the principle of complementarity makes it possible to assign 'jurisdiction to a subsidiary body [i.e., the ICC] when the main body [i.e., the domestic tribunal] fails to exercise its primary jurisdiction' (Philippe, 2006, p. 380). Universal jurisdiction and complementarity are therefore inherent to the implementation and enforcement of the Responsibility to Prosecute norm, to the extent that we consider them to form a norm cluster.

Concrete problems can arise, however, with complementarity, when it takes precedence over universal jurisdiction, as in the post-conflict context of Sri Lanka, but its implementation is compromised by domestic contestation practices. This may concern whether national processes meet standards of impartiality and reliability and are sufficiently depoliticised (Brown, 1998, p. 389). Or, considering that national courts have the right to grant pardons and amnesties, these tools can be ostensibly used to promote and prioritise reconciliation rather than justice in a post-conflict society, thus failing to uphold the norm of Responsibility to Prosecute. In such cases, there is very little that the ICC prosecutor can do to overturn the decision of the national court, although it does consider this a 'presumption of unwillingness' (Philippe, 2006, pp. 383, 391). Last but not least, the country in question must have an independent judicial system in place, which is often lacking, especially in post-conflict countries (Philippe, 2006, pp. 393–94). This led us to explore the role of post-conflict Sri Lankan government as a 'norm antipreneur' (Bloomfield, 2016,

p. 311; Bloomfield & Scott, 2018) by studying how both discursively and behaviourally it contests and resists the norm of the Responsibility to Prosecute as a cluster itself, thereby adversely affecting the norm's robustness. More specifically, we argue that alleged norm violators use the principle of complementarity to shield themselves from international interference to ensure full respect for the norm, as illustrated in the following sections.

Sri Lanka: International Calls for Accountability Brewing up After 'Victory'

The Sri Lankan Civil War was a 26-year-long violent conflict between the government and the Liberation Tigers of Tamil Eelam (LTTE) between 1983 and 2009. By the end of the war, the Sri Lankan army's crackdown resulted in over 100,000 deaths (Kingsbury, 2012, p. 298), to the point that international lawyer Francis Boyle (2016) even accused the Sri Lankan government of committing genocide. The historical reasons for this war were rooted in the country's colonial past when Sri Lanka—then known as British Ceylon—was a province of British India. The British colonial government encouraged Indian Tamils to migrate to the country to increase the number of indentured labourers for the coffee, tea, and rubber plantations (Liaras, 2015, p. 147; Wickramasinghe, 2006, p. 36). Without land, the migrants lived in enclaves on the plantations in the central highlands around Kandy with little social integration with the majority Sinhalese population. As soon as the country gained independence from the British in 1948, the Sinhalese-dominated government, dismayed by the British Tamilization of the island state, implemented discriminatory policies against the Tamils, making Sinhala the sole official language and giving Sinhalese preference in university admissions and government jobs (Liaras, 2015, pp. 142, 148; Sriram, 2013, p. 63).

The Sinhalese-Tamil conflict worsened in the second half of the 1970s when the nationalist politician J. R. Jayewardene[3] inflamed anti-Tamil sentiment and expanded the army by recruiting only Sinhalese (Rasaratnam, 2016, p. 176). In response, some Tamils demanded an independent homeland, which they called 'Eelam', and founded in 1976 the LTTE, under the leadership of Velupillai Prabhakaran, who was allegedly killed by the Sri Lankan army in May 2009 (Sriram, 2013, p. 63). The LTTE sought to create an independent Tamil-ruled state in the north and east of the country based on the principle of self-determination. It has led the Sri Lankan government to repeatedly justify its use of violence against the LTTE by arguing that it was a 'terrorist organisation' (Rasaratnam, 2016, p. 176) from which the government had to protect its people (Kurtz & Jaganathan, 2016). In 1979, the Prevention of Terrorism Act was passed, which was followed by major anti-Tamil riots in

[3] Jayewardene served as Prime Minister in July 1977–February 1978 and as President in February 1979–January 1989. The Prevention of Terrorism Act was passed in 1979 during his presidency.

Colombo in 1983—known as the 'July 1983 pogrom'—in which an estimated of 1000–3000 people were allegedly killed by the Sinhalese government forces (Weiss, 2012, p. xxiv). From then on, the civil war between the government and the LTTE began and lasted until 2009.

The civil war reportedly caused in total between 80,000 and 100,000 casualties (Sriram, 2013, pp. 64–65). The ceasefire agreement in Sri Lanka, mediated by Norway in 2002, temporarily ended the conflict and led to rounds of peace negotiations. These were broken by the rise of a coalition of Sinhalese nationalist parties, which were opposed to the peace process, in the parliamentary elections in 2004, when violence resumed. Subsequent events, including the victory of Mahinda Rajapaksa in the 2005 presidential election and the designation of the LTTE as a terrorist organisation also by Canada and the European Union (EU) in 2006, marked a shift in the conflict dynamics. The 'Fourth Eelam War' began in 2006, with the West initially backing the government's campaign against the LTTE (Price, 2022). As the conflict escalated, international oversight declined, allowing both sides to commit mass atrocities (Nackers, 2016, p. 877; Rasaratnam, 2016, p. 198). The LTTE was eventually defeated in May 2009 after a brutal offensive by government forces, marked by serious human rights violations and crimes against humanity. Despite the widespread violence, the UN Human Rights Council (UNHRC), shortly after the end of the civil war, in May 2009 passed a resolution (UNHRC, 2009), commending the Sri Lankan government's actions to: conclude 'hostilities', 'liberate' tens of thousands of citizens held by the LTTE against their will as 'hostages', and 'bring permanent peace to the country' while urging the government to end the discrimination against ethnic minorities (Cronin-Furman, 2020, p. 135; Sriram, 2013, p. 79).

Only after August 2009 did the international community, especially the West, begin to be sceptical about the Sri Lankan official narrative, recognise the scale of the atrocities, especially in the final months of the civil war, and put increasing pressure on the national government to address accountability for war crimes committed during the civil war. In response to mounting evidence, in June 2010 UN Secretary-General Ban Ki-moon appointed a panel of international experts to investigate alleged violations (Price, 2022, p. 69; Weiss, 2012, pp. 142–43). The release of reports and documentaries about these atrocities (see, e.g., Channel 4 News, 2014) provoked strong reactions from Western governments and human rights activists. In 2014, the UNHRC adopted Resolution 25/1 (UNHRC, 2014), which led to the establishment of the Office of the High Commissioner for Human Rights (OHCHR) Investigation on Sri Lanka (OISL) to look into the suspected human rights violations committed by both parties during the civil war. The resulting report detailed widespread human rights violations, including unlawful killings, enforced disappearances and sexual violence, committed primarily by the Sri Lankan government against Tamil combatants and civilians (OHCHR, 2015a, September, p. 219). The report also called for the establishment of a hybrid special court to prosecute those responsible. Despite international pressure and UNHRC resolutions, including Resolution 30/1 in 2015 (UNHRC, 2015), which urged for the inclusion of foreign judges and prosecutors in a Sri Lankan justice mechanism, progress towards accountability has been slow. The Sri Lankan government has been criticised for delaying the establishment of a promised special court when demands for accountability have continued, with the UN High Commissioner for Human Rights urging action and warning against backtracking on previous commitments. In 2020, the UNHRC still reiterated its concern about the lack of progress and the potential for a recurring cycle of violence and human rights violations in Sri Lanka; the UN High Commissioner for Human Rights outlined options for advancing criminal accountability—including referral to ICC or investigations by national courts under the principle of universal jurisdiction (OHCHR, 2017; Wanigasuriya, 2021, pp. 243–244, 249–250). The need to strengthen accountability mechanisms was re-emphasised in the UNHRC Resolutions 46/1 (2021) and 51/1 (2022) (UNHRC, 2021, 2022). These developments have underlined the continuing international focus on the charges of breaches of international humanitarian law by the Sri Lankan government and its armed forces. Despite ongoing efforts to hold perpetrators accountable, significant challenges remain, underscoring the failure of the international community to address impunity for crimes committed during and after the civil war. In addition to this, the case has not been brought before the ICC. What has made this possible?

Sri Lanka's 'Home-Grown' Mechanisms of Accountability: An Empty Promise of Justice

International calls for accountability were met with both behavioural and discursive contestation on the part of the Sri Lankan government. This section deals with the behavioural contestation employed by the government over the years. We claim that the home-grown mechanisms set up by the Sri Lankan government represent its contestation of the norm of the Responsibility to Prosecute because they were aimed at showing the international community that, in line with the principle of complementarity, the government is both willing and able to ensure justice on its own. As explained above, they are a subtle form of behavioural contestation that is inextricably linked with the discursive contestation, and both seek to contest the Responsibility to Prosecute by leveraging on the principle of complementarity.

After the UN Secretary-General's decision to establish a Panel of Experts on Accountability in Sri Lanka in June 2010, the government of Sri Lanka has established several home-grown mechanisms through national commissions of inquiry (Cronin-Furman, 2020, p. 143) to contest the norm of the Responsibility to Prosecute and reject international accusations and interference. According to the Sri Lankan government, such mechanisms have followed the principle of complementarity, whereby the primary responsibility for ensuring post-war accountability rests with the state (Wanigasuriya, 2021). These home-grown mechanisms included the Lessons Learnt and Reconciliation Commission (LLRC), the Maxwell Paranagama Commission, the Consultation Task Force (CTF) on Reconciliation Mechanisms, the Office on Missing Persons (OMP), and more recently, the National Unity and Reconciliation Commission (NURC).[4]

Specifically, the LLRC was pre-emptively established by then President Mahinda Rajapaksa in May 2010 in response to international calls for accountability.[5] Tasked with investigating events from 2002 to 2009, the LLRC in its report, released in December 2011, attributed mass atrocities to the LTTE while exonerating the government and military of excessive violence against civilians (Rasaratnam, 2016, p. 221). The report was published in English only, suggesting that its primary audience was international observers. However, critics soon pointed out its shortcomings, citing its lack of adherence to international humanitarian law standards and its reliance on the testimony of government officials and detained Tamil doctors (Sriram, 2013, pp. 79–82; Wanigasuriya, 2021, p. 226; The UN Secretary-General's Panel of Experts, 2011, para v). In contrast, they blamed the LLRC and recommended the creation of an independent international mechanism that could guarantee the full respect of the norm of Responsibility to Prosecute.

Later, in January 2016 the CTF was set up in response to the UNHRC Resolution 30/1, sponsored by the new Maithripala Sirisena government (2015–2019) together with the US. The resolution welcomed the Sri Lankan government's proposal to establish a judicial mechanism with a special counsel to investigate allegations of violations and abuses of human rights and breaches of international humanitarian law, as applicable. Among the recommendations made by the CTF were the establishment of a hybrid court, Special Court and Office of Special Counsel, in which there would be national and international judges with the former being the majority, and of a Truth, Justice, Reconciliation and Non-Recurrence Commission (TJRNRC) (Wanigasuriya, 2021, pp. 230–231). As part of the process to defuse international pressure, the Sirisena administration, who succeeded to Rajapaksa in 2015, also decided to create the OMP (Kalanadan, 2020, p. 1212), after a delegation of the UN Working Group on Enforced or Involuntary Disappearances paid a visit to the country in November 2015 (OHCHR, 2015b). The Sri Lankan Parliament passed the bill for establishing the OMP in August 2016. It began its operation in February 2018. Similar to previous accountability mechanisms, the OMP was mandated to look at the enforced disappearances—notoriously known as 'white van' abductions (Asian Human Rights Commission, 2006)—that happened during and after the civil war.

---

[4] Due to space constraint, not all of them can be discussed in detail in this chapter. The Parnagama Commission, officially known as the Presidential Commission of Inquiry into Complaints of Abductions and Disappearances, was established by then President Mahinda Rajapaksa in August 2013. The Commission disagreed with the findings of the UN Secretary-General's Panel of Experts on four major areas. One of them was the Panel's 'emphasis on prosecutions as an essential aspect of any transitional justice process' (para. 23). After August 2015 when its mandate expired, its work was later taken over by the OMP. The Commission's report is available at https://groundviews.org/wp-content/uploads/2015/10/14-August-final-version-edited-on-30.9.15.pdf (accessed 4 April 2025).

[5] The LLRC was established a month *before* the Secretary-General's Panel of Experts on Accountability in Sri Lanka was appointed.

Despite having a couple of regional offices throughout the country to collect information, it was not granted any prosecutorial authority (Fernando, 2016).

Overall, these commissions were instituted in the face of international pressure to show that the government was taking responsibility for the accountability process, in line with the norm of the Responsibility to Prosecute. Nevertheless, these commissions have not only failed to silence critics in the West (Cronin-Furman, 2020, p. 141) but also demonstrated partial respect for that international norm, as they have mostly been used to punish political opponents, leaving those who are close to the government and potentially guilty of serious human crises unpunished. These commissions operated in line with Price's (2022, p. 66) argument that Sri Lanka's approach 'did not openly reject an obligation to the [international humanitarian] law'. It instead 'supplied a new set of facts to seal its conduct off the remit of the law' (Price, 2022, p. 66) and fell short of international standards for effective accountability mechanisms. In February 2020, Mahinda Rajapaksa, who had meanwhile become the Prime Minister during the presidency of his brother Gotabaya (2019–2022), went even further by declaring that the government would withdraw support for the UNHRC resolutions regarding Sri Lanka adopted in 2015–2019, to which the Sirisena administration was committed (Kalanadan, 2020, p. 1212; Wanigasuriya, 2021, p. 258). More recently, after the overthrow of the Rajapaksa government in July 2022 amid mass protests over the worst economic crisis since independence (Ducci & Lee, 2022), the succeeding Wickremesinghe government in May 2023 approved the proposal to establish a National Unity and Reconciliation Commission (NURC), modelled partly on the South African Truth and Reconciliation Commission (Keenan, 2023), but its credibility has been questioned by both Tamil political parties and human rights groups (Grewal, 2023, p. 326). The lack of a transparent and rightful prosecution shows that rather than being genuine attempts to ensure accountability, these home-grown mechanisms turned prosecutions and convictions of those responsible for war crimes very rare.

Contesting by Contrasting: The Inherent Clash Between Universal Jurisdiction and Complementarity

The establishment of domestic mechanisms shows that the Sri Lankan government has not, at least rhetorically, rejected the norm of Responsibility to Prosecute outright. Instead, it has contested it by exploiting the potential conflicts between the two inherent principles of universal jurisdiction and complementarity. Sri Lanka's contestation of the Responsibility to Prosecute has not been confined to the behavioural level, but also carried out discursively as a response to international calls for accountability. Calling for respect for universal jurisdiction, the UNHRC, the High Commissioner for Human Rights and even the Security Council (UNSC, 2011a) have pressed Sri Lanka for an international investigation into war crimes and possible crimes against humanity. In response to these calls for accountability, Sri

Lanka has constructed a hierarchy within the Responsibility to Prosecute norm by assigning a higher priority to complementarity than universal jurisdiction, performing a discursive type of contestation directed at the Responsibility to Prosecute.

To this end, the establishment of national commissions and the concomitant rejection of the involvement of the international community (e.g., overseas judges) were justified under the pretext of the principle of complementarity. In other words, according to the Sri Lankan government, investigations and prosecutions should be carried out at the domestic level, through what in this chapter we define as 'home-grown mechanism'. This is also evident from its representatives' speeches at UN fora. For example, speaking of the LLRC and the government's efforts to ensure justice, G.L. Peiris, then Minister for External Affairs, levelled criticism at 'unhelpful external pressures' that would only be detrimental to peace resolution on the ground in a plenary meeting of the UN General Assembly in October 2012 (UNGA, 2012). Condemning UNHRC Resolution 25/1, before the UN General Assembly in November 2014, the Sri Lankan government openly opposed the involvement of the international community by referring to complementarity. In the words of the representative of Sri Lanka:

> The resolution infringes on a fundamental principle of international law, which requires that national mechanisms need to be exhausted before resorting to international ones. The resolution and its mandate also challenge the sovereignty and independence of a State Member of the United Nations by calling for a comprehensive investigation of Sri Lanka's alleged human rights violations at a time when the country has launched its own inquiries with, inter alia, the assistance of eminent international personalities (UNGA, 2014, p. 9).

In the same vein, the state representative pointed to the LLRC and its report to demonstrate that his government was willing and able to carry out prosecutions by itself without any external interference (UNGA, 2014). Hence, 'solutions to the country's political problems [...] must necessarily have local resonance [...]' (UNGA, 2010, pp. 7–8). Addressing a UN Human Rights Committee in October 2014, a Sri Lankan official asserted that 'the Lessons Learnt and Reconciliation Commission [...] clearly demonstrated the Government's determination to investigate the matter' (United Nations Human Rights Committee, 2014, p. 2). According to the principle of complementarity, the international community did not have any right to interfere. Drawing on the principle of complementarity, Sri Lanka's representative said in UN Security Council meetings in May and November 2011 that 'it is the first and foremost responsibility of States to address infractions of the law' and, accordingly, the establishment of the LLRC has demonstrated the state's willingness to take responsibility for dealing with accountability in this respect (UNSC, 2011a, pp. 31–32; 2011b, p. 18).

According to the Sri Lankan government's logic, 'external interventions' in the process of attaining justice would only pose an obstacle to the peace negotiations and post-conflict reconciliation (UNSC, 2011a, pp. 31–32). Rejecting *ad hoc* tribunals and externally imposed mechanisms, it instead 'prioritised rehabilitation, reconstruction, reintegration, and reconciliation to achieve a sustainable peace' and favoured ‘an extremely conciliatory attitude towards former combatants’. This was also ‘consistent with [Sri Lanka’s] culture’ of which ‘forgiveness was the theme’ (UNSC, 2013, p. 33), which was already evident in the LLRC report emphasising the importance of post-conflict reconciliation (Government of Sri Lanka, 2011, chap. 9). It also echoed Rajapaksa’s discourses about the government, the military and Sinhalese Buddhists as ‘war heroes’, who could thus not be prosecuted for any crimes (Seoighe, 2016, p. 368). This further supported the trend towards impunity under the rhetoric of reconciliation over the pursuit of international justice.

To shore up the standing of the complementarity norm, eventually, the Sri Lankan regime sought to discursively contest the justifiability of universal jurisdiction by framing international interventions, the ICC and the principle of universal jurisdiction as neo-imperialist by the West. In May 2010, Sri Lanka’s ambassador to the UN, Patitha Kohona, told Channel 4, ‘The government has just appointed a Commission of Inquiry [i.e., the LLRC] to go into [allegation of war crimes]. It will have a wide mandate, and I think it’s appropriate for us to let that Commission of Inquiry do its job, … Sri Lanka has a history of a very highly respected judicial system. To suggest that anybody from outside can do a better job is simply … *colonialist*’ (Weiss, 2012, p. 143, emphasis added). This exemplifies the Sri Lankan government’s belief in the existence of a neo-imperialist agenda that denies the Sinhalese the right to national determination. Rather, the international community’s calls for accountability were interpreted as part of the West’s neo-imperialist agenda in South Asia, which was an extension from Africa and should thus be rejected (Mills & Bloomfield, 2018, p. 106). By analogy, Sri Lankan governments even consider the Responsibility to Prosecute—just like R2P—being invoked by the Western states to cover their ‘neo-imperialist’ (Kingsbury, 2012, p. 114) intentions in geopolitically strategic countries. In contrast, it appeals to the norm of national sovereignty and non-interference into the internal affairs of a sovereign state. During the civil war when the international community wanted to mediate, President Mahinda Rajapaksa re-emphasised the inviolability of national sovereignty and claimed that such assistance would imply interference in the domestic affairs of the country (Kingsbury, 2012, p. 120). As a result, both Presidents Rajapaksa and Sirisena boosted a climate of deep distrust of any international accountability movement by claiming neo-imperialist motives as well as arguing that they were funded and supported by the pro-LTTE forces (Seoighe, 2016, p. 367). The anti-colonialist/imperialist discourse, which contests the value of universal jurisdiction and safeguards the Westphalian understanding of national sovereignty and non-intervention, has resonated with many developing, post-colonial, non-Western states. Moreover, the selective invocation of the Responsibility to Prosecute norm by Western states has also served to mobilise a common criticism, particularly among Asian and African states. The validity of the norm in the non-Western world has met with increasing scepticism (Schroeder & Tiemessen, 2014, p. 62). More recently, this position has indeed been embraced by China, Russia, and other countries of the Global South.

Conclusion

To date, despite three UNHRC resolutions calling on Sri Lanka to ensure justice and accountability through an independent and impartial mechanism, the independent international mechanism has yet to be established; military and government officials alleged to have committed war crimes during the civil war remain unpunished. How has this impunity been made possible? We have argued that Sri Lanka's norm contestation of the Responsibility to Prosecute as a norm cluster has been a key factor. This contestation has been accompanied by a divided international community between those who condemn the lack of respect for the Responsibility to Prosecute norm, particularly Western countries, and those who support the Sri Lankan government. The latter include countries from the Global South, such as China, Russia, India, Pakistan, Cuba, and South Africa. This collective inaction has enabled impunity. The Sri Lankan case, indeed, is not unique; it is part of a wider pattern of impunity in Asia. Despite major genocides in Cambodia, Sri Lanka, Myanmar, and East Pakistan—now Bangladesh—accountability in Asia remains elusive, apart from the conviction of a few former senior Khmer Rouge leaders (Lee & Ducci, 2020). Asian countries, united by anti-colonial narratives, accuse the Global North of justifying its own history of colonialism and aggression, while seeking to impose international norms on others. In response, they make the notions of sovereignty and self-determination the cardinal principles of international politics.

In Sri Lanka, post-war reconciliation and accountability remain a distant goal, rendering the norm of the Responsibility to Prosecute not only toothless, but also hollowing out of its intrinsic objective of ensuring justice for serious violations of international humanitarian law. In the process, Sri Lankan political leaders devise a special strategy to comply with the Responsibility to Prosecute norm ostensibly but to not enforce the mechanisms of accountability in practice. It has meant rhetorically invoking the principle of complementarity while resisting the more intrusive principle of universal jurisdiction and creating home-grown mechanisms to contest the Responsibility to Prosecute norm behaviourally. This was done by constructing a hierarchy of the juxtaposing underlying principles that we can observe when conceptualising the Responsibility to Prosecute as a norm cluster itself (on norm hierarchy see also García Iommi, 2025, Chap. 8). In our study, indeed, we seek to advance the theoretical understanding of norm clusters beyond Winston's original conceptualisation. If Winston's idea of clustering norms into constitutive elements revolves around understanding the nature of the norm—namely, the problem, value, and prescribed behaviour that are intrinsic to it—we also discuss how some actors use a constituent element of a norm to contest the application and validity of another element of the same norm. This may render the norm as a whole ineffective in implementation. Sri Lanka's contestation of the Responsibility to Prosecute as a norm cluster demonstrates that both the structure of a norm and actors' interpretations or even manipulation of it matter for its robustness. Consisting of the inbuilt principles of complementarity and universal jurisdiction, the Responsibility to

Prosecute norm has been made vulnerable to contestation, ultimately undermining its implementation in Sri Lanka.

The value of this chapter is, however, not limited to the study of post-conflict Sri Lanka and as it may be advanced in other post-conflict situations. More importantly, exploring the internal structure of a norm and the contestation practices that affect its constituent principles can pave the way for future research on other norms beyond the Responsibility to Prosecute. It therefore draws the attention of scholars to further investigate the norm as a cluster in itself to see whether similar discursive and behavioural contestation, overt and subtle, are also carried out affecting the norm robustness. As in the scope of this volume, our approach aims to offer yet another insight and more dynamic perspective for researching norm's and norm clusters' resiliency and robustness.

References

Abbott, K. W., Keohane, R. O., Moravcsik, A., Slaughter, A. M., & Snidal, D. (2000). The concept of legalization. *International Organization, 54*(3), 401–419. https://doi.org/10.1162/002081800551271

Acharya, A. (2004). How ideas spread: Whose norms matter? Norm localization and institutional change in Asian regionalism. *International Organization, 58*(2), 239–275. https://doi.org/10.1017/S0020818304582024

Asian Human Rights Commission. (2006, September 12). *Sri Lanka: White vans without number plates; the symbol of disappearances reappear*. http://www.humanrights.asia/news/ahrc-news/AS-213-2006/

Birdsall, A. (2015). The responsibility to prosecute and the ICC: A problematic relationship? *Criminal Law Forum, 26*(1), 51–72. https://doi.org/10.1007/s10609-015-9244-5

Bloomfield, A. (2016). Norm antipreneurs and theorising resistance to normative change. *Review of International Studies, 42*(2), 310–333. https://doi.org/10.1017/S026021051500025X

Bloomfield, A., & Scott, S. V. (Eds.). (2018). *Norm antipreneurs and the politics of resistance to global normative change* (First issued in paperback 2018). Routledge.

Boyle, F. A. (2016). *The Tamil genocide by Sri Lanka: The global failure to protect Tamil rights under international law* (2nd ed.). Clarity Press.

Brown, B. S. (1998). Primacy or complementarity: Reconciling the jurisdiction of national courts and international criminal tribunals. *Yale Journal of International Law, 23*(2), 383–436. https://openyls.law.yale.edu/handle/20.500.13051/6385

Channel 4 News. (2014, March 27). *Sri Lanka 'war crimes': The evidence*. https://www.channel4.com/news/sri-lanka-united-nations-inquiry-evidence-war-crimes-abuse

Cronin-Furman, K. (2020). Human rights half measures: Avoiding accountability in postwar Sri Lanka. *World Politics, 72*(1), 121–163. https://doi.org/10.1017/s0043887119000182

Deitelhoff, N., & Zimmermann, L. (2020). Things we lost in the fire: How different types of contestation affect the robustness of international norms. *International Studies Review, 22*(1), 51–76. https://doi.org/10.1093/isr/viy080

Ducci, C., & Lee, P. K. (2022, July 16). Opinion – The demise of the Rajapaksa dynasty and prospects for peace and justice in Sri Lanka. *E-International Relations*. https://www.e-ir.info/2022/07/16/opinion-the-demise-of-the-rajapaksa-dynasty-and-prospects-for-peace-and-justice-in-sri-lanka/

Ducci, C., & Lucenti, F. (2022). 'Contestation from within': US escalating aversion to the International Criminal Court and the non-impunity norm in the Trump era. *Interdisciplinary Political Studies, 8*(2), 281–297. https://doi.org/10.1285/i20398573v8n2p281

Fehl, C. (2018). *Navigating norm complexity: A shared research agenda for diverse constructivist perspectives* (PRIF Working Papers No. 41). Peace Research Institute Frankfurt. https://www.prif.org/en/publications/publication-search/publication/navigating-norm-complexity

Fernando, R. (2016, June 14). Sri Lanka's 65,000 disappeared: Will the latest missing persons' office bring answers? *The Wire*. https://thewire.in/world/sri-lankas-disappeared-will-the-latest-missing-persons-office-bring-answers

García Iommi, L. (2025). Exceptions as contestation: Understanding norm withdrawal. In F. Lucenti, C. Ducci, C. Wunderlich, & J. S. Lantis (Eds.), *Contestation in prism: The evolution of norms and norm clusters in contemporary global politics* (pp. 143–161). Springer.

Government of Sri Lanka. (2011, December 16). *The report of the Commission of Inquiry on Lessons Learnt and Reconciliation*. https://reliefweb.int/report/sri-lanka/report-commission-inquiry-lessons-learnt-and-reconciliation

Grewal, K. K. (2023). The epistemic violence of transitional justice: A view from Sri Lanka. *International Journal of Transitional Justice, 17*(2), 322–338. https://doi.org/10.1093/ijtj/ijad016

Hall, I., & Jeffery, R. (2021). India, the Rome Statute, and the International Criminal Court: Negotiating to no. *Global Governance: A Review of Multilateralism and International Organizations, 27*(3), 460–482. https://doi.org/10.1163/19426720-02703001

Hofmann, G. P., & Zimmermann, L. (2019). Introduction: Norm contestation and its effects: Challenges to the responsibility to protect and the responsibility to prosecute. *Global Responsibility to Protect, 11*(2), 137–148. https://doi.org/10.1163/1875984X-01102002

Huelss, H. (2025). Contestation of normativity in military practices and the AI transformation . In F. Lucenti, C. Ducci, C. Wunderlich, & J. S. Lantis (Eds.), *Contestation in prism: The evolution of norms and norm clusters in contemporary global politics* (pp. 107–124). Springer.

ICC. (n.d.). *How the Court works*. https://www.icc-cpi.int/about/how-the-court-works

ICC. (2002). *The Rome Statute of the International Criminal Court*. Retrieved March 23, 2025, from https://www.icccpi.int/sites/default/files/Publications/Rome-Statute.pdf

Kalanadan, S. (2020). Combating impunity in Sri Lanka: Searching beyond the United Nations. *Journal of International Criminal Justice, 18*(5), 1207–1228. https://doi.org/10.1093/jicj/mqaa042

Keenan, A. (2023, September 7). *Sri Lanka needs truth, but not (yet) a truth commission*. International Crisis Group. Retrieved April 16, 2025, from https://www.crisisgroup.org/asia/south-asia/sri-lanka/sri-lanka-needs-truth-not-yet-truth-commission

Kersten, M. (2016). *Justice in conflict: The effects of the International Criminal Court's interventions on ending wars and building peace*. Oxford University Press. https://doi.org/10.1093/acprof:oso/9780198777144.001.0001

Kingsbury, D. (2012). *Sri Lanka and the responsibility to protect: Politics, ethnicity and genocide*. Routledge.

Knapp, A., & Fritzler, J. (2025). 'Soft contestation' of the responsibility to protect? Assessing Canada and Sweden's norm diplomacy. In F. Lucenti, C. Ducci, C. Wunderlich, & J. S. Lantis (Eds.), *Contestation in prism: The evolution of norms and norm clusters in contemporary global politics* (pp. 65–85). Springer.

Kurtz, G., & Jaganathan, M. M. (2016). Protection in peril: Counterterrorism discourse and international engagement in Sri Lanka in 2009. *Global Society, 30*(1), 94–112. https://doi.org/10.1080/13600826.2015.1092421

Lantis, J. S., & Wunderlich, C. (2018). Resiliency dynamics of norm clusters: Norm contestation and international cooperation. *Review of International Studies, 44*(3), 570–593. https://doi.org/10.1017/S0260210517000626

Lantis, J. S., & Wunderlich, C. (2022). Reevaluating constructivist norm theory: A three-dimensional norms research program. *International Studies Review, 24*(1). https://doi.org/10.1093/isr/viab059

Lee, P. K., & Ducci, C. (2020). No humanitarian intervention in Asian genocides: How possible and legitimate? *Third World Quarterly, 41*(9), 1575–1594. https://doi.org/10.1080/01436597.2020.1774358

Liaras, E. (2015). Settlers, immigrants, colonists: The three layers of settler-induced conflict in Sri Lanka. In O. Haklai & N. Loizides (Eds.), *Settlers in contested lands: Territorial disputes and ethnic conflicts* (pp. 141–167). Stanford University Press. https://doi.org/10.1515/9780804796521-009

Mende, J. (2024). Liberal-democratic norms under contestation: Norm relations and their decoupling in the US Supreme Court's decisions on abortion. *Global Constitutionalism*, 1–25. https://doi.org/10.1017/S204538172400004

Mills, K. (2015). *International responses to mass atrocities in Africa: Responsibility to protect, prosecute, and palliate*. University of Pennsylvania Press.

Mills, K., & Bloomfield, A. (2018). African resistance to the International Criminal Court: Halting the advance of the anti-impunity norm. *Review of International Studies, 44*(1), 101–127. https://doi.org/10.1017/S0260210517000407

Nackers, K. (2016). Sri Lanka. In A. J. Bellamy & T. Dunne (Eds.), *The Oxford handbook of the responsibility to protect* (pp. 876–894). Oxford University Press. https://doi.org/10.1093/oxfordhb/9780198753841.013.47

OHCHR. (2015a, September 28). *Comprehensive report of the Office of the United Nations High Commissioner for Human Rights on Sri Lanka* (A/HRC/30/61). https://digitallibrary.un.org/record/805731?v=pdf

OHCHR. (2015b, November 18). *Preliminary observations of the Working Group on Enforced or Involuntary Disappearances at the conclusion of its visit to Sri Lanka (9–18 November 2015).* https://www.ohchr.org/en/statements/2015/11/preliminary-observations-working-group-enforced-or-involuntary-disappearances

OHCHR. (2017, September 11). *Darker and more dangerous: High Commissioner updates the Human Rights Council on human rights issues in 40 countries.* https://www.ohchr.org/en/statements/2017/09/darker-and-more-dangerous-high-commissioner-updates-human-rights-council-human

Panke, D., & Petersohn, U. (2012). Why international norms disappear sometimes. *European Journal of International Relations, 18*(4), 719–742. https://doi.org/10.1177/1354066111407690

Philippe, X. (2006). The principles of universal jurisdiction and complementarity: How do the two principles intermesh? *International Review of the Red Cross, 88*(862), 375–398. https://doi.org/10.1017/S1816383106000580

Price, M. (2022). The end days of the fourth Eelam war: Sri Lanka's denialist challenge to the laws of war. *Ethics & International Affairs, 36*(1), 65–89. https://doi.org/10.1017/S0892679421000654

Ralph, J. (2007). *Defending the society of states: Why America opposes the international criminal court and its vision of world society*. Oxford University Press. https://academic.oup.com/book/7017.

Ralph, J. (2016). The international criminal court. In A. J. Bellamy & T. Dunne (Eds.), *The Oxford handbook of the responsibility to protect* (pp. 638–654). Oxford University Press. https://doi.org/10.1093/oxfordhb/9780198753841.013.34

Rasaratnam, M. (2016). *Tamils and the nation: India and Sri Lanka compared.* Oxford University Press. https://doi.org/10.1093/acprof:oso/9780190498320.001.0001

Sandholtz, W. (2008). Explaining international norm change. In W. Sandholtz & K. Stiles (Eds.), *International norms and cycles of change* (pp. 1–26). Oxford University Press.

Sandholtz, W. (2019). Norm contestation, robustness, and replacement. *Journal of Global Security Studies, 4*(1), 139–146. https://doi.org/10.1093/jogss/ogy042

Sandholtz, W., & Stiles, K. (Eds.). (2008). *International norms and cycles of change.* Oxford University Press. https://doi.org/10.1093/acprof:oso/9780195380088.001.0001

Schabas, W. A. (2004). United States hostility to the International Criminal Court: It's all about the Security Council. *European Journal of International Law, 15*(4), 701–720. https://doi.org/10.1093/ejil/15.4.701

Schabas, W. A. (2009). *Genocide in international law: The crime of crimes*. Cambridge University Press. https://doi.org/10.1017/CBO9780511575556

Schabas, W. A. (2017). *An introduction to the International Criminal Court* (5th ed.). Cambridge University Press. https://doi.org/10.1017/9781316459997

Schroeder, M. B., & Tiemessen, A. (2014). Transnational advocacy and accountability: From declarations of anti-impunity to implementing the Rome Statute. In A. Betts & P. Orchard (Eds.), *Implementation and world politics* (pp. 50–67). Oxford University Press. https://doi.org/10.1093/acprof:oso/9780198712787.003.0003

Seoighe, R. (2016). Discourses of victimization in Sri Lanka's civil war: Collective memory, legitimacy and agency. *Social & Legal Studies, 25*(3), 355–380. https://doi.org/10.1177/0964663915614097

Sriram, C. L. (2013). Sri Lanka: Atrocities, accountability, and the decline of rule of law. In R. Jeffery & H. J. Kim (Eds.), *Transitional justice in the Asia-Pacific* (pp. 61–86). Cambridge University Press. https://doi.org/10.1017/CBO9781139628914.003

Stimmer, A., & Wisken, L. (2019). The dynamics of dissent: When actions are louder than words. *International Affairs, 95*(3), 515–533. https://doi.org/10.1093/ia/iiz019

Teitt, S. (2017). Sovereignty as responsibility. In T. Dunne & C. Reus-Smit (Eds.), *The globalization of international society* (pp. 325–344). Oxford University Press. https://doi.org/10.1093/acprof:oso/9780198793427.003.0017

The UN Secretary-General's Panel of experts on accountability in Sri Lanka. (2011, March 31). *Report of the Secretary-General's panel of experts on accountability in Sri Lanka*. Security Council Report. Retrieved April 16, 2025, from https://www.securitycouncilreport.org/atf/cf/%7B65BFCF9B-6D27-4E9C-8CD3-CF6E4FF96FF9%7D/POC%20Rep%20on%20Account%20in%20Sri%20Lanka.pdf

Turan, G. (2016). 'Responsibility to prosecute' in an age of global governmentality: The international criminal court. *Cooperation and Conflict, 51*(1), 20–37. https://doi.org/10.1177/0010836715597946

UNGA. (2010). Summary record of the 34th meeting: 3rd Committee, held at Headquarters, New York, *on Thursday, 28 October 2010, General Assembly, 65th session* (A/C.3/65/SR.34). https://digitallibrary.un.org/record/698324?v=pdf

UNGA. (2012). *General Assembly official records, 67th session: 19th plenary meeting, Monday, 1 October 2012, New York* (A/67/PV.19). https://digitallibrary.un.org/record/737642?v=pdf

UNGA. (2014). *General Assembly official records, 69th session: 54th plenary meeting, Monday, 17 November 2014, New York* (A/69/PV.54). https://digitallibrary.un.org/record/787463?v=pdf

UNHRC. (2009). *S-11/1 Assistance to Sri Lanka in the promotion and protection of human rights* (A/HRC/RES/S-11/1). Retrieved April 16, 2025, from https://www.securitycouncilreport.org/un-documents/document/sri-lanka-ahrc-s11-l1-rev2.php

UNHRC. (2014). *Promoting reconciliation, accountability and human rights in Sri Lanka* (A/HRC/RES/25/1). https://www.ohchr.org/en/hr-bodies/hrc/regular-sessions/session25/res-dec-stat

UNHRC. (2015). *Promoting reconciliation, accountability and human rights in Sri Lanka* (A/HRC/RES/30/1). https://www.ohchr.org/en/hr-bodies/hrc/regular-sessions/session30/res-dec-stat

UNHRC. (2021). *Promoting reconciliation, accountability and human rights in Sri Lanka* (A/HRC/RES/46/1). https://www.ohchr.org/en/hr-bodies/hrc/regular-sessions/session46/res-dec-stat

UNHRC. (2022). *Promoting reconciliation, accountability and human rights in Sri Lanka* (A/HRC/RES/51/1). https://www.ohchr.org/en/hr-bodies/hrc/regular-sessions/session51/res-dec-stat

United Nations Human Rights Committee. (2014). Summary record of the 3099th meeting, held at the Palais Wilson, Geneva, *on Wednesday, 8 October 2014: Human Rights Committee, 112th session* (CCPR/C/SR.3099). https://digitallibrary.un.org/record/784844?v=pdf

UNSC. (2011a, May 10). *Protection of civilians in armed conflict* (S/PV.6531). https://research.un.org/en/docs/sc/quick/meetings/2011

UNSC. (2011b, November 9). *Protection of civilians in armed conflict* (S/PV.6650, Resumption 1). https://research.un.org/en/docs/sc/quick/meetings/2011

UNSC. (2013). *Threats to international peace and security caused by terrorist acts* (S/PV.6900, Resumption 1). https://research.un.org/en/docs/sc/quick/meetings/2013

Wanigasuriya, A. (2021). Justice delayed, justice denied? The search for accountability for alleged wartime atrocities committed in Sri Lanka. *Pace International Law Review, 33*(2), 219–260. https://doi.org/10.58948/2331-3536.1409

Weiss, G. (2012). *The cage: The fight for Sri Lanka & the last days of the Tamil Tigers*. Vintage/Random House.

Wickramasinghe, N. (2006). *Sri Lanka in the modern age: A history of contested identities*. C. Hurst.

Wiener, A. (2014). *A theory of contestation*. Springer. https://doi.org/10.1007/978-3-642-55235-9

Wiener, A. (2018). *Contestation and constitution of norms in global international relations*. Cambridge University Press. https://doi.org/10.1017/9781316718599

Winston, C. (2018). Norm structure, diffusion, and evolution: A conceptual approach. *European Journal of International Relations, 24*(3), 638–661. https://doi.org/10.1177/1354066117720794

Zimmermann, L. (2017). *Global norms with a local face: Rule-of-law promotion and norm translation*. Cambridge University Press. https://doi.org/10.1017/9781316771341

Chapter 6
Contestation of Normativity in Military Practices and the AI Transformation

Hendrik Huelss

AI Transformation and Norm Contestation

The launch of accessible generative artificial intelligence (AI) applications in 2022 suddenly boosted major interest in AI. It seemed as if the academic, political, and public communities had just woken up to a world where humans were no longer alone in their achievements and failures. In the spring of 2023, open letters by prominent figures at the intersection of research and Big Tech, as well as countless media contributions, warned of the risks associated with the speed of AI development. One international non-profit organisation, the Future of Life Institute, issued an open letter in which they argued that 'Contemporary AI systems are now becoming human-competitive at general tasks, and we must ask ourselves: […] *Should* we develop nonhuman minds that might eventually outnumber, outsmart, obsolete, and replace us? *Should* we risk loss of control of our civilization?' (Future of Life Institute, 2023).

Today's warnings and considerable hype about the opportunities and pitfalls of AI arguably transforming, or even revolutionising, all parts of life spearheaded by large language models such as ChatGPT are just the very visible tip of an iceberg that has been growing for years. Research in AI machine learning (ML) is advancing, and applications in the public policy domain such as education, healthcare, justice and policing, military, and security are ever-increasing. AI advancements also have profound implications for international politics and norms. These advances raise important normative and regulatory questions based on ethical and legal considerations. They range from questions of accountability and responsibility of

H. Huelss (✉)
Center for War Studies, Department of Political Science and Public Management, University of Southern Denmark, Odense, Denmark
e-mail: huelss@sam.sdu.dk

F. Lucenti et al. (eds.), *Contestation in Prism*, Norm Research in International Relations, https://doi.org/10.1007/978-3-031-83639-8_6

algorithmic decision-making to more fundamental aspects, such as human dignity in the face of life and death decisions.

The increasing importance of AI in decision-support systems that are meant to assist human operators in processing more data and making decisions faster and more accurately represents a crucial case for research on norms, broadly understood as standards of appropriateness (see Bode & Huelss, 2018). First, national, supranational, and global attempts to regulate or even prohibit the use of certain AI applications are growing. The adoption of the EU AI Act in 2024 (European Parliament, 2024), after years of deliberation, testifies to these conventional, legal norm-making endeavours. Second, the pace and complexity of technological developments in this field constitute a legal-normative void. As in other areas of transformative technologies, the political-deliberative method of creating norms to govern an issue area typically lags behind practices of developing, testing, or using AI. AI practices represent sites where the emergence of social norms, in contrast to the legal norms of formal deliberation mentioned above, fuses with the contestation of existing legal and social normative frameworks. What makes the case of AI particularly important is that human control is infringed by decision-support applications, which is especially a problematic issue in the military domain (see Bode & Watts, 2021) as it pertains to life and death decisions at the normative core.

In this chapter, I explore what the AI transformation means for the contestation of norms, drawing on conceptual arguments of norm robustness and norm cluster resiliency and validity and applicatory contestation that are introduced in detail in the introductory chapter of this volume (Wunderlich et al., 2025, Chap. 1). Given that human agency is transforming in relation to AI technology, I am investigating what this implies for the emergence, impact, and contestation of norms. Research on military AI is particularly suitable for demonstrating the contribution and challenges of contestation research in the light of novel, important technological developments. While the use of AI in the military has been a political and academic focal point for more than a decade, also regarding international norms (Bode & Huelss, 2022), the recent armed conflicts in the Gaza Strip and Ukraine have further highlighted the importance of military technology in the context of norms.

This chapter also examines two empirical illustrations of these relationships. First, it probes the announcement of the US military AI company Palantir that generative AI—the most popular civilian example is known as ChatGPT—is now integrated into a warfare decision 'support' system, which is called artificial intelligence platform (AIP). Palantir made headlines for its applications being used by the Ukrainian military in the ongoing war (Bergengruen, 2024). The second illustration focuses on the discussion about the AI components of the Israeli Habsora and Lavender systems that were reportedly used in the military campaign in the Gaza Strip following the 7 October 2023 attack by Hamas on Israeli territory. Both the design and testing of AI-based decision support in these cases, as well as reports about their usage in military targeting, underline changes to how a contestation of norms and norm clusters might take place in practices.

The analysis proceeds as follows: Section "Contestation and the Meaning-*of*-Use of Norms identifies the main contributions and challenges of contestation research as a basis for outlining its contribution. Section "Normative Structures, Norm Clusters, and Norms of Armed Conflict" discusses the concept of normative structure and norm clusters using the example of International Humanitarian Law (IHL), which sets out the legal norms of protecting civilians in armed conflict. Sections "Military AI and Challenges to Norms" and "Generative AI and Use of Force Norms" analyse illustrations of AI transformation and norm development using the examples of the Palantir decision-support system and the Habsora and Lavender target identification systems. The chapter concludes by emphasising that the increasing role of AI in military decision-making is shifting norm-making from human deliberation to AI-driven standards, challenging traditional legal norms and leading to 'hybrid contestation', where social norms partly contest and partly generate normative meaning. This is a transformation that demands a closer examination of the implications of AI on the resiliency of legal norms and norm clusters, as it alters perceptions of the appropriate use of force without public input.

Contestation and the Meaning-*of*-Use of Norms

Research on norms has become a prominent subfield of IR studies, building on the early constructivist literature of the late 1980s and 1990s. In the context of Wendt's theorising of the influential 'agency-structure' problem (Wendt, 1987) that made its way into IR from sociology, norms are conceptualised as factors that are useful for understanding the structuring but also structured quality of the ideational dimension. Norms can therefore provide a crucial theoretical link between agency and actions and structural forces. A widely accepted definition of norms is that they are 'standards of appropriate behaviour for actors with a given identity' (Katzenstein, 1996, p. 5) or standards of appropriateness in a broader perspective.

Research on norms has produced substantial conceptual contributions to understanding the institutionalisation and codification of norms into law and how these impact international relations. The role of legal norms as well as their emergence and existence in official documents served simultaneously as the analytical starting and end points of early norm studies. Thus, the structural side of norms is represented by a normative structure that is widely conceptualised as identical to the structure of international law. The idea is that once norms become institutionalised in this regard, their impact expands. The main research interest of norm studies in the late 1990s and 2000s was hence an exploration of norm compliance and of relevant processes such as diffusion, internalisation, and socialisation (Finnemore & Sikkink, 1998; Keck & Sikkink, 1998; Risse et al., 1999).

However, in the last two decades, norm research has especially delivered diversified viewpoints on the influential assumption that 'norms are contested by default' as 'social constructs' (Wiener, 2007, p. 58), as it is also succinctly summarised in the introduction to this volume (Wunderlich et al., 2025, Chap. 1). For example, research has recently conceptualised norm robustness (Deitelhoff & Zimmermann, 2018, 2019; Zimmermann et al., 2023) and norm resiliency in the context of norm clusters

(Lantis & Wunderlich, 2018) as well as reflected on different types of contestation such as validity and applicatory contestation (Deitelhoff & Zimmermann, 2019). Together with research on localisation (Acharya, 2004; Zimmermann, 2016), there is hence a strong tendency to differentiate a declaratory-discursive level of norm establishment from a level of norm usage, where implementation and contestation take place. Wiener (2009) calls the latter level the structure of 'meaning in use', highlighting that the normative substance of norms as the actual content of meaning might only be shaped—or re-shaped—in the context of norm usage. Contestation studies thus bridge the sequential gap between agreed norms and their implementation by emphasising that normative meaning can also be constituted at the level of practices that may refine or even contest the meaning initially attached to norms.

At the same time, the productive research agenda on contestation faces conceptual challenges. First, it has not focused extensively on norm emergence outside of the contestation framework. While the above-mentioned literature at least implicitly highlights the importance of the practice level to understand the emergence of normative substance, this is only conceptualised with reference to an existing normative structure, which is typically understood as a legal structure. The question is then if we can further think of norms that emerge on the practice level without reacting to the declaratory, structural level in terms of a direct contestation—that is, responsive vs. creative norm emergence. In this regard, the chapter includes a perspective on the generative meaning-*of*-use, where it is less about the application of meaning *in use* but more about investigating the meaning that emerges by engaging in practice, including practices *of* using and interacting with technology.

Second, the sites—and, by extension, the practices—of contestation are underspecified, so that the relationship between discourse and practice is often not sufficiently clear in the existing literature. In particular, Wiener (2004, p. 190) refers to 'social practices' and to 'the role of discursive interventions as social practices that entail and re/construct the meaning of norms'. She understands contestation as 'an interactive social practice' that 'may be performed either explicitly (by contention, objection, questioning, or deliberation) or implicitly (through neglect, negation, or disregard)' (Wiener, 2014, p. 2). However, as Wiener (2014, p. 1) argues, while norm contestation is 'mostly expressed through language not all modes of contestation involve discourse *expressis verbis*. Thus, among the distinct modes of contestation, including justification, deliberation, arbitration, or contention, especially the latter does not necessarily involve language'. This means that the approach of contestation studies has so far been mainly discursive in terms of written language and requires a certain extent of public performance to be of analytical significance. Indeed, contestation seems to require a public act of work that translates meaning into discourses—documented verbalisation—and is then analytically accessible.

Such an emphasis on discourses arguably leads to an under-conceptualisation of practices and, in particular, of norm-generative performances. Although contestation research provides a solid conceptual basis for examining variances in how existing, to a certain extent stable, norms discernible from discourses—as discursive normative structures—are contested in discourses understood as practices. In that, contestation is a meaning-generative practice by default that is, however, largely thought of as relational, i.e., with relation to existing norms as a top-down view. But the bottom-up perspective of norm generation in practices that are not publicly verbalised (Bode, 2023) or codified and that might lead to a relatively stable normative (co-)structure with broader impact remains understudied. In sum, this is an important challenge and gap for norm research and thus sets up the research question: Could we also broaden the perspective to different, non-public, perhaps even non-verbalised practices?

This theme is not completely new to norm research, of course, and has most recently received more attention—Orchard and Wiener (2023, p. 55) mention the concept of 'hidden norms', while Drubel and Mende (2023) explore 'hidden discursive contestation'. Tholens (2025, Chap. 9) discusses the idea of 'hidden transcripts' of contestation, while Bode (2023, p. 1009) differentiates between 'non-public practices and public deliberation' in the context of norms. If contestation is not only the typically studied public act of unfolding one's understanding of what norms mean in discourses, and if norms are not only what is to be found in public, written documents, this may lead us to rethink how contestation processes work. Particularly, the concepts of validity and applicatory contestation might be relevant—for a more detailed review of these concepts, see the introduction to this volume (Wunderlich et al., 2025, Chap. 1).

Third, in contrast to the conceptualisation of a normative structure, the agency or actorness dimension remains less theorised beyond the dichotomy of 'norm entrepreneur' (Finnemore & Sikkink, 1998; Sunstein, 1996) and 'norm antipreneur' (Bloomfield, 2016), which are more of an abstract ideal type than nuanced conceptions of the human actor. I find this aspect particularly pertinent to a normative analysis of AI, as re-thinking human–machine interaction and its consequences for agency is one of the major challenges of emerging AI applications. While the general, abstract idea of 'agency' is based on a rather unidimensional conception of human actors, the question of how agency becomes 'distributed' (Rammert, 2008) in the interaction of humans and AI is crucial and of relevance for norm research concepts. As Rammert (2008, p. 83) outlines, distributed agency 'is the hybrid constellation of people, machines, and programs'. It is the mode in which the agencies of the heterogeneous instances are distributed and connected with one another and the level of agency that is given to them in certain situations. It is neither the single or the collective human actor, nor the technical artefact alone, nor the combined technical system. It is the mixed ensemble made of all elements on both sides of the border. With the increasing use of AI, not least in the military context, practices in the above-mentioned sense become especially important because norms are contested or shaped in the distribution of agency.

The following section introduces protection of civilians' cluster norms as the overarching empirical context of this chapter. The conceptual discussion of the role of norm clusters and mechanisms of contestation will also be integrated.

Normative Structures, Norm Clusters, and Norms of Armed Conflict

This section discusses how the contribution of norm contestation research can offer perspectives on the impact of norms in the context of using force. I will first discuss the idea of a normative-legal structure that provides guidelines for how humans, especially civilians, are protected in use of force scenarios. Second, I will also draw connections in these arguments to norm cluster research.

As argued above, research on norms takes a traditional starting point in accepting the existence and meaningfulness of a normative structure that is often located in international law, such as human rights. Against this awareness, humans in armed conflict are protected by an overarching legal-normative structure of *jus ad bellum* and *jus in bello*. While *jus ad bellum* specifies rules of when an armed conflict is generally lawful—including Article 2, paragraph 4 of the United Nations (UN) Charter (United Nations, 1945), which prohibits the use of force in international relations, as well as Article 51 that defines the right of individual or collective self-defence—*jus in bello* is concerned with the lawful conduct of armed conflict. Under the latter structure fall International Humanitarian Law (IHL) and International Human Rights Law (IHRL).

While the level of specification differs, IHRL and IHL can be considered as comprising several, interrelated norm complexes. However, IHRL is universal in scope, whereas IHL is specifically concerned with humanitarian aspects of armed conflict, which means that the human right to life in IHRL is universal but depends on the 'category of person' in armed conflict under IHL. The purpose of IHL is indeed to protect humans in armed conflict and to restrict the means and methods of warfare to a permitted set of practices. The primary sources of IHRL and IHL are international treaties and customary law. IHRL is most notably defined by the Universal Declaration of Human Rights and the International Covenants on Economic, Social and Cultural Rights and on Civilian and Political Rights as well as their Optional Protocols. IHRL is also grounded in customary international law that is binding on all states, even if they are not party to a specific treaty. Furthermore, some legal norms of customary law are peremptory and cannot be derogated. Among these are the prohibitions of torture, slavery, genocide, racial discrimination, and crimes against humanity, and the right to self-determination. Instead, the treaties at the heart of IHL are the Hague Regulations and the Geneva Convention and its Additional Protocols.

Research on norm clusters helps link understandings of legal-normative structures, contestation, and norm impact. As Lantis and Wunderlich (2018, pp. 575–76) contend, 'authors have supplemented the traditional focus on norms as structuring units of world politics by reference to an overarching "normative structure" as the broadest layer in world politics. [They] argue that norm clusters represent a third or intervening layer, located between the intersection of norms (lowest layer) and normative structures (broadest layer)'. In this investigation, international humanitarian law and its legal norms may be closest to the idea of a cluster of norms, with central provisions and principles concerning the protection of civilians constituting the protection of civilians' legal norm cluster. This frame is grounded in the Fourth Geneva Convention and its two Additional Protocols of 1977. In contrast to IHRL, there is no universal protection of civilians in armed conflict under IHL, which considers the killing or injuring of civilians as permitted under specific rules. The best-known and research-relevant principles of IHL are the principles of distinction, necessity and proportionality, principle of humane treatment, principle of non-discrimination, and protection of women and children (Bode, 2023). Among these, the principles of distinction, necessity, and proportionality form a highly interrelated norm cluster. The basic rule of Article 48 of the Protocol Additional to the Geneva Conventions (AP I) states: 'In order to ensure respect for and protection of the civilian population and civilian objects, the Parties to the conflict shall at all times distinguish between the civilian population and combatants and between civilian objects and military objectives and accordingly shall direct their operations only against military objectives' (United Nations, 1977a). Article 51 (5) (b) AP I further states that 'an attack which may be expected to cause incidental loss of civilian life, injury to civilians, damage to civilian objects, or a combination thereof, which would be excessive in relation to the concrete and direct military advantage anticipated'. Article 57: 2 expands this by arguing, 'With respect to attacks, the following precautions shall be taken: (a) those who plan or decide upon an attack shall: (i) do everything feasible to verify that the objectives to be attacked are neither civilians nor civilian objects and are not subject to special protection but are military objectives within the meaning of paragraph 2 of Article 52 and that it is not prohibited by the provisions of this Protocol to attack them' (United Nations, 1977a). While the provisions cited above are at the heart of the IHL protection of civilians, further rules provide substance specifying this aspect. Overall, Articles 48, 51-52, 57 of AP I as well as Articles 13-16 of AP II (United Nations, 1977b) build a significant norm cluster around the protection of civilians in armed conflict.

It can be argued that the existence of these IHL provisions in combination with IHRL such as the 'right to life, liberty and security of the person' (United Nations, 1948) constitutes a powerful legal-normative force or super-cluster. Hence, the discursive contestation of the protection of civilians in armed conflict cluster is very low. Actors generally agree that civilians must be protected—the contestation takes place rather on a lower level regarding the practical interpretation of what proportionality and necessity mean in practice and especially what distinction between civilians and combatants implies.

In addition, there are domestic and international legal norms regarding state and individual responsibility for IHRL and IHL violations (United Nations, 2011, pp. 70–86). Individual actors, commanders, or other superiors have a responsibility for acts that constitute international crimes under international criminal law. The Rome Statute of the International Criminal Court (ICC) inter alia mentions, for example, in Article 8 as 'War crimes' the 'extensive destruction and appropriation of property, not justified by military necessity and carried out unlawfully and wantonly (ICC, 2002, section 2, paragraph a, iv) and 'Other serious violations of the laws and customs applicable in international armed conflict, within the established framework of international law, namely, any of the following acts' (ICC, 2002, section 2, paragraph b), such as 'Intentionally launching an attack in the knowledge that such attack will cause incidental loss of life or injury to civilians or damage to civilian objects or widespread long-term and severe damage to the natural environment which would be clearly excessive in relation to the concrete and direct overall military advantage anticipated' (ICC, 2002, section 2, paragraph b, iv). These provisions add another powerful collection of norms to the IHRL and IHL legal norms that share widespread global acceptance: 123 countries are states parties to the Rome Statute. While major military actors such as China, India, Israel, Russia, and Saudi Arabia are not state parties, a mutually re-enforcing interrelation between the ICC and IHRL/IHL cluster exists.

The subsection has established that there is evidence of three layers of significant legal-normative substance regarding laws of war; it can also be argued that the above legal norm cluster enjoys robustness. Like Lantis and Wunderlich (2018, p. 575) write: 'generally speaking, norms are considered robust when they are regarded as legitimate, endorsed, ratified, and followed by a critical mass of players'. It follows that the two norm clusters are also resilient— resiliency referring to 'the ability of systems to recover from or adjust to (external) challenges while retaining essential functions' (Lantis & Wunderlich, 2018, p. 575). Moreover, this analysis suggests that, when contested, the validity of the protection of civilians' legal norm cluster[1] has retained its essential meaningfulness by being discursively supported and maintained in legal frameworks. Furthermore, the applicatory contestation present in these cases, which involves providing different verbalised and non-verbalised interpretative practices of interpreting actors and processes (e.g., who are combatants and non-combatants, or what is necessary and proportional in the use of force), has not fundamentally undermined the discursive resiliency on a public level. This supports the idea that norm clusters can promote robustness and resiliency.

However, this inquiry assumes that human deliberations and interpretations are driving public processes. What does it mean for the arguments about norm contestation and the theoretical-conceptual models, when practices that should take place within a norm application framework are substantially using AI-generated decisions? I explore these themes in the next section.

[1] See also Knapp and Fritzler (2025, Chap. 4)'s definition of 'wider protection cluster' and Lucenti et al. (2025, Chap. 5)'s formulation humanitarian cluster. In contrast to this chapter, Lee et al. also comprises responsibility to protect, the responsibility to prosecute, the protection of civilians, and the prohibition of genocide, war crimes, and crimes against humanity, and women, peace, and security. Knapp and Fritzler instead include the responsibility to protect, protection of civilians, and women, peace, and security as norms guaranteeing the subsidiary international responsibility to prevent or respond to mass atrocities.

Military AI and Challenges to Norms

AI ML applications may have a profound impact on IR in the future, not least of which will emerge in the military realm. While the meaning of 'artificial intelligence' as a public and academic term is understood in different ways and not universally defined along the same lines, it should be noted that the applications most relevant for this chapter are from the field of ML—that is also central for many of the attention-grasping civilian applications such as generative AI, like ChatGPT.

In general, the way ML acquires data is by supervised and unsupervised learning (Brownlee, 2016; IBM, 2024). In the former case, ML is trained on labelled data. The supervisor gives the system concrete examples with attached meaning and the expected outcome is known. By that, the input and the output or performance of a model can be compared, and the system can learn to predict the outcome for new data. In unsupervised learning, the data is unlabelled and unstructured, which means that the input is unknown and not linked to a desired output. The ML model learns to find patterns and correlations in the data.

Both these general processes can be used in practical applications, for example in the security and military contexts. Supervised learning is an approach that is typical for image recognition applications in terms of surveillance or target identification based on photographic images or video footage. But there is also significant testing of unsupervised learning applications that are particularly used for pattern detection in data. Here, ML seeks to spot anomalies in the data. A frequently cited example is the US SKYNET programme, which, among other things, used mobile phone data to scan movement patterns to identify possible members of terrorist organisations in Afghanistan through the use of ML. SKYNET flagged the movements of what turned out to be an Al-Jazeera journalist as a data anomaly and, therefore, most likely member of a militant group. In the critical security studies literature (Aradau & Blanke, 2018; Huelss, 2020; Suchman, 2022), this is mentioned as a prominent example of ML failure.

Data and Norms

Yet, the implications of data and learning algorithms that can generate their own decision-making standards or norms have not yet received a great deal of scholarly attention. It is important to recognise that neither supervised nor unsupervised learning is value-free, neutral, or normatively blank. This means that normative substance is installed in algorithms by way of design, or rather through the data on which they are trained. Recently, Chandler (2021, pp. 15–18) brought attention to the work of ImageNet, which is one of the most important, publicly available sources for images and that is used for training ML models designed for image recognition. Chandler shows the various sources of biases that become part of ML in the different processes of distributed agency, including conceptual, development, testing, and deployment phases. But even other civilian applications such as ChatGPT basically work like black-box algorithms, because OpenAI does not disclose what kind of training data it uses and how its learning approach works in detail.

There are many examples of algorithmic bias from different societal contexts. But how does this matter for research on norms, agency, and interactions with AI or ML? As mentioned above, I find the concept of distributed agency well fitting for the ongoing transformation that is the incorporation of AI in decision-making structures. To give an example of what this can mean: in the case of military AI, much attention is directed to the concept of 'Meaningful Human Control' (MHC) (Article 36, 2015; Schwarz, 2021) that plays a role in the political debate on emerging technologies in the area of Lethal Autonomous Weapons System (LAWS), which has been taking place since 2014 in the framework of the UN Convention on Certain Conventional Weapons. This frame is grounded on the assumption that normatively driven standards (read: human standards) would guide the use of LAWS.

While there is no universally shared definition of what MHC is, there is evidence that human control can be increasingly limited and even become rather 'meaningless' in the interaction with AI (Bode & Watts, 2021). If human control indeed becomes *meaningless* in the interaction between human and ML, the interpretation or contestation of norms by way of human application turns into an unintentional process and outcome. Decision-making predominantly influenced by algorithmic output would then be based on a normative substance that is potentially outside and beyond the influence of an existing human normative structure. Norms as standards of appropriate action might then become perceptible in the light of action outcomes but inaccessible at the decision-making point.

The argument that AI systems represent a 'black box' in terms of the predictability and understandability of algorithmic decision-making (Holland Michel, 2020) is important in this analysis, also in combination with the data bias mentioned above. Specifically, it is relevant to discuss the emergence of a practice of meaning-*of*-use, described as the meaning generating practice of using AI, which is less approachable with existing models of norm study because they are profoundly anchored in the human agency-structure framework. The next section illustrates these conceptual-theoretical arguments using two current examples: the 2023 release of a military decision-support platform by the US company Palantir using generative AI and the use of the Israeli Gospel (Habsora) and Lavender systems in the military conflict with the Palestinian Hamas starting in the autumn of 2023.

Generative AI and Use of Force Norms

The increasing importance of a distributed human-technological agency raises the possibility of an emergence of a normative co-structure, which is neither legally codified nor necessarily public-discursively established. While the outcome of practices of using AI for military purposes can contest norms and norm clusters in the same way non-AI-based use of force does, the distributed form of agency may also erode the very fundamentals of how norms have been conceptualised throughout human history.

The most recent trend in the defence industry using AI focuses on integrating visual interfaces with emerging generative AI models, such as ChatGPT and similar applications in civilian domains. Palantir, a leading US company in this field, showcased its artificial intelligence platform (AIP) in April 2023, which combines large language models with an interface.[2] Users can interact with AIP through questions and prompts, simulating human-like chat interactions.

What sets AIP apart is its ability to provide actionable recommendations alongside these interactions. This seamless integration provides a clear and efficient situational assessment akin to removing the 'fog of war' (Owens & Offley, 2001), which is synonymous for the military importance of gaining the most complete 'situational awareness' (Suchman, 2020, 2022). However, AIP provides a reconstruction of the reality on the battlefield that comes with certain limitations and challenges. Although the interface offers a clear and clean overview of the situation 'on the ground' as well as the 'best' options for actions, the 'black-box' problem of ML remains. It is unclear what data has been used to arrive at this visual representation, how the data has been processed, and why certain courses of action are recommended while others are excluded—and remain invisible. The distinction between combatants and non-combatants, military targets, and civilian objects, as well as the assessment of the proportionality of an attack, is at the core of the protection of civilians. In the API interface, these issues are already resolved by sensor input, algorithmic processing, and potentially without any human intervention. Friends and enemies are clearly identified by blue and red symbols, but the nuances in between are invisible. AIP and its visual presentation via the interface offer putative clarity amidst complexity, while eradicating the ability to 'doubt' the algorithmic situational assessment (Amoore, 2019), thereby streamlining decision-making processes. This illustrates a broader trend towards realising the US Joint All-Domain Command and Control (JADC2) vision, which aims to minimise human involvement in rapid decision-making processes (DoD, 2022). However, it also risks overlooking nuanced situational distinctions, such as the identification of combatants and non-combatants, which may be better addressed by slower, more deliberate methods.

Despite the limitations, the arguably much greater efficiency of AI, such as ML, in dealing with high data loads under time and speed constraints is one of the main reasons given for the use of AI in the military. The influential US National Security Commission on Artificial Intelligence (NSCAI) suggests in its concluding report in 2021 that '[t]he best human operator cannot defend against multiple machines making thousands of manoeuvres per second potentially moving at hypersonic speeds and orchestrated by AI across domains. Humans cannot be everywhere at once, but software can' (NSCAI, 2021, p. 23). This perspective supports the notion of AI 'solutionism' (Morozov, 2014), wherein AI is viewed as the *panacea* for complex

[2] A presentation of the AIP can be found on Palantir's website (see Palantir, 2023).

military challenges. Former Department of Defence (DoD) electronic warfare executive William Conley emphasises that 'a future battlespace will contain threat signals not previously observed, [so] it will be essential for many platforms to be executing real time decision algorithms' (Hoehn et al., 2020, p. 15). The vision of real-time algorithmic decision-making means basically a complete subordination of human agency—supposed to represent certain deliberative norms—to AI decision-making standards, however, opaque they are. The practice of developing, testing, and using AI described above sets new social norms of what appropriate use of force is.

A similar development in the actual use of AI in a combat situation, where the protection of civilians is a crucial aspect, is the Israeli AI system 'Habsora' (which translates to 'Gospel' in English language). Insights into the architecture and recent use of the Israeli Gospel system have been produced by an extensive investigation conducted by +972 Magazine[3] with the news site Local Call (*Sikha Mekomit* in Hebrew),[4] which led to the publication of an online article published by Yuval Abraham on 30 November 2023 (Abraham, 2023). The article includes conversations with seven members, or former members, of the Israeli intelligence community. In the article, it is argued that 'Compared to previous Israeli assaults on Gaza, the current war [...] has seen the army significantly expand its bombing of targets that are not distinctly military in nature. These include private residences as well as public buildings, infrastructure, and high-rise blocks' (Abraham, 2023). Those sources report that Habsora is used to 'generate' targets almost automatically at a rate that far exceeds what was previously possible' (Abraham, 2023). Arguably, the article asserts that the criteria regarding the killing of civilians—or the distinction and proportionality requirements of international legal norms—are significantly relaxed to eliminate 'as many Hamas operatives as possible' (Abraham, 2023).

Apart from the change of Israeli policy regarding the protection of civilians—such as refraining from prior warnings about attacks that is also described in this article—the selection of targets moves into the centre of attention. Israel has likely attacked targets in Gaza on an unprecedented scale: approximately 15,000 targets in the first 35 days of fighting. It is reported that the rate was much lower in previous operations and there was previously a possibility of running out of targets. The article also cites a statement by the Israeli Defence Forces (IDF) from 2 November 2023, where Habsora is presented as a solution to the target identification problem. The interviewee declares that '(Hasbora) enables the use of automatic tools to produce targets at a fast pace, and works by improving accurate and high-quality intelligence material according to [operational] needs' (Abraham, 2023). It is further explained how Habsora even recommends automatically the attacking of private residences where suspected militants live and can recommend bombing sites in 'real time' by processing vast amounts of data that immensely surpasses human capacities.

---

[3] https://www.972mag.com

[4] https://www.mekomit.co.il

Following the publication of this article, +972 Magazine and the Local Call also investigated the Israeli targeting software 'Lavender', which may be playing an equally important role in the Gaza Strip. Findings on Lavender were published in April 2024 (Abraham, 2024), this time supported by interviews with six Israeli intelligence officers who had served with the Israeli army in the ongoing operation. As explained, the difference between Habsora and Lavender is that the former targets buildings, while the latter targets 'people' in the sense of a kill list and has presumably resulted in the practice of destroying private residences in night attacks. Lavender reportedly works by using ML algorithms to put together vast amounts of data such as '[v]isual information, cellular information, social media connections, battlefield information, phone contacts, photos' (Abraham, 2024) and create a list of most probable targets. The report underlines the heavy reliance on Lavender, particularly at the beginning of the use of force. Like Abraham (2024) writes: 'During the first weeks of the war, the army almost completely relied on Lavender, which clocked as many as 37,000 Palestinians as suspected militants—and their homes—for possible air strikes'. The conclusion is that Lavender's 'influence on the military's operations was such that they essentially treated the outputs of the AI machine "as if it were a human decision"' (Abraham, 2024). While a more detailed discussion of the technical features and use of Lavender is beyond the limitations of this chapter, this case underscores the reality of meaning-generating military AI is not about some futuristic scenario. These findings confirm what has been argued above about the military reasons for using AI in terms of efficiency, speed, and data load, where human control may only be formal and become meaningless. As confirmed in the 2023 article, where the source cited admits: 'We work quickly and there is no time to delve deep into the target. The view is that we are judged according to how many targets we manage to generate' (Abraham, 2023).

Regarding the volume's intention to investigate 'the spillover effect of norm contestation in norm clusters' resiliency' (Wunderlich et al., 2025, Chap. 1), I suggest going a step beyond this perspective and consider how the three layers of normative structure, norm cluster, and norms are interrelated and the contestation of one of these layers can also erode the other layers. Moreover, all layers can be thought of as being embedded in a human-centred supra-structure of agency. In other words, the function of the three normative layers depends on human agents as co-constitutive pendants in line with the basic idea of structuration theory.

By zooming in on the case of military applications of AI, a twofold contestation comes into play. First, distributed agency contests the foundation of norm research—not least of contestation studies. Responding to this challenge requires a thorough consideration and reconceptualisation of how the relation of structure and agency, as well as of norms as co-constituted, can be understood. The general decision to use force lies still with human actors. But lower levels of how force is used and what it means for norms when the decision-making is being taken over by AI, like in the Israeli example, are not sufficiently studied yet. Second, and relatedly, distributed agency in decision-making fills the legal-normative void of, in this case, norms of the protection of civilians' legal norm cluster. While the meaning of legal norms such as distinction, proportionality, and necessity is, and was, always up for interpretative contestation and disagreement, the lack of human agency and deliberation creates a new, parallel normative structure defining conditions of possibility in practices. Distributed agency—what is also portrayed as 'meaningless human control' (Bode & Watts, 2021)—erodes the important aspect of human responsibility and accountability fundamental for the legal-normative structure. It means that it is not so much the conventional contestation that is the outcome of these practices but new understandings of what is appropriate use of force and how appropriateness is decided in distributed agency. How norms and their contestation depend on human agency is another sub-question to be considered by future research.

Norm generation of practices that involve distributed agency is in line with the argument about the silent, non-public changing and making of norms. Thus, I also highlight a double conceptual challenge of norm contestation studies. On the one hand, this refers to the lacking conceptual inclusion of norm generation in practices that are not necessarily a contestation of norms and, in the other hand, to the emergence of distributed agency in the interaction between humans and AI, which means an unprecedented interrelationship between forms of agency and structure.

Conclusion

The empirical illustrations show that AI becomes increasingly part of making life and death decisions in the military. While the extent to which agency is distributed between humans and AI systems differs and is not always analytically accessible without insights into classified processes, there is a discernible tendency that demonstrates the important role of AI in generating meaning-*of*-use by setting standards of appropriate use of military force. The normativity as the product of deliberative, public processes of human agency is gradually replaced by the normality of using AI in practices, such as those illustrated above. Here, the expectation of conventional norm research of normativity shaping practices—or being contested by them—is reversed in a shaping of normativity by what is functionally normal and appropriate. The chapter thus contributes to the volume by exploring the interaction between practices and norm dynamics.

The theoretical and practical incompatibility of the idea of distributed agency or non-human agency with epistemological and ontological foundations of legal norms creates an alternative structure that might be best characterised by a form of hybrid contestation: protection of civilians' legal norm cluster, including also the IHL, is contested by the social norms emerging in practices because they arguably violate dominant meanings of norms—even though it is unclear whether we see the contestation, or rather the concretisation of normative meaning. It can also be argued that distributed agency constitutes a contestation cluster because it puts into question the basic foundation of human-centred legal norms. The existence of norm clusters does not improve the resiliency of norms as long as there is no accommodation of changing conditions such as the emergence of elements of AI agency. If resiliency is also about the ability to adapt to external challenges, the challenge of distributed agency is not yet accommodated, putting resiliency under pressure.

Conversely, the emergence of new standards for applied distributed agency could create social norms that run parallel to the established legal-normative framework, without being informed by it or contesting it, because the interpretive void of perpetual contestation is not meaningful enough. Therefore, while the protection of civilians' norm cluster appears to be robust and strongly anchored in the normative structure of IHRL and international law, this robustness might be rather discursive than practical. Apart from the aspect of AI, there is evidence that understandings of appropriate use of force are changing in circumstances such as the Gaza war without public deliberation. The transferral of normative decision-making on AI is a contributing factor in this development. The question of what happens if the norm *entre-* and *antipreneur* is very much represented by an AI agency remains so far understudied. Again, the question is also to what extent contestation or affirmation depends on human agency and aspects such as intention.

The theoretical discussion in this chapter together with the introduction of practices underlines that the emergence of different and complex applications of AI in social practices poses potentially a major challenge for our conceptualisation of what norms are and do, and of how they relate to actors/agency. Social science has only started to respond to this challenge. Given the importance of the AI transformation of the present, a closer examination of its implications seems to be, however, highly important in different contexts of IR theorising and publishing.

References

Abraham, Y. (2023, November 30). "A mass assassination factory": Inside Israel's calculated bombing of Gaza. *+972 Magazine*. Retrieved February 4, 2025, from https://www.972mag.com/mass-assassination-factory-israel-calculated-bombing-gaza/

Abraham, Y. (2024, April 3). '"Lavender": The AI machine directing Israel's bombing spree in Gaza'.*+972 Magazine*. Retrieved February 4, 2025, from https://www.972mag.com/lavender-ai-israeli-army-gaza/

Acharya, A. (2004). How ideas spread: Whose norms matter? Norm localization and institutional change in Asian regionalism. *International Organization, 58*(02), 239–275.

Amoore, L. (2019). Doubt and the algorithm: On the partial accounts of machine learning. *Theory, Culture & Society, 36*(6), 147–169. https://doi.org/10.1177/0263276419851846

Aradau, C., & Blanke, T. (2018). Governing others: Anomaly and the algorithmic subject of security. *European Journal of International Security, 3*(01), 1–21. https://doi.org/10.1017/eis.2017.14

Article 36. (2015). *Killing by machine: Key issues for understanding meaningful human control*. Retrieved February 4, 2025, from https://www.stopkillerrobots.org/wp-content/uploads/2021/09/KILLING_BY_MACHINE_6.4.15.pdf

Bergengruen, V. (2024, February 8). How tech giants turned Ukraine into an AI war lab. *TIME*. https://time.com/6691662/ai-ukraine-war-palantir/

Bloomfield, A. (2016). Norm antipreneurs and theorising resistance to normative change. *Review of International Studies, 42*(2), 310–333. https://doi.org/10.1017/S026021051500025X

Bode, I. (2023). Practice-based and public-deliberative normativity: Retaining human control over the use of force. *European Journal of International Relations, 29*(4), 990–1016. https://doi.org/10.1177/13540661231163392

Bode, I., & Huelss, H. (2018). Autonomous weapons systems and changing norms in international relations. *Review of International Studies, 44*(03), 393–413. https://doi.org/10.1017/S0260210517000614

Bode, I., & Huelss, H. (2022). *Autonomous weapons systems and international norms*. McGill-Queen's University Press.

Bode, I., & Watts, T. (2021). *Meaning-less human control: Lessons from air defence systems for lethal autonomous weapons*. Drone Wars UK.

Brownlee, J. (2016). *Supervised and unsupervised machine learning algorithms*. Machine Learning Mastery. Retrieved February 4, 2025, from https://machinelearningmastery.com/supervised-and-unsupervised-machine-learning-algorithms/

Chandler, K. (2021). *Does military AI have gender? Understanding bias and promoting ethical approaches in military applications of AI*. UNIDIR.

Deitelhoff, N., & Zimmermann, L. (2018). Things we lost in the fire: How different types of contestation affect the robustness of international norms. *International Studies Review*. https://doi.org/10.1093/isr/viy080

Deitelhoff, N., & Zimmermann, L. (2019). Norms under challenge: Unpacking the dynamics of norm robustness. *Journal of Global Security Studies, 4*(1), 2–17. https://doi.org/10.1093/jogss/ogy041

DoD. (2022). *U.S. Department of Defense responsible artificial intelligence strategy and implementation pathway*. Retrieved February 4, 2025, from https://media.defense.gov/2022/Jun/22/2003022604/-1/-1/0/Department-of-Defense-Responsible-Artificial-Intelligence-Strategy-and-Implementation-Pathway.PDF

Drubel, J., & Mende, J. (2023). The hidden contestation of norms: Decent work in the International Labour Organization and the United Nations. *Global Constitutionalism, 12*(2), 246–268. https://doi.org/10.1017/S2045381722000259

European Parliament. (2024). Artificial Intelligence Act. *13 March 2024*. Retrieved February 4, 2025, from https://www.europarl.europa.eu/doceo/document/TA-9-2024-0138_EN.pdf

Finnemore, M., & Sikkink, K. (1998). International norm dynamics and political change. *International Organization, 52*(4), 887–917.

Future of Life Institute. (2023). *Pause Giant AI Experiments: An Open Letter*. Retrieved Feburary 4, 2025, from https://futureoflife.org/open-letter/pause-giant-ai-experiments/

Hoehn, J. R., Gallagher, J. C., & Sayler, K. M. (2020). *Overview of department of defense use of the electromagnetic spectrum* (R46564). Congressional research service. Retrieved February 4, 2025, from https://sgp.fas.org/crs/natsec/R46564.pdf

Holland Michel, A. (2020). *The black box, unlocked: Predictability and understandability in military AI*. United Nations Institute for Disarmament Research. https://doi.org/10.37559/SecTec/20/AI1

Huelss, H. (2020). Norms are what machines make of them: Autonomous weapons systems and the normative implications of human-machine interactions. *International Political Sociology, 14*(2), 111–128. https://doi.org/10.1093/ips/olz023

IBM. (2024). *What Is Machine Learning (ML)?* Retrieved February 4, 2025, from https://www.ibm.com/topics/machine-learning

ICC. (2002). *The Rome Statute of the International Criminal Court*. Retrieved April 23, 2025, from https://www.icc-cpi.int/sites/default/files/Publications/Rome-Statute.pdf

Katzenstein, P. J. (Ed.). (1996). *The culture of National Security: Norms and identity in world politics*. Columbia University Press.

Keck, M. E., & Sikkink, K. (1998). *Activists beyond Borders: Advocacy networks in international politics*. Cornell University Press.

Knapp, A., & Fritzler, J. (2025). Soft contestation' of the responsibility to protect? Assessing Canada and Sweden's norm diplomacy. In F. Lucenti, C. Ducci, C. Wunderlich, & J. S. Lantis

(Eds.), *Contestation in prism: The evolution of norms and norm clusters in contemporary global politics* (pp. 65–85). Springer.
Lantis, J. S., & Wunderlich, C. (2018). Resiliency dynamics of norm clusters: Norm contestation and international cooperation. *Review of International Studies, 44*(3), 570–593. https://doi.org/10.1017/S0260210517000626
Lucenti, F., Ducci, C., & Lee, P. K. (2025). Conceptualising the responsibility to prosecute norm as a cluster: Impunity for war crimes in Sri Lanka. In F. Lucenti, C. Ducci, C. Wunderlich, & J. S. Lantis (Eds.), *Contestation in prism: The evolution of norms and norm clusters in contemporary global politics* (pp. 87–105). Springer.
Morozov, E. (2014). *To save everything, click here: Technology, solutionism, and the urge to fix problems that don't exist.* Penguin Books.
NSCAI. (2021). *National Security Commission on artificial intelligence final report.*
Orchard, P., & Wiener, A. (2023). Norms and norm contestation. In P. A. Mello & F. Ostermann (Eds.), *Routledge handbook of foreign policy analysis methods* (pp. 51–66). Routledge.
Owens, W. A., & Offley, E. (2001). *Lifting the fog of war.* Johns Hopkins University Press.
Palantir. (2023). *Palantir AIP for defense.* Retrieved April 17, 2025, from https://www.palantir.com/aip/defense/
Rammert, W. (2008). Where the action is. Distributed agency between humans, machines, and programs. In U. Seifert, J. H. Kim, & A. Moore (Eds.), *Paradoxes of interactivity. Perspectives for media theory, human-computer interaction, and artistic investigations* (pp. 62–91). https://doi.org/10.25969/mediarep/2718
Risse, T., Ropp, S., & Sikkink, K. (1999). *The power of human rights: International norms and domestic change.* Cambridge University Press.
Schwarz, E. (2021). Autonomous weapons systems, artificial intelligence, and the problem of meaningful human control. *Philosophical Journal of Conflict and Violence, 5*(1), 53–72. https://doi.org/10.22618/TP.PJCV.20215.1.139004
Suchman, L. (2020). Algorithmic warfare and the reinvention of accuracy. *Critical Studies on Security, 8*(2), 175–187. https://doi.org/10.1080/21624887.2020.1760587
Suchman, L. (2022). Imaginaries of omniscience: Automating intelligence in the US Department of Defense. *Social Studies of Science., 53*, 761. https://doi.org/10.1177/03063127221104938
Sunstein, C. R. (1996). Social norms and social roles. *Columbia Law Review, 96*(4), 903–968.
Tholens, S. (2025). Hidden transcripts and normative transformations. In F. Lucenti, C. Ducci, C. Wunderlich & J. S. Lantis (Eds.), *Contestation in prism: The evolution of norms and norm clusters in contemporary global politics* (pp. 163–181). Springer.
United Nations. (1945). *United Nations Charter.* Retrieved February 4, 2025, from https://www.un.org/en/about-us/un-charter/full-text
United Nations. (1948). *Universal Declaration of Human Rights.* Retrieved February 4, 2025, from https://www.un.org/sites/un2.un.org/files/2021/03/udhr.pdf
United Nations. (1977a). *Protocol additional to the Geneva Conventions of 12 August 1949 and relating to the protection of victims of international armed conflicts (Protocol I).* Retrieved February 4, 2025, from https://www.un.org/en/genocideprevention/documents/atrocity-crimes/Doc.34_AP-I-EN.pdf
United Nations. (1977b). *Protocol additional to the Geneva Conventions of 12 August 1949 and relating to the protection of victims of international armed conflicts (Protocol II).* Retrieved February 4, 2025, from https://www.ohchr.org/en/instruments-mechanisms/instruments/protocol-additional-geneva-conventions-12-august-1949-and-0
United Nations. (2011). *International legal protection of human rights in armed conflict.* United Nations Publications.
Wendt, A. (1987). The agent-structure problem in international relations theory. *International Organization, 41*(3), 335–370.
Wiener, A. (2004). Contested compliance: Interventions on the normative structure of world politics. *European Journal of International Relations, 10*(2), 189–234. https://doi.org/10.1177/1350661040429 34

Wiener, A. (2007). The dual quality of norms and governance beyond the state: Sociological and normative approaches to 'Interaction'. *Critical Review of International Social and Political Philosophy, 10*(1), 47–69.

Wiener, A. (2009). Enacting meaning-in-use: Qualitative research on norms and international relations. *Review of International Studies, 35*(1), 175–193. https://doi.org/10.1017/S0260210509008377

Wiener, A. (2014). *A theory of contestation*. Springer.

Wunderlich, C., Lucenti, F., Ducci, C., & Lantis, J. S. (2025). Contestation in prism: An introduction. In F. Lucenti, C. Ducci, C. Wunderlich, & J. S. Lantis (Eds.), *Contestation in prism: The evolution of norms and norm clusters in contemporary global politics* (pp. 1–21). Springer.

Zimmermann, L. (2016). Same same or different? Norm diffusion between resistance, compliance, and localization in post-conflict states. *International Studies Perspectives, 17*(1), 98–115. https://doi.org/10.1111/insp.12080

Zimmermann, L., Deitelhoff, N., Lesch, M., Arcudi, A., & Peex, A. (2023). *International norm disputes: The link between contestation and norm robustness*. Oxford University Press. https://doi.org/10.1093/oso/9780198873235.001.0001

Chapter 7
Gender Equality Norm Cluster in Action: The Resiliency of Sexual and Reproductive Health and Rights in the EU

Diego Badell

Contesting Sexual and Reproductive Health and Rights in the EU Context

International norms related to gender equality exhibit a particular characteristic as they demonstrate significant synergy and an intrinsic interdependence among them (Zwingel, 2020, p. 52). This implies that a contestation exerted against one of the norms that make up the gender equality norm cluster may have an effect on the rest of the norms that compose it (Lantis & Wunderlich, 2018). Gender equality involves three interconnected norms: Sexual and Reproductive Health and Rights (SRHR), women's full economic and social parity, and distinguishing between biological sex and socially constructed gender roles (Sanders, 2018). This chapter particularly focuses its attention on one of such norms: SRHR, which applies human rights principles to matters of bodily autonomy, reproductive control, and sexual freedom. SRHR was officially endorsed as a soft law norm during the 1994 Fifth International Conference on Population and Development and the 1995 Fourth World Conference on Women. Over the years, the norm of SRHR has gained global acceptance. As a result, many countries have expanded the legal circumstances for abortion, allowing it in cases where it was previously prohibited.[1] This norm, however, still faces

[1] The issue of abortion is one of the SRHR core features. From the 1994 and 1995 conferences to the present day 'almost 50 countries around the world [enacted] laws expanding the circumstances in which abortion is legal' (Center for Reproductive Rights, 2021). For example, 15 countries have reformed their national legislation to permit abortion—e.g. Ireland, Spain, Portugal, Mozambique—and 18 countries have repealed the total ban on abortion—e.g. Nepal, Chile, Colombia, Iran, Angola.

D. Badell (✉)
Facultat de Ciències Polítiques i Sociologia, Autonomous University of Barcelona, Bellaterra, Cerdanyola del Vallés, Spain
e-mail: diego.badell@uab.cat

F. Lucenti et al. (eds.), *Contestation in Prism*, Norm Research in International Relations, https://doi.org/10.1007/978-3-031-83639-8_7

opposition from state and non-state actors, particularly the Holy See and Republican presidential administrations in the US (e.g. Barbé & Badell, 2023), who contest the norm based on reframing arguments related to culture, religion, abortion, family, and homosexuality. Of particular interest to this contribution is the case of the European Union (EU), which is defined as a 'liberal normative community' (Badell, 2023, p. 1). Within the EU, SRHR has been broadly supported, and it is internalised and embedded in various initiatives, including the European Consensus on Development (European Union, 2006, 2017) and the EU Gender Action Plans (European Commission, 2016, 2020). Such support is based on a constant norm's re-enactment based on an institutionalisation of the EU's promotion of SRHR abroad and the reassertion of national sovereignty by some member states at home (Badell, 2024). This is also known as the existence of a 'permissive consensus ' (Hooghe & Marks, 2009),[2] suggesting that not all member states are socialised with the norm in equal terms.

In detail, the chapter examines the contestation of SRHR within EU foreign policy from 1995, when it was first introduced as part of EU-promoted norms, until 2023. In line with the aims of the volume (see Wunderlich et al., 2025, Chap. 1), it delves into how the SRHR has been contested, by distinguishing between applicatory and validity contestation (Deiteholff & Zimmermann, 2020) and whether such contestation has eroded the gender equality norm cluster. Applicatory contestation is therefore observed as the dominant type of contestation in this issue area, creating an agreed channel for the expression of challenging views on the norm based on the premise of permissive consensus (Barbé & Badell, 2020; Wiener, 2014). However, in 2020, there was also a case of contestation of validity during the negotiations of GAP III. Two member states, Poland and Hungary, contested the need to uphold SRHR, but also widened the focus of their contestation by focusing on other gender equality norms such as the socially constructed definition of gender. Instead of eroding the norm, as it could have been expected, most member states opted for a staunch defence of the gender equality norm cluster. This resulted in the creation of a clear division within the EU, with the in-group continuing to support the norms and the out-group not only opposing GAP III but also being ostracised. Later, in 2021, Hungary and Poland re-joined the in-group by reinstating SRHR in the Team Europe Conclusions (Council of the European Union, 2021). The type of contestation carried out also has an impact on the gender equality cluster, with the contestation in Hungary and Poland going beyond the norm and escalating to question other fundamental norms that are similar in principles, values, and orientations within the issue area covered (Lantis & Wunderlich, 2018, p. 571). In particular, it impinged on the norm that represents the social construction of gender (Sanders, 2018).

Given these premises, the chapter proceeds as follows. To begin with, it traces the inclusion of the SRHR on the EU's agenda as well as its norm internalisation. Next, the chapter analyses how the norm has been contested within the EU through the prism of applicatory and validity contestation and its impact on the norm

[2] Permissive consensus refers to a historical phase within European integration during which both citizens and political elites exhibited substantial support for the integration process without active opposition. This era stands in stark contrast to the contemporary period, which is characterised by constraining dissensus, wherein European integration has become increasingly politicised and subject to contestation by both citizens and political elites alike.

robustness within the EU system. This analysis employs the qualitative case study research method and is based on fieldwork conducted by the author mostly in Brussels, but also online, mainly between 2020 and 2021 and partially enriched with reference to the present information. The empirical evidence comes from 32 semi-structured interviews with EU officials from the European Commission and the Diplomatic Service of the European Union (EEAS), representatives from member states' permanent representations,[3] and civil society organisations (see Table 7.1).

The chapter also employs document analysis,[4] examining references to SRHR in Council Conclusions, as well as other documents where SRHR plays a significant role, such as the European Consensus on Development and GAPs. Finally, the concluding section reflects on the findings of this study and outlines new avenues for research on SRHR and gender equality norms.

The EU and Gender Equality Norms: A Strong Defender of SRHR

In 2015, the EU underscored its enduring dedication to advancing gender equality norms, regarding them as a fundamental aspect of its identity (EEAS, 2015). Indeed, the EU's commitment to eliminating inequalities and promoting equality between men and women is enshrined in Article 8 of the Treaty on the Functioning of the EU. This has led scholars to refer to the EU as a gendered actor, highlighting its active role in shaping gender policies (Elgström, 2017; Guerrina & Wright, 2016).

The importance of reducing gender disparities in the EU's external action has been recognised since the 1995 Council Resolution on integrating gender issues in development cooperation. The adoption of gender norms as part of the EU's framework of action is twofold. Firstly, the accession of Nordic countries such as Sweden and Finland in 1995 strengthened the Union's support for gender equality norms by creating a critical mass of states in favour of such measures (Finnemore & Sikkink, 1998, p. 901). Second, the catalyst for the EU's inclusion of gender as a policy priority was the 1995 Beijing Conference (Elgström, 2000, p. 462). The presence and prominence of gender norms at the international level has also influenced the internal consensus within the EU. However, the European Consensus on Development (ECD) of 2006 and 2017 are among the most important documents that have enshrined the EU's commitment to promoting SRHR globally. The ECDs have played a crucial role in the institutionalisation of the SRHR norm within the EU

[3] The interviewee sample encompasses representatives from both big and small member states. Despite efforts to engage all member states' permanent representations, some responses to requests for interviews were not positive. It is noteworthy that there is an imbalance, with underrepresentation of Central and Eastern European member states. Their representatives politely declined participation. Additionally, Members of the European Parliament uniformly declined interview invitations.

[4] Document analysis refers to a systematic review and evaluation of documents guided by the research question. Documents were read to uncover the underlying meanings and to understand the context of these documents.

Table 7.1 List of Interviews

#	Position	Date
1.	Member state representative (UN in New York)	11/9/2020
2.	Member state representative (UN in New York)	15/9/2020
3.	EU official (UN in New York)	18/9/2020
4.	Member state representative (UN in New York)	22/9/2020
5.	Member state representative (UN in New York)	2/10/2020
6.	Member state representative (UN in New York)	12/11/2020
7.	Member state representative (UN in New York)	26/10/2020
8.	Member state representative (UN in Geneva)	16/10/2020
9.	Member state representative (UN in Geneva)	23/10/2020
10.	EU official	10/11/2020
11.	EU official	2/10/2020
12.	EU official	2/10/2020
13.	EU official	2/10/2020
14.	EU official	10/11/2020
15.	EU official	10/11/2020
16.	EU official	10/11/2020
17.	CSO	23/9/2020
18.	CSO	19/10/2020
19.	CSO	19/10/2020
20.	CSO	22/10/2020
21.	Member state representative in the EU	22/9/2020
22.	Member state representative in the EU	8/10/2020
23.	Member state representative in the EU	15/10/2020
24.	Member state representative in the EU	16/10/2020
25.	Member state representative in the EU	30/10/2020
26.	Member state representative in the EU	23/11/2020
27.	Member state representative in the EU	26/11/2020
28.	Member state representative in the EU	26/11/2020
29.	Member state representative in the EU	15/1/2021
30.	Member state representative in the EU	1/2/2021
31.	Member state representative in the EU	9/2/2021
32.	Member state representative in the EU	7/5/2021

This work was supported by Spanish Ministry of Science, Innovation and Universities, Research Project: A contested European Union in a fragmenting international order (COURAGE), Grant Agreement: PID2023-147735NB-I00

until its implementation in the Lisbon Treaty, but it is important to note that the institutionalisation of SRHR predates these documents. Already in 1997, Council Regulation 1484/97 on aid to populations and programmes in developing countries was the first document to address SRHR issues and served to socialise the 15 member states with the norm (Council of the European Union, 1997). Similarly, the 2006 ECD promoted the socialisation of the 25 member states on SRHR, and the

2017 ECD achieved the same objective with the 27 member states. This process was based on the premise that the EU would not force member states to change their own national positions on SRHR but would instead ask them to allow the EU to promote SRHR externally. More specifically, the language agreed in the ECDs, which together with the 2015 Council Conclusions on Gender in Development (Council of the European Union, 2015) will become the reference point for SRHR, is referred to in various Council Conclusions, such as those of the Human Rights Council and the Commission on the Status of Women, as well as in thematic documents such as the EU Gender Action Plans.

Yet, while on the surface it may appear that the EU normative community is composed of actors who share a common set of values and expectations (Hoffmann, 2010), this chapter shows that within the EU there is instead a fragmentation between member states. Despite the requirement that any country wishing to join the EU must adhere to the Copenhagen principles, which creates expectations of appropriate behaviour (March & Olsen, 2011), not all countries adhere to the EU's existing and emerging standards, principles, and norms on respect for human rights, democracy, and the rule of law. This leads to the assumption of the existence of an in-norm community, i.e. an in-group of member states that fully endorse the norms and values of the EU, and the possible emergence of an out-community, i.e. an out-group of member states that deviate from the expected appropriate behaviour (Katzenstein, 1996). The potential emergence of an out-group can be found in weak norm socialisation. This is relevant because norm socialisation has the ultimate goal of internalising the norms and values of a given normative community (Checkel, 2001, p. 554), where actors who join the normative community are assumed to adopt them as their own (Badell, 2024; Schimmelfennig, 2000). As Checkel (2005) argues, there are two forms of norm internalisation: one (type I) in which an actor adopts the norm without reflective consideration, and another (type II) where the norm is internalised because it is perceived as the morally correct path of action. The former is relevant to this chapter as it bears the inherent risk of contestation escalating to its validity form since it does not involve a thought-through internalisation of norms (Juncos & Pomorska, 2006, p. 4). In this respect, a case in point is the 2004 Malta Accession Agreement, which mainly contrasts with the EU context of promoting sexual and reproductive health and rights as an international norm. The Agreement stipulated that while the EU would respect Malta's decision to ban abortion domestically, the country would also allow the EU to promote gender equality norms, including SRHR, globally (Badell, 2024). Such socialisation of Malta within the EU, and its promotion of the SRHR norm, echoes Type I norm socialisation, and by extension, the norm can be subject to validity contestation at any point (Deitelhoff & Zimmermann, 2020). Not only that, but it also posits that the EU's engagement with gender equality norms, including SRHR, would take place primarily in its external relations. In other words, when it comes to human rights, the EU is mainly seen as an exporter of norms (Barbé et al., 2009), which further reflects the EU's identity as a liberal normative power (Wagner, 2017), but which can also provoke controversy, primarily from states or entities that perceive its norms as imposing unwanted standards.

Currently, however, the EU uses various main approaches to promote and advocate for SRHR. First, it establishes close partnerships with Civil Society Organisations (CSOs) by collaborating with representatives from CSOs like ACT Alliance EU and Women in Development Europe. The European Commission's Directorate-General for International Cooperation and Development (DG DEVCO/DG INTPA) works with these CSO representatives to address gender issues. The Commission also organises the annual European Development Days in Brussels and improves its external relations and aid programmes in this direction. Within the European Commission, for example, two Directorates-General (DGs) have played a crucial role in advancing gender equality norms, including SRHR. DG IB—external relations, responsible for aid to Latin America and Asia, and DG VIII—development—responsible for aid to African, Caribbean, and Pacific countries, have been instrumental in shaping the EU's engagement with gender issues. As a result, the Commission rebranded the Women in Development Desk, which focused on women's projects, as the Gender and Development Desk (Elgström, 2000), with an emphasis on gender role analysis in all development aid projects. Second, the EU's gender action plans specify the areas where the SRHR norm, and other gender equality norms, should be applied, and they identify several United Nations forums for its expansion, including the UN General Assembly, the UN Human Rights Council, and the UN Security Council. The EU considers the UN Security Council a crucial institution for promoting gender equality norms and strives to implement Resolution 1325 on 'Women, Peace and Security' (WPS). The EU's WPS Strategy emphasises the need to incorporate mechanisms for providing access to reproductive health services to survivors of sexual violence in future UN Security Council resolutions on WPS (Council of the European Union, 2018).

Third, the EU expands the socialisation of SRHR through international institutions, endorsing a more progressive language on SRHR at the international level compared to the UN (Interview 3, Table 7.1). While the EU advocates for 'sexual and reproductive health and rights' (Interview 3, Table 7.1), which encompasses aspects of bodily autonomy such as contraception and abortion, the UN uses the term 'sexual and reproductive health and reproductive rights' (Interview 3, Table 7.1). The differentiation of reproductive rights from sexual and reproductive health in the UN's language clarifies that abortion is not promoted as part of bodily autonomy rights at the UN level (Interview 1 and 2, Table 7.1). The EU is aware that advocating for abortion rights directly at the UN could be counterproductive and even jeopardise existing support for the SRHR norm (Interview 3, Table 7.1). However, the EU has been proud to advocate for more progressive language on SRHR at the UN and to defend the norm when it faces opposition.

All things considered, the EU can be considered a relevant actor in the field of SRHR, aiming to promote a progressive stance on the norm at the international level. This actorness is built on a permissive consensus, which relies on an institutionalisation of the norm that enables the EU to accommodate the divergent views of its member states. When member states express disagreement with SRHR, the EU refers to agreed language to address contestation, where member states are reminded that they are not asked to domestically abide by but to pragmatically enhance the EU to promote the norms abroad. Rather, the EU encourages the global outward promotion of the norm through its key institutions. However, this way of institutionalising the norm runs the risk of transforming the consensus into a constraining dissensus in the future, both in the EU and in the international context.

Contesting SRHR Within the EU

Institutionalising Contestation (1995–2017)

The opposition to SRHR within the EU is not a recent development. As early as 1997, during the first attempt to internalise the norm (Finnemore & Sikkink, 1998), Italy objected to the term 'sexual and reproductive health' due to concerns that it could be interpreted as taking a stance on abortion at the national level. Ultimately, after consultation with the national capital, the Italian representative withdrew the threat of entering a reservation on the wording since it was clear that the EU was not enforcing changes at the national level but building external actorness on the issue (Elgström, 2000, p. 468; see also Badell, 2023, 2024). A similar situation occurred in 2004 during the negotiations for Malta's accession to the EU. As mentioned before, it was specified in the accession agreement that the EU would not interfere in Maltese policy regarding women's reproductive rights, while the EU could advocate for the norm globally.

Both the Italian and Maltese cases illustrate that when non-enthusiastic member states are socialised into SRHR, they tend to express their opposition to the norm's implementation through established negotiation channels, emphasising that they are not obliged to adhere to the norm domestically. This has led to the development of a particular norm institutionalisation within the EU that touches upon the norm's application. It acknowledges that the member states are not mandated to alter their national laws and policies, but this does not prevent the EU from advocating for SRHR internationally. This institutionalisation is reaffirmed over time, such as during the 2006 ECD, where SRHR was given a prominent position.

Moreover, it is worth noting that in 2015 member states with a longstanding opposition to or those newly acquainted with SRHR—for instance, after the enlargements in 2004 and 2007—had the opportunity to shape the consensus on the matter. Despite negotiations, no significant alterations were made. The Council Conclusions on Gender and Development revitalised the institutionalisation of SRHR within the EU, serving as the official document that encapsulates the collectively agreed language and stance on SRHR. Crucially, these Conclusions would develop into the established reference point for the EU's position on SRHR. This language played a similar role to that of the 2006 ECD in acquainting new member states with SRHR terminology, albeit this time with the added ownership and endorsement of all 28 member states. This implies that the contestation based on the constant re-enactment of the boundaries within which the norm applies has ended up reinforcing it over time. This is because each time the EU has enlarged, it has coincided with the negotiation of a text specifying the expected appropriate behaviours of the actors. In line with debates on applicatory contestation (Wunderlich et al., 2025, Chap. 1), applicatory contestation seems to have reinforced the norm.

In the context of the process of institutionalising the norm, a progressive group of member states therefore welcomed the European Commission's reports on SRHR, while the more reluctant actors took note of them. The existence of a group of reluctant actors vis-à-vis SRHR led to the progressive group of countries to gather in informal meetings. That is, an informal network of like-minded countries was established to establish a negotiating tactic to protect the SRHR consensus from unexpected setbacks (Interview 22, 25, and 30, Table 7.1). The European Parliament, recognised as the most progressive European human rights institution and a strong advocate for SRHR, also has raised concerns regarding the potential setback due to existing weak norm socialisation processes (European Parliament, 2021a, 2021b, 2021c). The first occurred in 2012 when the first European Citizens' Initiative, known as 'One of Us', targeted SRHR cutting off EU funding to organisations (Badell, 2022), like the International Planned Parenthood Federation, a prominent civil society organisation working in this field. This initiative, coordinated by the European Religious Right, mirrored the US Gag Rule (Badell, 2022) by targeting funding activities of organisations specialising in SRHR. However, the European Commission rejected their claim after a public hearing in Parliament, asserting that the existing funding framework, previously agreed upon by EU member states and the European Parliament, was appropriate (European Commission, 2014).

The second concerning signal emerged in 2013 when the Estrela Report, addressing both the external and internal aspects of SRHR, failed to be adopted. This report recommended that member states ensure the legality, safety, and accessibility of high-quality abortion services within their public health systems while urging the EU to adopt a human rights-based approach and concrete targets on SRHR, including family planning services, maternal and infant mortality, safe abortion, and contraceptives. However, an alternative report drafted by the far-right and right-wing factions passed, emphasising that action related to SRHR speaks directly to national sovereignty, thus falling under the competence of member states (European Parliament, 2013a, 2013b). Despite this, the Commission's approach to SRHR remained unchanged.

Such developments culminated in a critical moment in 2017 when Malta, during its presidency, challenged the assumption that contestation against SRHR could always be channelled effectively. Indeed, the negotiation of the new ECD took place under Malta's chairmanship of the Working Party on Development Cooperation (CODEV). This opened the debate on redefining the common position on SRHR, causing significant strain (Interview 21, Table 7.1). Two plausible options emerged for member states. Malta supported a less ambitious SRHR language, while progressive parties pushed for a significantly more progressive stance. Faced with the risk of deadlock that could severely impact the EU's commitment to the norm abroad, it was decided to revert to the language agreed upon in 2015. The 2015 Council Conclusions on Gender and Development (Council of the European Union, 2015), which were upheld, contained the following provisions:

> The Council remains committed to the promotion, protection and fulfilment of all human rights and to the full and effective implementation of the Beijing Platform for Action and the Programme of Action of the ICPD and the outcomes of their review conferences and remains committed to sexual and reproductive health and rights (SRHR), in this context.

And the 2017 ECD replicated the Council Conclusions SRHR (Council of the European Union, 2017) language stating the following:

> The EU remains committed to the promotion, protection and fulfilment of all human rights and to the full and effective implementation of the Beijing Platform for Action and the Programme of Action of the ICPD and the outcomes of their review conferences and remains committed to sexual and reproductive health and rights (SRHR), in this context.

In essence, Malta's contestation of SRHR resulted in maintaining the *status quo* of the norm, without significant progress or regression. Subsequent meetings have since then revolved around re-enacting the norm's previous status. Therefore, Malta's opposition ended up strengthening the norm but left SRHR in a precarious position. Indeed, according to some interviewees, the diplomatic efforts invested in reaching this agreement have led the EU to focus more on solving internal conflicts related to SRHR rather than diffusing the norm externally (Interview 25 and 30, Table 7.1).

In parallel, Ireland, which had been Malta's staunchest ally in opposing SRHR, completely reversed its position with the legalisation of abortion through a referendum in May 2018. But also, later on, Malta itself embarked on a path towards a more proactive role in the SRHR domain by legalising same-sex marriage in July 2017. While abortion remains prohibited in Malta, the country's shift towards recognising sexual rights made it easier for them to abandon their obstructive stance in such negotiations. The changes at the domestic level suggested that the EU could develop a comprehensive SRHR policy encompassing both internal and external dimensions. Yet, international developments in January 2017 fuelled intensified struggles. It is important to note that the EU is highly dependent on the Liberal International Order and its norms, where changes in this order significantly impact the EU's commitment to it (Badell, 2023). This speaks to another aspect of contestation, which is very relevant for the EU: the role of external contestation—i.e. outside-in contestation (Badell, 2022). As we will see in the following lines, internal and external contestation is frequently intertwined (Thevenin et al., 2020).

The Limits of Contestation: The Emergence of Validity Contestation (2017–2020)

In 2017, the election of a new US administration posed a substantial setback to the EU's steady progression towards becoming a significant global player in the realm of SRHR. The Trump Administration's policies contributed to a polarisation of views towards SRHR on the world stage, deliberately undermining its universalistic nature in favour of putting forward an illiberal alternative (Barbé & Badell, 2023). As a result, contestation against SRHR within the EU appeared to arise from both internal and external sources.

Examining the inside aspect, we observe a positive aspect, the transformation of Malta and Ireland into progressive or less-reluctant actors. This involves internalising SRHR because it is perceived as the morally correct course of action (Checkel, 2005). However, two other member states persisted in playing an obstructing role. According to one interviewee for this study, Poland and Hungary consistently opposed SRHR. The timing of Trump's election coincided with the emergence of Hungary and Poland's distinctive form of contestation, contrasting with that of Malta and Ireland. Indeed, both Hungary and Poland were ruled, at that time, by populist far-right parties, which made women's rights and abortion one of their main political battles. As we will see later in this chapter, opposition to SRHR led the US, Hungary, and Poland to collaborate in the emergence of an alternative international norm to SRHR. This period also saw the UK withdrawing from the EU. Several interviewees noted the UK's significant role in bridging gaps between member states supporting and opposing SRHR (Interviews 4, 5, and 14, Table 7.1). The EU was confronted with a dual challenge: the departure of a key consensus-building actor and ongoing efforts by the Trump Administration to establish an alternative norm.

However, as noted above, Hungary and Poland have taken a different approach from Ireland and Malta in the past. On the one hand, Maltese and Irish contestation was channelled in a way that the countries' concerns were heard. For instance, in the case of Malta a note was added that the EU's position on SRHR did not include the country. On the other hand, according to multiple interviewees, Hungary and Poland began to vehemently question the need to include SRHR on the COHOM (Working Party on Human Rights) and CODEV agenda (Interviews 21, 23, 28, and 30, Table 7.1). In other words, while Ireland and Malta had exerted contestation based on the norms, Hungary and Poland started to exert contestation by questioning the norm's validity. Yet, Hungary's and Poland's contestation of SRHR did not immediately disrupt the EU consensus. The institutional processes that ensure that the EU's international stance on SRHR does not compel domestic compliance remained intact (e.g. Badell, 2024). However, tensions surfaced during the negotiations for the post-Cotonou agreements, which were concluded in April 2021, as progressive and opposing member states clashed over the issue. Countries such as Finland, Sweden, and Denmark advocated for stronger women's rights through an updated SRHR section, while Hungary, Malta, and Poland raised concerns about the link between reproductive rights and abortion—with Malta quickly withdrawing its opposition but Poland entering a reservation on the EU mandate. This reservation was later lifted after an official statement clarified that the SRHR provisions would not oblige member states to amend their national laws (Carbone, 2019, p. 145).

As a result, despite Poland's initial resistance, the EU's stance on SRHR remained intact with the post-Cotonou agreement adopting language consistent with the 2015 conclusions. While Poland prioritised safeguarding its national interests, Hungary focused on building a broader coalition against SRHR. One notable example was Hungary's hosting of the World Congress of Families (WCF) in 2017, an event that united SRHR opponents from Islamic, Catholic, and post-Soviet states. During the event, Hungarian Prime Minister Viktor Orbán emphasised the distinct cultural identity of Central Europe, stating, 'Central Europe [...] has a special culture. It is different from Western Europe' (Hungary, 2017 in Badell, 2024, p. 8). He further asserted that 'every European country has the right to defend its Christian culture and the right to reject the ideology of multiculturalism [...] and to defend the traditional family model' (Hungary, 2017 in Badell, 2024, p. 8).

In other words, the Hungarian President perceives SRHR as a threat to the survival of the nation and is therefore seeking to reshape European policy on SRHR. More to the point, the US inclination to undermine the international norm resulted in a further polarisation within CODEV. Initially, this had a beneficial effect, prompting silent actors—those whose foreign policy doesn't prioritise women's rights—to express their position on the matter. It demonstrated that a considerable number of member states, including traditionally silent and reluctant ones like Romania or Cyprus, aligned with the EU's language on SRHR (Interviews 13 and 14, Table 7.1). That is how, in successive CODEV meetings focusing on SRHR, a pattern emerged where 25 countries consistently supported the agreed language, while Hungary and Poland initially dissented. However, by the end of each meeting, both these countries eventually aligned themselves with the majority. It may indicate that the US actions at that stage seemed to trigger a new wave of contestation that ultimately did not substantially undermine the norm within the EU. During this phase, hence, member states became increasingly vocal in defending the norm and a clear boundary started to emerge: the EU's commitment to SRHR could not be questioned.

Differently, the contestation of SRHR culminated when Trump offered Hungary and Poland an alternative SRHR on the international stage, allowing them to openly push for the reshaping of the norm in EU foreign policy. This was the case of the Geneva Consensus Declaration presented by the US in October 2020 (Barbé & Badell, 2023; United States, 2020). The Geneva Consensus reframed reproductive health, emphasising that under no circumstances should abortion be promoted as a method of family planning. In essence, supporters of the Geneva Consensus promoted an illiberal version of SRHR, seeking to exclude women's rights from public discourse and policies, thereby diminishing their autonomy and depriving them of the ability to make decisions about their reproductive health in a private and personal setting. Moreover, there has also been a resurgence of national sovereignty sentiments in the area of reproductive rights, leading to a renationalisation of the norm, driven by an anti-multilateralist stance. The argument posited was that such rights could only be guaranteed by the sovereign state and should not be subject to international discussion. Particularly significant for the EU was that this illiberal alternative regarding SRHR prompted Hungary and Poland to openly contest the validity of their commitment to SRHR. This is evident from Hungary's co-sponsorship of the Consensus, with Poland also endorsing it by adding their signature.

Within the EU, the immediate repercussions of the Geneva Consensus were striking. Shielded by an illiberal international norm, Hungary and Poland shifted their attention towards the GAP, which is an EU multiannual framework of action to promote gender equality norms, including SRHR. The negotiations of GAP III coincided with a period when SRHR was not only prominent at the international level but also highly significant in Poland due to the Constitutional Tribunal's ruling imposing an almost complete ban on abortion. In a virtual meeting necessitated by the COVID-19 pandemic, Poland, and to a greater extent Hungary, obstructed CODEV from endorsing the GAP as Council Conclusions (Interview 18). This signified the demise of the permissive consensus on SRHR (Hooghe & Marks, 2009).

During negotiations, SRHR was not the only object of validity contestation. Indeed, contestation escalated as Hungary and Poland drove a revisionist agenda, focusing on the need to redefine gender. These two countries, joined by Bulgaria, argued that gender should be understood as equality between men and women, and rejected the idea of gender as a social construct. In essence, Hungary and Poland were contesting the validity of another fundamental norm within the gender equality cluster (Sanders, 2018). It was precisely this escalation in the contestation strategy of these countries that led the large group of progressive actors to make the decision for the first time in the realm of external action to not approve Council Conclusions. Such a decision was made for fear of eroding the norm's status. This prompted Germany, then holding the chairmanship of CODEV, to downgrade the final document by approving the GAP as Presidency Conclusions. This decision was unprecedented, as the German delegate initially planned to address the issue at the ambassadorial level but hesitated due to concerns that doing so might necessitate accommodating the perspectives of the two opposing countries at that level. However, this coincided with the already packed agenda at higher levels, including discussions on the EU's COVID-19 recovery plan, which favoured the tactic of retaining the GAP at the CODEV level. It is also worth noting that another rationale cited to justify the ostracisation of Hungary and Poland was the minimal impact their development budget would have had on the successful implementation of GAP II (Interview 18). Even more significant was the Commission's perspective, which regarded the Conclusions as a mere formality given its autonomy in drafting and implementing many of the GAP provisions (Interviews 1, 2, and 3, Table 7.1). Ultimately, adopting GAP III as Presidency Conclusions in December 2020 was seen as the only option found to preserve the content of the Plan without yielding to the views of the two contesting countries. In this regard, GAP III echoed the 2015 common position on SRHR. These events can be seen as further evidence of the resiliency of SRHR within the EU. In essence, contesting the norm has not only strengthened its content but also showcased its resiliency as actors openly questioning its validity were symbolically expelled—i.e. ostracised—from the EU normative community. It marks, in the words of Ouwerkerk et al. (2005), the social death penalty in terms of an actor's exclusion from a community.

A symbolic expulsion was therefore highlighted in the Presidency Conclusions, marking the first instance of an analysis of the current state of the norm. It gathered the signatures of 24 member states, with Bulgaria initially abstaining from adherence. Consequently, the Conclusions emphasised the necessity to 'safeguard achievements made on gender equality and women and girls' full enjoyment of all human rights and their empowerment against any deterioration and backlash' norm (Council of the European Union, 2020). For the first time, an EU document expressed deep concern and regret that gender equality, the empowerment of women and girls, and their full enjoyment of all human rights, including SRHR, were under threat, questioned, and faced setbacks amid shrinking civil, democratic, and civic space globally (Council of the European Union, 2020). Essentially, the Presidency Conclusions showcased the collective readiness of the vast majority of member states, the European Commission, and the European Parliament to defend and protect SRHR.

The Return of Applicatory Contestation (2021–Ongoing)

In 2021, the international scenario took a different direction. The Trump factor disappeared, and in January 2021, Joseph Biden assumed the US presidency, expressing a willingness to recommit the country to multilateralism and reinstate its support for SRHR. Among the various decisions made by the new administration, it was decided that the US would withdraw from the Geneva Consensus. Consequently, the illiberal alternative to SRHR lost a significant supporter, and Poland and Hungary no longer had this international backing. With a less polarised international environment, the EU was able to re-enact the normative consensus on SRHR. This was evident in the unanimously adopted Team Europe 2021 Conclusions (Council of the European Union, 2021), which stated the following:

> The Council recalls the EU's commitment, under the European Consensus on Development, to remain committed to the promotion, protection and fulfilment of all human rights and to the full and effective implementation of the Beijing Platform for Action and the Programme of Action of the International Conference on Population and Development (ICPD) and the outcomes of their review conferences and remains committed to sexual and reproductive health and rights (SRHR), in this context.

The Conclusions of Team Europe demonstrate that EU foreign policy on SRHR has been stronger than initially anticipated. It is evident that there has always been an ongoing debate about SRHR within the EU. However, the shift of Hungary and Poland from the December 2020 Gender Action Plan III to the April 2021 Team Europe indicates that contestation does not always weaken SRHR but rather strengthens the norm over time.

Along these lines, the Neighbourhood, Development, and International Cooperation Instrument, which established a new coherent financing architecture for the EU's relationships with partner countries, was adopted in 2021. Among one of its most controversial issues was making gender equality as a cross-cutting priority. While Hungary opposed this movement, it was not successful in blocking it (Lundgren et al., 2022). Indeed, in subsequent meetings that included references to gender equality norms, Hungary and Poland decided not to question the reasons why the EU should uphold such norms but contested how the norm should be implemented, hence showing an applicatory rather than a validity contestation. A very relevant and more recent example is found in November 2023, where the Council addressed various Conclusions on the Team Europe approach, on social, green, and digital transitions, and on the Spotlight initiative, which were approved with statements made by Hungary and Poland opposing the socially constructed definition of gender and references to SRHR. The statement by Hungary is quite relevant since it seems to speak again to the kind of contestation that abides by the rules of the game, as the country clarified that SRHR issues 'are interpreted and promoted by Hungary [...] in line with relevant national legislations' (Council of the European Union, 2023). In short, the EU returned to its traditional role as an exporter of human rights, where member states are not forced to change their behaviour at national level.

Conclusion

This chapter analyses the evolution of norm contestation within the EU foreign policy of SRHR. It identifies two main types of contestation: applicatory contestation exerted during the period 1995–2017 and 2021-ongoing and validity contestation exerted in the period 2017–2020.

During the periods 1995–2017 and 2021-ongoing, contestation was focused on the application of the norm. It consisted in the following norm institutionalisation: member states were not asked to implement certain aspects, such as abortion, related to SRHR at the domestic level, while they continued supporting the EU's external promotion of the norm. Examples include the Italian contestation in 1997 and subsequent objections from Malta. But also, this speaks to how still nowadays Poland and Hungary contest the norm's implementation by making clear member states' emphasis on national sovereignty to clarify they are not constrained by the EU's support for SRHR. It suggests a socialisation of norms that has enabled the EU to institutionalise SRHR in various external action documents and plans, and such constant re-enactment of SRHR has ended up reinforcing the norm (Wiener, 2014). Yet, the existence of a critical stance within the EU also implies the possibility of contestation going beyond mere applicatory contestation to a validity contestation (Deitelhoff & Zimmermann, 2020). In this respect, changes at the international level can influence the EU's position, as demonstrated by the EU's response to the US's attempts to weaken the norm mostly during the Trump Administration (Barbé & Badell, 2023).

Indeed, the period 2017–2020 was dominated by a validity contestation (Deitelhoff & Zimmermann, 2020). This scenario reached its peak in 2020. In October, the US presented the international alternative norm to SRHR, the Geneva Consensus Declaration, on which Hungary and Poland were key stakeholders contributing to the document.

This time, their strategy differed from previous instances of contestation in that they sought to revise the SRHR norm by dismantling individual rights and returning authority to sovereign states. The two countries' contestation thus went beyond the norm and escalated to question another fundamental norm contained in the gender equality cluster, namely the social construction of gender (Sanders, 2018). This could have led to a weakening of the EU consensus on SRHR and gender equality at large since the Gender Action Plan III was not adopted as Council Conclusions. Yet, Germany, holding the presidency at the time, bypassed the demands of Hungary and Poland and opted for a strategy of normative entrenchment, symbolically ostracising the two countries from the EU normative community. In 2021, Hungary and Poland, no longer receiving external support from the US and the Geneva Consensus, decided to re-enact the EU's consensus on SRHR.

Nevertheless, it can be argued that the EU's external policy on SRHR has been stronger than expected, with the EU advocating and committing to the norm. Contestation by some member states, whether in terms of application or validity, has not led to a change in the SRHR norm, as the contesting actors run the risk of being excluded from the EU's normative consensus. The EU foreign policy system has effectively managed contestation and turned it into a factor that strengthens the norm. Still, the interplay between the international and national levels can weaken SRHR within the EU if an alternative international norm is proposed, making it easier for contesters to abandon the consensus. Faced with this challenge, the European Commission, while lacking internal competence on gender equality norms, is gaining implementing powers in this area. President Von der Leyen's commitment to gender equality, exemplified by the appointment of the first Commissioner for Equality Helena Dalli, indicates a drive to make gender equality a salient issue in the EU. Accession to the Council of Europe Convention on Preventing and Combating Violence Against Women and Domestic Violence—the so-called Istanbul Convention—was a crucial step that could also address internal contestation over the gender equality norm cluster—including ensuring international adherence to the norm of social construction of gender. However, there is a risk that efforts to maintain the *status quo* of norms within the EU will be mostly at the expense of the EU' international actor. Two events may account for this statement. The first event is Turkey's withdrawal from the Istanbul Convention, where the country argued that internal contestation within the EU was one of the reasons that prompted it to pull out of the agreement. The second event pertains to a meeting that took place in February 2022 between the EU and the African Union, during which the president of the Council decided to omit mentions of SRHR to secure a joint declaration. This chapter therefore paves the way for future studies on the EU's international actorness in relation to this and other norm clusters.

References

Badell, D. (2022). *Normative contestation in EU foreign policy. Lessons from the arms control, migration and gender equality regimes*. [Doctoral dissertation, Universitat Autònoma de Barcelona].

Badell, D. (2023). Norm contestation in EU foreign policy: Understanding the effects of opposition and dissidence. *Cambridge Review of International Affairs, 1-20*, 592. https://doi.org/10.1080/09557571.2023.2287078

Badell, D. (2024). Contesting EU foreign policy: The case of sexual and reproductive health and rights. *Journal of Common Market Studies*. https://doi.org/10.1111/jcms.13622

Barbé, E., & Badell, D. (2020). The European Union and lethal autonomous weapons systems: United in diversity? In E. Johansson-Nogués, M. Vlaskamp, & E. Barbé (Eds.), *European Union contested* (pp. 133–152). Springer.

Barbé, E., & Badell, D. (2023). Chasing gender equality norms: The case of sexual and reproductive health and rights. *International Relations, 37*(2), 274–297. https://doi.org/10.1177/00471178221136994

Barbé, E., Costa, O., Surrallés, A. H., & Natorski, M. (2009). Which rules shape EU external governance? Patterns of rule selection in foreign and security policy. *Journal of European Public Policy, 16*(6), 834–852. https://doi.org/10.1080/13501760903087845

Carbone, M. (2019). The calm after the storm: Plurilateral challenges to the post-2020 EU–ACP partnership. *Journal of Common Market Studies, 57*(1), 141–151. https://doi.org/10.1111/jcms.12933

Centre for Reproductive Rights. (2021). *Accelerating progress: Liberalization of abortion laws since ICPD.*

Checkel, J. T. (2001). Why comply? Social learning and European identity change. *International Organization, 55*(3), 553–588. https://doi.org/10.1162/00208180152507551

Checkel, J. T. (2005). International institutions and socialization in Europe: Introduction and framework. *International Organization, 59*(4), 801–826. https://doi.org/10.1017/S0020818305050289

Council of the European Union. (1997). *Aid for population policies and programmes in the developing countries* (1484/97).

Council of the European Union. (2015). *Council conclusions on gender in development* (9242/15).

Council of the European Union. (2017). *European Consensus on Development - 'our world, our dignity, our future'.*

Council of the European Union. (2018). *EU strategy on women, peace and security* (15086/18).

Council of the European Union. (2020). *Presidency conclusions on the Gender Action Plan III 2021–2025.*

Council of the European Union. (2021). *Team Europe* (7742/21).

Council of the European Union. (2023). *Draft minutes* (15885/23).

Deitelhoff, N., & Zimmermann, L. (2020). Things we lost in the fire: How different types of contestation affect the robustness of international norms. *International Studies Review, 22*(1), 51–76. https://doi.org/10.1093/isr/viy080

EEAS. (2015). Statement by first vice-president Timmermans, High Representative/Vice-President Mogherini and Commissioners Mimica, Avramopoulos, Thyssen, Stylianides and Jourová on the occasion of international women's day.

Elgström, O. (2000). Norm negotiations: The construction of new norms regarding gender and development in EU foreign aid policy. *Journal of European Public Policy, 7*(3), 457–476.

Elgström, O. (2017). Norm advocacy networks: Nordic and like-minded countries in EU gender and development policy. *Cooperation and Conflict, 52*(2), 224–240.

European Commission. (2016). *EU gender action plan II.*

European Commission. (2020). *EU gender action plan III.*
European Commission. (2014). *European citizens' initiative: European Commission replies to 'One of Us'.*
European Parliament. (2013a). *Report on sexual and reproductive health and rights* (2013/2040(INI)).
European Parliament. (2013b). *Sexual and reproductive health and rights* (P7_TA (2013)0548).
European Parliament. (2021a). *Challenges ahead for women's rights: More than 25 years after the Beijing Declaration and platform for action* (P9_TA (2021)0058).
European Parliament. (2021b). *25th anniversary of the International Conference on Population and Development (ICPD25) (Nairobi Summit)* (P9_TA (2021)0315).
European Parliament. (2021c). *Sexual and reproductive health and rights in the EU, in the frame of women's health* (P9_TA (2021)0314).
European Union. (2006). *European consensus on development.*
European Union. (2017). *The new European consensus on development: Our world, our dignity, our future.*
Finnemore, M., & Sikkink, K. (1998). International norm dynamics and political change. *International Organization, 50*(4), 887–918. https://doi.org/10.1162/002081898550789
Guerrina, R., & Wright, K. (2016). Gendering normative power Europe: Lessons of the women, peace and security. *International Affairs, 92*(2), 293–312. https://doi.org/10.1111/1468-2346.12555
Hoffmann, M. J. 2010. Norms and social constructivism in international relations. In *Oxford research encyclopedia of international studies* (pp. 1–24).
Hooghe, L., & Marks, G. (2009). A postfunctionalist theory of European integration: From permissive consensus to constraining dissensus. *British Journal of Political Science, 39*(1), 1–23. https://doi.org/10.1017/S0007123408000409
Hungary. (2017). *PM Orbán at World Congress of Families XI summit: 2018 will be the year for families.*
Juncos, A., & Pomorska, K. (2006). Playing the Brussels game: Strategic socialisation in the CFSP council working groups. *European Integration Online Papers, 10.*
Katzenstein, P. J. (1996). *The culture of national security: Norms and identity in world politics.* Columbia University Press.
Lantis, J. S., & Wunderlich, C. (2018). Resiliency dynamics of norm clusters: Norm contestation and international cooperation. *Review of International Studies, 44*(3), 570–593. https://doi.org/10.1017/S0260210517000626
Lundgren, M. S., Tallberg, J., & Pedersen, P. (2022). *Member state influence in the negotiations on the neighbourhood, development and international cooperation instrument (NDICI)* (EBA Report, 7).
March, J. G., & Olsen, J. P. (2011). The logic of appropriateness. In R. Goodin (Ed.), *The Oxford handbook of political science*. https://doi.org/10.1093/oxfordhb/9780199604456.013.0024.
Ouwerkerk, J. W., Kerr, N. L., Gallucci, M., & Van Lange, P. A. M. (2005). Avoiding the social death penalty: Ostracism and cooperation in social dilemmas. In K. D. Williams, J. P. Forgas, & W. von Hippel (Eds.), *The social outcast: Ostracism, social exclusion, rejection, and bullying* (pp. 321–322). Psychology Press.
Sanders, R. (2018). Norm spoiling: Undermining the international women's rights agenda. *International Affairs, 94*(2), 271–291. https://doi.org/10.1093/ia/iiy023
Schimmelfennig, F. (2000). International socialisation in the new Europe: Rational action in an institutional environment. *European Journal of International Relations, 6*(1), 109–139.
Thevenin, E., Liedlbauer, L., & Petri, F. (2020). Conclusions on contestation of EU foreign policy: Diverse causes, various modes and multiple effects? *Global Affairs, 6*(4–5), 451–459.
United States. (2020). *US signs Geneva consensus declaration*. Retrieved April 10, 2025, from https://editorials.voa.gov/a/u-s-signs-geneva-consensus-declaration/5691772.html
Wagner, W. (2017). Liberal power Europe. *Journal of Common Market Studies, 55*(6), 1398–1414. https://doi.org/10.1111/jcms.12572

Wiener, A. (2014). *A theory of contestation*. Springer.
Wunderlich, C., Lucenti, F., Ducci, C., & Lantis, J. S. (2025). Contestation in prism: An introduction. In F. Lucenti, C. Ducci, C. Wunderlich, & J. S. Lantis (Eds.), *Contestation in prism: The evolution of norms and norm clusters in contemporary global politics* (pp. 1–21). Springer.
Zwingel, S. (2020). Gender equality norms in international governance: Actors, contexts, meanings. In L. Engberg-Pedersen, A. Ferjerskov, & S. M. Cold Ravnkilde (Eds.), *Rethinking gender equality in global governance: The delusion of norm diffusion* (pp. 41–70). Palgrave.

Chapter 8
Exceptions as Contestation: Understanding Norm Withdrawal

Lucrecia García Iommi

Norm Withdrawal: Exceptions as Contestation

Norm withdrawal (NW) occurs when actors seek an exception to the behaviour prescribed by a norm by appealing to the competing demands of another. In doing so, NW embodies a relational understanding of the norms. Specifically, it presupposes a complex and often incongruous normative system within which actors interact with one another facing competing normative demands. The contestation literature has not yet sufficiently addressed the impact of such normative systems, despite notable exceptions, such as the work on norm collisions (Gholiagha et al., 2020). NW provides an entry point to further explore this issue. Accordingly, this chapter situates NW in relation to other types of norm contestation and assesses its impact on norm robustness, with special attention to the impact of NW on norm clusters, as in the scope of this volume. It also develops a typology of states' use of NW based on the type—political or legal—and the level—domestic or international—at which NW takes place, which speaks directly to larger debates about withdrawal and exceptionalism in normative systems (see also Panke et al., 2025, Chap. 3).[1]

[1] Although in both Chaps. 2 and 3 norm withdrawal is defined as a type of norm contestation, in this chapter the author contends that norm withdrawal constitutes not a rejection of a norm but the establishment of an exception. In contrast, Panke et al. (2025, Chap. 3) use the concept of norm withdrawal to discuss the resiliency of RIOs' cluster of community norms in the face of contestation.

L. G. Iommi (✉)
Fairfield University, Fairfield, CT, USA
e-mail: lgarciaiommi@fairfield.edu

F. Lucenti et al. (eds.), *Contestation in Prism*, Norm Research in International Relations, https://doi.org/10.1007/978-3-031-83639-8_8

We can better understand the scope of NW using Winston's tripartite definition of norms as a combination of *problem, value, and behaviour* (Winston, 2018, p. 641). NW does not implicate the diagnosed problem or the values that inform the norm's behavioural prescription; it addresses only the behaviour component. Furthermore, an actor who engages in NW is not challenging the validity of this prescription; it only seeks to carve out an exception for itself on the basis of competing normative demands. Yet in doing so it critically engages with the norm in question and, when the norm is part of a norm cluster, with the corresponding cluster. Accordingly, it constitutes an instance of contestation.

Echoing other kinds of contestation that emphasise discursive practices, the justification of the exception is the defining feature of NW. Specifically, NW creates, explicitly or implicitly, a hierarchy between the competing norms that provides the reason for the exception. This hierarchy is not pre-existing; it is determined by individual actors. Although there may be agreement between some actors on the hierarchy of norms, in a world of persistent differences, we should expect significant discrepancies.

Despite involving deviant behaviour, NW differs from non-compliance. Those who engage in norm-violating behaviour often seek to justify their actions and contend that their behaviour does not amount to a violation of the norm. For example, in the context of the War on Terror, the US claimed its use of 'enhanced interrogation' did not constitute torture (Bush in Birdsall, 2016, p. 181). These actors might even reference other norms in the process of justifying their behaviour just like withdrawing actors would. For example, the US government argued that the president can resort to any measures, including enhanced interrogation, in order to fulfil their 'primary responsibility [...] to protect the security of the United States' (Yoo, 2003, p. 4). However, this behaviour does not amount to NW. As the 'enhanced interrogation' example illustrates, ad hoc justifications of non-compliant behaviour manipulate the scope or even validity of a norm to legitimise the violation. NW does not. Instead, it carves out an exception by appealing to norms that sit higher in the hierarchy of competing normative demands.

NW also presents important similarities and differences with other types of norm contestation. For example, unlike reactive contestation, NW does not involve objection to a norm, yet like reactive contestation it entails both discursive and behavioural contestation (Orchard & Wiener, 2022, p. 54). Similarly, NW does not seek to alter the meaning of a particular norm like proactive contestation does (Wiener, 2017, p. 3). It is only when NW is widespread or not perceived as legitimate that it can change the meaning of the norm. Furthermore, while reactive contestation usually takes effect at the implementing stage and proactive contestation at the constitutive stage, NW can happen at any stage of the norm cycle.

Comparing NW with Applicatory and Validity Contestation

Norm withdrawal can also be compared with applicatory and validity types of contestation. In contrast with applicatory contestation, NW is more likely to take place when a norm enjoys a high degree of validity (Deitelhoff & Zimmermann, 2020, p. 57). More significantly, unlike applicatory contestation, NW engages with the core of a norm. For instance, the US making a reservation to the Convention Against Torture (CAT) regarding the proper interpretation of cruel, inhuman, and degrading treatment is an instance of NW that targets the core of the norm that prohibits this behaviour. When the US indicated that it would interpret the CAT in light of the Fifth, Eighth, and Fourteenth Amendments of its constitution (United States, 1990), it narrowly defined the behaviour it committed itself not to engage in. In other words, this reservation did not address the situational boundaries of the norm in question but its fundamental meaning.

The fact that NW engages critically with the core of a norm begs the question of whether it constitutes an instance of validity contestation. It does not. When an actor engages in NW, it is not trying to challenge the validity of the norm but the behavioural implications of that norm for itself in a specific context. In this sense, it is aimed at creating an exception while not fundamentally changing the meaning of the norm, nor challenging its validity. There are multiple reasons—principled or strategic—why an actor would choose to do so but it is important to remember that NW does not entail a denial of a norm's validity (see Table 8.1).

The reaction of third-party actors to NW is critical to its impact on norm robustness, that is, the facticity and validity of a norm (Deitelhoff & Zimmermann, 2019). While NW does not entail a rejection of a norm, if a critical number of actors emulate the behaviour of the withdrawing actor or if other stakeholders perceive NW as illegitimate, NW may undermine the robustness of a norm. Specifically, widespread emulation of NW would impact the facticity of the norm. In turn, rejection would characterise withdrawing as a challenge to the validity of the norm. Both scenarios negatively affect norm robustness. In contrast, if NW remains circumscribed to one actor—or a small number of actors—and NW is successful, that is if NW is accepted as an exception by third parties, there should be no negative impact on norm robustness. Furthermore, successful NW might even reinforce it by underscoring the exceptionality of the withdrawing actor's behaviour.

Third parties' reactions to NW by one or more actors may be shaped by factors, such as procedural legitimacy and the perception that the justification has merit. Regarding the first criterion, NW is more likely to be perceived as legitimate if it entails measures within the generally recognised boundaries of the actor's authority. With regard to the second criterion, it can be posited that NW is more likely to be regarded as legitimate if third-party actors acknowledge the conflict and deem the normative hierarchy underlying NW to be reasonable—even if they do not concur with it. The justification withdrawing actors' offer is thus critical to their success.

In addition, access to NW might be necessary for a norm to acquire legitimacy and become an asset for norm robustness, thereby fostering its validity and facticity

Table 8.1 Contestation types comparison

	Validity contestation	Applicatory contestation	Proactive contestation	Reactive contestation	Norm withdrawal
Purpose	Undermine validity	Modify scope	Critical engagement (norm validation)	Rejection	Exception
Focus	Norm (core)	Norm in context (meaning-in-use)	Norm in context (meaning-in-use)	Norm in context (meaning-in-use)	Behavioural expectations for withdrawing actor (what counts as compliance)
Relation to norm core	Challenges core	Does not challenge core	N/A	N/A	May challenge core behavioural expectations (for withdrawing actor)
Norm Specificity	The *more* precise the norm, the more likely validity contestation is	The *less* precise the norm, the more likely applicatory contestation is	N/A	N/A	The *more* precise the norm, the more likely norm withdrawal is
Type of practices	Discourse	Discourse	Discourse	Discourse and behaviour	Discourse and behaviour
Norm dimension	Single norm	Single norm	Normative configurations	Normative configurations	Normative configurations

(Hansen-Magnusson et al., 2018). It can be argued that access to contestation for the largest possible number of stakeholders is a necessary condition of norm legitimacy (Wiener, 2014, p. 50). This is because stakeholders' engagement leads to norm 'ownership', which increases the perception of the appropriateness of the norm (Park & Vetterlein, 2010). This then facilitates negotiation and compromise over the meaning and proper interpretation of norms (Wiener, 2014, p. 30). Finally, while a complex and incongruous normative system creating competing normative demands is a precondition for NW, this does not account for timing. Actors don't withdraw all the time; they choose NW when competitive normative demands come into the fore.

Scope Conditions for Norm Withdrawal

Why do actors choose NW? While the norm contestation literature suggests a wide range of factors that foster norm contestation, this study identifies four scope conditions that increase the likelihood of an actor withdrawing, namely (1) how precise the norm is, (2) whether the norm at play is a single norm or it is part of a norm cluster, (3) actors' relative resourcefulness, and (4) actors' commitment to the norm. The first two are characteristics of the norm; the latter two are characteristics of the actor.

First, the more precise a norm the more likely an actor will withdraw in response to a norm collision (Gholiagha et al., 2020). When colliding norms are precise their competing demands are apparent, conditioning actors to take action. While NW is not the only option available to actors, its likelihood increases with precision like it does for other forms of contestation. As legalised norms enjoy a higher degree of precision—reducing the ambiguity around the conduct the norm requires, authorises, or proscribes (Abbott et al., 2000)—actors are more likely to withdraw from them.

Second, norm clusters reduce, in principle, the likelihood of NW. The existence of a norm cluster gives actors 'relative freedom of choice within the cluster to determine for itself what constitutes "appropriate behaviour" in its own specific context' (Winston, 2018, p. 647). If an actor can choose a norm within the cluster that does not create competing behavioural demands with others, it can avoid norm conflict altogether. This might preclude the development of NW, even if it remains a possibility. Norm clusters do not necessarily acquire formal validity as such. In some instances, it is specific combinations within the cluster that create legal obligations for actors, limiting actors' freedom of choice as legal norms might create a stronger sense of obligation and increase the cost of non-compliance. Moreover, if there is a hierarchy within a cluster, associated or not with the legalisation or institutionalisation of specific norms, actors' ability to choose also decreases. Certain circumstances may also prevent actors from accessing all the options within a cluster. All of this increases the probability of NW and, arguably, of other forms of contestation.

Third, actors will choose NW over other forms of contestation that seek to undermine or alter the scope of the norm if they believe the norm is valid or if it is in their interest to foster its robustness. The reason is that NW does not undermine the validity or challenge the scope of the norm. Finally, the less resourceful an actor is, the more likely it will choose NW over other forms of contestation. NW is a less costly option than other forms of contestation due to its limited scope. However, we must also consider the interaction between commitment and resources. While a committed, resourceful actor might still choose NW, a less resourceful actor who does not recognise the validity of the norm or seeks to alter its boundaries might attempt to engage in more costly forms of contestation regardless of the cost.

State Norm Withdrawal: A Typology

While any actor can engage in NW, this chapter focuses on states. Specifically, it admits that typology of state norm withdrawal derived from two criteria: (1) the *type* of measure used to withdraw and (2) the *level* at which this action takes place. Regarding the first condition, a state can engage in NW formally, i.e. relying on the

Table 8.2 Typology of State Norm Withdrawal

		Level	
		Domestic	International
Measure	Law	Type 1: Domestic legal withdrawal Laws, administrative rules and regulations, court decisions	Type 2: International legal withdrawal Treaty reservations
	Policy	Type 3: Domestic policy withdrawal Domestic policy decisions	Type 4: International policy withdrawal Foreign policy decisions

legal instruments, or informally, i.e. by means of policy decisions, which are often led by the executive branch. Regarding the second criterion, a state can take action at the international or domestic level. At the international level, treaty reservations constitute a legal approach to creating an exception,[2] and any number of policy decisions can be used to that end as well. At the domestic level, legal NW can take the form of laws, administrative rules, and regulations, and even court decisions, while policy NW includes a range of government decisions. The distinctive feature of all withdrawing measures is that they acknowledge competing normative demands and create an exception for the state on the basis of a hierarchy between them (Table 8.2).

While the four types of state NW in this typology are different, they are not mutually exclusive. States may choose to engage in one or more of them depending primarily on whether the norm operates primarily at the domestic or international level and the availability and expediency of legal and policy options—e.g. reservations are not available after ratification, limiting the options for states.

The next section illustrates this typology with four case studies that are highly relevant in contemporary global politics. These are the Colombian peace accord, Tunisia's reservations to CEDAW, South Africa's refusal to arrest Al-Bashir, and the US bombing of Serbia. They involve contestation of different norms, namely non-impunity in the case of Colombia and South Africa, gender equality in the case of Tunisia, and the norm regulating the use of force in the case of the US bombing of Serbia.

Exploring State Norm Withdrawal

Type 1: Domestic Legal Withdrawal: Colombia's Peace Accord

In 2016, after 50 years of armed struggle and 4 years of negotiations, the Colombian government concluded a peace agreement with the *Fuerzas Armadas Revolucionarias de Colombia-Ejército del Pueblo* (FARC-EP). Colombia, an early ratifier of the Rome Statute for the International Criminal Court (ICC), had also implemented cooperation and complementarity legislation to better fulfil its commitments to the

[2] Not all reservations to treaties constitute an instance of norm withdrawal. Only those reservations made on the grounds of competing normative demands are instances of norm withdrawal.

Court (Parliamentarians for Global Action, 2024). However, Colombia had also been under preliminary examination by the ICC Office of the Prosecutor (OTP) for over a decade. Specifically, the OTP focused on alleged crimes against humanity and war crimes in the context of the Colombian conflict. With a mandate to ensure accountability for these crimes, the ICC closely observed the peace process and sought to ensure Colombia fulfilled its obligations under the Rome Statute (Wojciak, 2014).[3]

Consistent with its culture of legalism (Espinosa, 2005) and the legal expertise that comes with it, Colombia did not deny these and other obligations under International Humanitarian Law (IHL) and human rights law during the peace negotiation. Instead, it embraced them, asserting its sovereignty over the justice process, while also advancing an interpretation of the relevant rules that allowed for the use of amnesties, without which a peace agreement with the FARC-EP was not possible. In this way, Colombia carved out an exception for itself vis-à-vis the anti-impunity norm, which calls for the use of criminal proceedings to ensure accountability in response to grave breaches to IHL (Han & Rosenberg, 2021, p. 2). While it seeks to manage the expectations of the international community, notably the ICC, the peace agreement is essentially a domestic legal instrument. Accordingly, the 2016 Peace Accord constitutes an instance of domestic legal withdrawal.

The Peace Accord created a novel hierarchy within the category war crimes, defining ‘serious war crimes’. By stipulating that these war crimes could not be subject to amnesties, it implicitly established that other ‘lesser’ war crimes could (Urueña, 2016, p. 366). Furthermore, the Peace Accord explicitly privileged the value of peace over that of accountability, which underlines the anti-impunity norm. Indeed, in its Preamble the Accord states that ‘Article 22 of the Political Constitution of the Republic of Colombia establishes peace as a right and as a mandatory duty’ and emphasises that ‘peace has come to be universally described as a superior human right and as a prerequisite for the exercising of all other rights and duties incumbent upon individuals and citizens’ (Peace Accord, 2016). Relatedly, High Commissioner for Peace, Jaramillo (2013 in Hillebrecht et al., 2018, p. 311) explains that the situation in Colombia was exceptional and made the argument that the peace process should be understood not from the perspective of a ‘normal’ justice system, but rather the specific framework of transitional justice following an armed conflict. In other words, because there was no peace without amnesties and the right to peace is paramount, an exception to the anti-impunity norm is justified.

In addition, drawing from the jurisprudence of the Inter-American Human Rights System, the agreement emphasised victims’ rights, notably the right to truth and reparations, over criminal prosecution as the main response to crimes occurred during the conflict (Hillebrecht et al., 2018, p. 323). In doing so, Colombia’s ‘vernacularized’ international justice (Easterday, 2015, p. 432) challenged the hierarchy of values and behaviours in the transitional justice norm cluster. This cluster of

[3] While the issue of amnesties is not directly addressed in the Rome Statute and some experts initially argued for their compatibility with the Statute (Bassiouni, 2005), the prevailing interpretation has come to exclude that possibility (Naqvi, 2018).

international humanitarian norms includes truth and accountability—values—as well as criminal proceedings, reparations, and truth commissions—behaviour—(Winston, 2018, p. 653), and the international community has come to privilege the anti-impunity norm in recent years (Carvajalino & Davidovic, 2023, p. 1). By engaging in NW, Colombia thus challenged the transitional justice cluster hierarchy.

The reaction by the international community and domestic players to Colombia's withdrawal was mixed, with some questioning both its procedural legitimacy and the merit of the justification, the two elements previously identified as affecting the success of NW. Multiple domestic and international actors responded negatively to the possible use of amnesties as the price for peace. Domestically, this was one of the factors that led to the government's defeat in the plebiscite on the Peace Accord (Huneeus and Urueña, 2016, p. 161). Yet the public also took to the streets after this defeat to support peace and ensure the negotiation of a new agreement (Marcos, 2016). A new, similar agreement was concluded in November and promptly ratified by Congress without a new plebiscite, a move the opposition criticised (BBC, 2016).

Internationally, the efforts of President Santos to bring about peace were recognised with the Nobel Peace Prize the following month, validating the project as well as its normative implications. Furthermore, after manifesting concerns and unsuccessfully seeking to more directly influence the process,[4] ICC Prosecutor Bensouda (2016) came to support the Peace Accord and, disregarding the space it had created for amnesties, noted 'with satisfaction, that the final text of the peace agreement excludes amnesties and pardons for crimes against humanity and war crimes under the Rome Statute', while restating that '[t]he paramount importance of genuine accountability—which by definition includes effective punishment—in nurturing a sustainable peace cannot be overstated'. In this way, the Prosecutor opted to underplay the norm collision between the right to peace and the anti-impunity norm, while reinforcing the prevailing hierarchy in the norm cluster. This reaffirmed the extraordinary nature of the Colombian case and strived to minimise its impact on the robustness of the anti-impunity norm.

Type 2: International Legal Withdrawal: Tunisia's Reservations to CEDAW

In spite of widespread ratification, the Convention on the Elimination of All Forms of Discrimination Against Women (CEDAW), which embodies the gender equality norm, has been subject to extensive reservations, including reservations from

[4] In 2013, ICC Prosecutor Fatou Bensouda sent two confidential letters to the president of the Colombian Constitutional Court, the body responsible for reviewing the Framework for Peace Law. In the first of these letters, she spoke strongly against the possibility of suspending prison sentences for crimes under the jurisdiction of the ICC, explaining that by precluding punishment it would be in violation of the Statute (Bensouda, 2013). These letters were leaked to the press and public opinion strongly criticised ICC's interference (Hillebrecht et al., 2018, p. 298).

governments of numerous Muslim countries. These countries made their reservations mainly on the basis of competing normative demands emanating from Islamic law, as reflected in their domestic legislation. This is the case of Tunisia. Despite Tunisia's understanding that 'women's rights' and Islam are compatible (Mashhour, 2005, p. 587), there was a tension between domestic legislation and specific obligations in the CEDAW, creating the need to carve out an exception. Accordingly, Tunisia issued reservations to the CEDAW, an instance of international legal withdrawal. The reservations concerned issues such as nationality, family names, inheritance, and women's right to choose their place of residence (United Nations, 2006). Specifically, Tunisia's reservations focused on Articles 9 and 16 of the Convention, and the government also made a declaration on Article 15 and a general declaration on the primacy of Chapter I of the Tunisian Constitution, which was of particular concern.

However, the CEDAW Committee did not address the issue of the compatibility of this declaration with the Convention, and only three countries—Germany, the Netherlands, and Sweden—raised objections to Tunisia's reservations (United Nations, 2006, p. 55). In other words, most third parties confirmed the procedural legitimacy of Tunisia's reservations. Krivenko (2009, pp. 203–4) argues that this lack of backlash was a result of Tunisia's first and second reports, which persuaded the Committee of its commitment to the eventual full implementation of the Convention. Arguably, an additional reason for accepting the reservations and finding merit in the justification was the trajectory of Tunisia on women's rights. Indeed, 'State Feminism' was integral to Tunisia's post-colonial nation-building project (Kallander, 2021). Tunisia's 1959 Constitution regarded women as full citizens and stated that '[a]ll citizens have equal rights and obligations, they are equal before the law' (Article 6 of the 1959 Tunisian Constitution), thus enshrining the gender equality norm. Furthermore, issues like polygamy, child custody, and inequality regarding the dissolution of marriage, which were invoked in the reservations of other Muslim states, were not part of Tunisia's reservations because the 1957 Personal Code Status had already dealt with these issues (Krivenko, 2009, p. 172). Tunisia also recognised women's reproductive rights (Brandt & Kaplan, 1995, p. 130). Tunisia's reservations and the exception they carved were interpreted in this context.

In its third and fourth reports, the Tunisian government explained that changes to the Personal Code Status meant that '[t]he position of head of household is no longer a right granted to a husband to the detriment of his wife but an economic function and a responsibility linked to the duty incumbent on him to provide for the needs of his wife and children' (UN Committee on the Elimination of Discrimination Against Women, 2000, p. 212, para. 1068). In this report, Tunisia also provided data on women's low participation in the job market in that country (Combined third and fourth periodic reports of Tunisia 2000, p. 212, para. 1063) to explain the importance of protecting the notion of the man as the head of the household, who is responsible for supporting his family, to protect women and families. It also expressly recognised that women can be the head of the household as in the case of single mothers (Combined third and fourth periodic reports of Tunisia 2000, p. 212, para. 1065). It follows that it was not a lack of commitment to gender equality, but the socio-economic context that prevented Tunisia from fully complying with CEDAW, despite moving in that direction.

Tunisia's reservations, combined with states' objections and responses and questions from the CEDAW Committee, helped to foster a productive national dialogue (Universal Rights Group, 2019). Following the 2011 revolution, this process culminated in the lifting of Tunisia's reservations in 2014 (United Nations, 2014). However, Tunisia's general declaration still stipulates that no measures will be taken to comply with CEDAW that contradict Chap. I of the Constitution, which remains in force.

Type 3: Domestic Policy Withdrawal: South Africa's Refusal to Arrest Al-Bashir

In 2009, the ICC issued an arrest warrant against Sudanese President Omar al-Bashir for crimes against humanity and war crimes; then, in 2010, the Court issued a second arrest warrant adding changes of genocide and ethnic cleansing (ICC, 2009, 2010). The Arab League (Al Jazeera, 2009a) and the African Union (Al Jazeera, 2009b) both criticised this decision and several countries refused to arrest Al-Bashir, the sitting president of a non-party state. South Africa's refusal to arrest al-Bashir stands out because of its early and consistent support for the creation of the ICC. South Africa was one of only two African members of the original—pre-Rome Conference—Like-Minded Group that spearheaded the creation of the ICC, and it was an early ratifier of the Rome Statute. South Africa also implemented cooperation and complementarity legislation and refused to sign a Bilateral Immunity Agreement with the US at a great cost (García Iommi, 2023, p. 23). This commitment to the ICC, and by extension the norm of anti-impunity, makes South Africa's refusal to arrest al-Bashir when he visited South Africa in 2015 more remarkable. In those circumstances, South Africa chose not to challenge the validity or scope of the norm, but instead to carve out an exception. This exception was built on the basis of the pre-eminence of competing normative imperatives, specifically those emanating from the pan-African solidarity and sovereignty norms. Thus, without rejecting its commitment to the anti-impunity norm, South Africa interpreted the conflicting norms in a manner that justified the violation of its obligation to arrest al-Bashir. While South Africa's actions were conditioned by international actors and their expectations, its decision to exempt itself from executing the arrest warrant is fundamentally a domestic policy decision. In other words, South Africa engaged in domestic policy withdrawal—NW Type 3.

To justify his decision to let al-Bashir leave the country, President Zuma explained that al-Bashir was in South Africa as 'the guest of the African Union (AU)', stating to Parliament that if he had visited as an individual, rather than as a state delegate to an AU summit, he would have been detained (Radio Tamazuj, 2015). In doing so, Zuma attempted to justify the refusal to arrest al-Bashir by invoking his immunity as a representative of the state, thus invoking the norm of sovereignty. Obed Bapela (Hunter et al., 2015), the head of the African National Congress' international relations sub-committee and deputy co-operative governance minister, restated South Africa's commitment to the ICC but further justified the decision not to arrest al-Bashir by stating that if they had arrested him, South Africa 'would have been seen as lackeys of the West', adding that '[w]e had to choose between the unity of Africa and the ICC and we chose Africa'. This statement speaks to the prevalence of sovereignty and pan-African solidarity, both critical to the anti-colonial discourse the AU embodies (Labuda, 2013, p. 310–311) and to South Africa's foreign policy (Nathan, 2010), over the anti-impunity norm (see also Lucenti et al., 2025, Chap. 5). While South Africa would go on to consider more costly forms of contestation, specifically a failed attempt to withdraw from the ICC,[5] its choice to engage in NW makes sense based on its historical commitment to the anti-impunity norm and the ICC, despite privileging other normative commitments in the context of the Court's case against al-Bashir. It also speaks to South Africa's lack of access to the full range of options in transitional justice. Despite South Africa participating in regional peace efforts in Sudan, its involvement in the conflict did not translate into the freedom to choose peace as the most prominent value in the transitional justice cluster.

South Africa's refusal to arrest Al-Bashir was controversial both at the domestic and international levels (García Iommi, 2020, pp. 115, 117) For instance, some domestic actors strived to have the government fulfil its obligation to the Rome Statute and arrest al-Bashir. Specifically, the Southern African Litigation Centre, a South African human rights organisation, asked the Gauteng High Court to call for al-Bashir's arrest and surrender to the ICC. The High Court agreed but the government still allowed al-Bashir to leave the country (Amnesty International, 2015). A few months later, the South African parliament unsuccessfully voted on whether to investigate President Zuma for allowing al-Bashir to avoid arrest and leave the country (Reuters, 2015). This speaks to domestic audiences challenging the procedural legitimacy of South Africa's actions. Internationally, multiple actors, including the ICC Assembly of States Parties, legal scholars, human rights organisations, and state representatives (CICC, 2016), condemned South Africa's actions. Yet, South Africa's refusal to arrest al-Bashir was part of a broader regional rejection to the arrest warrants, backed by the AU and a number of other African states, like Kenya and Nigeria, which also refused to cooperate with the ICC (Boehme, 2017, p. 51). In sum, while South Africa's NW was acceptable to regional stakeholders, both because of its procedural legitimacy and the merit of the argument, globally it was seen as a violation to the anti-impunity norm. As African states constitute the largest regional bloc in the ICC and, more importantly, were the countries best

[5] In 2016, South Africa submitted its instrument of withdrawal from the Court to the UN Secretary General, specifically referring to the question of whether head-of-state immunity—Campbell precludes ICC indictments (Campbell, 2016). However, the South African High Court would declare this decision unconstitutional, leading the government to revoke it (Onishi, 2017).

placed to execute the arrest warrant, this behaviour posed a significant challenge to the robustness of the norm.

Type 4: International Policy Withdrawal: US Bombing of Serbia

In 1999, the US and its NATO allies engaged in a three-month bombing campaign against Serbia without the authorisation of the United Nations Security Council (UNSC), in violation of the United Nations Charter rules on the use of force. Its goal was to end the violence that Serbian forces were perpetrating against civilians during the Kosovo war. This decision was justified as an instance of humanitarian intervention, where the US and NATO allies prioritised the protection of human rights over the use of force norm. This humanitarian intervention norm was in no small part a product of US leadership and the US continues to have a vested interest in fostering it to ensure order in the international system (Henderson, 2022, pp. 84–87, 98). The policy nature of the decision and the fact that it operated at the international level make the bombing of Serbia a case of international policy NW.

In its justification of the need to use force even in the absence of UNSC authorisation, NATO allies, specifically the UK citing former Ambassador Ivor Roberts who had been sent as an emissary to Belgrade (Select Committee on Foreign Affairs, 1999), referred to the need to avert a 'humanitarian catastrophe'. NATO (2022) also stated that the goals of the bombing campaign included ending 'all military action, violence and repression' and the 'unconditional and safe return of all refugees and displaced persons and unhindered access to them by humanitarian aid organizations'. To domestic and international audiences, President Clinton (1999) explained that ending Serbian atrocities against the Kosovar people was a 'moral imperative'. While he also referred to regional stability and peace, President Clinton emphasised that 'the most important thing is that our children will understand it, years from now, if we stand against ethnic cleansing and we can turn the world against it. And they will not forgive us, years from now, if we do not' (Washington Post, 1999a). This justification did not seek to undermine or redefine the scope of the use of force norm but effectively to create an exception. In his analysis of the decision, Whippman (2001, p. 130) explains that NATO did not attempt to justify its actions in legal terms—e.g. a self-defence argument—because this would have undermined the UN Charter or contested the scope of the use of force norm. In the context of competing normative imperatives and faced with the impossibility that the UNSC would take action, the US established a normative hierarchy in response to a specific situation and created an exception for itself. Significantly, Whippman (2001, p. 137) suggests that a genuine humanitarian intervention, such as this one, could be understood as an 'acceptable breach' to international law. According to Ellis (2007, p. 23) morality and legality constitute two distinct normative systems and when the tension between them becomes too great an acceptable breach becomes a possible solution. In the aforementioned case, it allowed for NATO's exceptional unauthorised, without undermining broader support for the norm against the use of force in the short term.

Multiple actors criticised the US decision to bomb Serbia, primarily in terms of procedural legitimacy as NATO did not have the authority to bypass the UNSC. These critics insisted on a diplomatic solution or a UNSC response to the crisis (United Nations Security Council Press Release, 1999a). For example, UN Secretary General Kofi Annan (United Nations Secretary General Press Release, 1999), while sympathetic to the goals of the intervention, and thus the merit of the justification, criticised NATO for acting outside the authority of the UNSC. Possibly NATO's harshest critic, Russia, called for a UNSC meeting to consider NATO's unilateral action on the very day the bombing started. However, a draft resolution was defeated with only three votes in favour, namely those of Russia, China, and Namibia (United Nations Security Council Press Release, 1999b). In Latin America, Asia, Africa, the Middle East, and other regions not directly engaged in the conflict there was widespread, albeit not homogenous, opposition to the bombing (Washington Post, 1999b). In contrast, Europe was more supportive of NATO's actions. The European Council, for instance, justified them as necessary to end the humanitarian crisis, even if it did not endorse the bombing itself (Rees, 2000, p. 66). Arguably, widespread rejection of the bombing of Serbia did not immediately undermine the robustness of the use of force norm. However, US actions set a dangerous precedent, which was cited by Russia's Vladimir Putin (2014) as part of his propaganda to justify the interference and offensive during the 2014 crisis in Ukraine, followed by the annexation of Crimea a year later and the full-scale invasion in 2022. This suggests that the US precedent may have weakened the robustness of the use of force norm in the long run.

Summary of Findings

The cases examined here help illustrate NW and help us further understand this type of contestation. Comparing evidence across the cases yields several patterns. First, in all the cases, actors faced a norm collision brought to the fore by particular circumstances and carved out an exception on the basis of justifications that referenced other norms, creating an implicit or explicit hierarchy between them. While Colombia alluded to the right to peace and South Africa to sovereignty and pan-African solidarity, Tunisia's reservations pointed to incompatibilities with domestic legislation, and the US invoked human rights. Even though, Colombia and South Africa referenced the law—to different degrees—in their justifications and Tunisia took advantage of the legal possibility of treaty reservations, the US chose not to make a legal argument for the bombing of Serbia. Yet, although countries' justifications varied, they all reflected a fundamental commitment to the norm from which they were withdrawing from (for a different perspective on this dynamic, see Panke et al., 2025, Chap. 3).

Second, as predicted, all cases entail contestation of legalised norms with a high degree of precision. Indeed, the anti-impunity norm, the use of force norm, and the gender equality norm are all embodied in international treaties. Interestingly, some of the norms privileged by withdrawing states were also legal rules. Colombia referenced its Constitution and human rights law, Tunisia invoked domestic laws, and South Africa underscored official immunities rules. This speaks to the tensions and contradictions that exist not just between legal rules and moral rules, like Ellis' 'acceptable breach' argument suggests, but also between legal rules. Despite efforts to present the law as a coherent system, it is not. The competing demands of the ICC and the AU on South Africa speak of the additional difficulties that norm collisions present when norms are backed by international institutions.

Third, the fact that the anti-impunity norm belongs to the transitional justice norm cluster did not prevent NW. The Colombian case indicates that hierarchical clusters might be conducive to contestation. Indeed, the dominance of the anti-impunity norm in this cluster limited Colombia's access to all options within it and made contestation necessary. Yet hierarchies are not immutable. Colombia's NW challenged the cluster's hierarchy, defying the prevailing understanding of the relation between peace and accountability, both values within the transitional justice cluster. This has the potential to revert the cluster to previous hierarchies, which privileged peace over accountability (Engle, 2016, pp. 26–28). The fact that the anti-impunity norm is part of the transitional justice cluster did not prevent South Africa's NW either. South Africa did not have access to a range of legitimate options because it was not undergoing a transition. While South Africa did participate in regional peace efforts in Sudan, its involvement in the conflict did not appear to grant it the same goodwill that Colombia had received.

Fourth, in all cases the withdrawing actor, either out of conviction or self-interest, seemed committed to the norm they were contesting. This helps us understand why the countries studied chose NW over more ambitious forms of contestation, even when they had the necessary resources. This suggests that actors' resources as a scope condition are only relevant when commitment is low enough to make more ambitious forms of contestation, such as validity or applicatory contestation, desirable.

Fifth, the analysis indicates that legal forms of state NW, such as Colombia's and Tunisia's, are unsurprisingly more likely to gain procedural legitimacy than policy ones. A plausible reason is that modern societies perceive the law as legitimate (Kratochwil, 1989, pp. 15, 95–129). However, the cases also suggest that, even without the benefit of procedural legitimacy, the merit of the justification can go a long way. This is indeed the case with the US bombing of Serbia on humanitarian grounds, which had almost universal appeal even among some of its harshest critics. By contrast, the limited regional appeal of South Africa's justification on the basis of sovereignty and Pan-Africanism further undermined its ability to successfully withdraw. Accordingly, from all the cases analysed in this chapter, South Africa's NW represents the most dangerous challenge to norm robustness.

Finally, the case of Tunisia's reservations to CEDAW indicates that history and reputation matter. When credible actors—actors with proven support for a norm—create an exception, they are more likely to succeed—i.e. have others accept the exception. Additionally, this case suggests that access to contestation, in this case NW, can strengthen norms. Reservations, and the domestic and international dialogue that followed, ameliorated the implications of the open norm collision between the gender equality norm and Tunisia's domestic legislation, providing actors with the necessary tools to manage it without undermining the gender equality norm. However, the usefulness of reservations to prevent or manage open norm collisions is limited by the ability of states to anticipate conflict at the time of ratification. Accordingly, access to all forms of state NW, not just international legal withdrawal, is necessary.

Lessons for Norm Withdrawal

NW creates an exception for an actor vis-à-vis the behavioural expectations emanating from a norm on the basis of an implicit or explicit subjective hierarchy that privileges another. Unlike other forms of contestation, NW understands norms and norm dynamics in a relational manner, presupposing not just diversity but a complex and incongruous normative structure that frequently leads to norm collisions.

The analysis of the four cases discussed in the previous section helps us better understand the likelihood of NW and the relation between the different scope conditions of NW. While precision increases the likelihood of contestation as norm collisions come to the fore, commitment to the norm—out of conviction or self-interest—may influence states to choose NW. In turn, resources are secondary to an actor's commitment. If an actor is highly committed, they will favour NW even if they are powerful. This helps us understand why, even though NW is less ambitious and costly than other forms of contestation, it is not a 'weapon of the weak'. Lastly, norm clusters can decrease the likelihood of NW, but only when they are not hierarchical and are fully accessible to the relevant actors.

This study suggests that, like other forms of contestation, NW does not necessarily undermine norm robustness and that it can foster a norm's legitimacy. The cases discussed in the previous section appear to validate the argument that procedural legitimacy and the merit of the justification are both conducive to successful NW, leaving the robustness of the norm fairly intact. Beyond affecting their robustness, NW can also alter perceived hierarchies between single norms or within norms clusters.

Finally, the concept of NW and the analysis of cases underscore the inconsistencies that exist between legal rules and other norms as well as within the law itself. Regarding the first type of inconsistencies, the literature on norm dynamics, which is very much focused on legalised norms, has not sufficiently explored this tension. Accordingly, studying instances of NW where actors privilege non-legalised norms—e.g. pan-African solidarity—over legalised norms— e.g. the anti-impunity norm—could be particularly useful to foster our understanding of norm dynamics in complex normative configurations. Regarding inconsistencies within the law, we need to problematize the assumption of internal coherence in international law. International law does offer some guidelines to establish an objective hierarchy among rules to avoid conflict—e.g. international law prevails over domestic law—but actors, informed by a broader understanding of norm validity and legitimacy that includes social and cultural validity (Wiener, 2014) and conditioned by their circumstances, are likely to challenge them.

References

Abbott, K. W., Keohane, R. O., Moravcsik, A., Slaughter, A. M., & Snidal, D. (2000). The concept of legalization. *International Organization, 54*(3), 401–419. https://doi.org/10.1162/002081800551271

Al Jazeera. (2009a, March 30). *Arab leaders snub al-Bashir warrant*. Retrieved April 1, 2025, from https://www.aljazeera.com/news/2009/3/30/arab-leaders-snub-al-bashir-warrant

Al Jazeera. (2009b, July 4). *AU nations 'will not arrest Bashir'*. Retrieved March 1, 2025, https://www.aljazeera.com/news/2009/7/4/au-nations-will-not-arrest-bashir

Amnesty International. (2015). *Impunity vs Immunity: Africa and the ICC*. Retrieved March 1, 2025, https://www.amnesty.org/en/latest/news/2015/06/impunity-vs-immunity-africa-and-the-icc/

Bassiouni, M. C. (2005). *The legislative history of the International Criminal Court: Introduction, analysis and integrated text*. Transnational Publishers.

BBC. (2016). *Colombia: el Congreso aprueba el nuevo acuerdo de paz con las FARC y las divisiones se trasladan a las presidenciales de 2018*. Retrieved March 1, 2025, from https://www.bbc.com/mundo/noticias-america-latina-38165978

Bensouda, F. (2013). Letter to Jorge Iván Palacio Palacio. *Heavy Metal Colombia*. Retrieved March 1, 2025, from http://www.ips.org/blog/cvieira/2013/08/16/documento-fiscalia-cpi-sobre-cero-carcel-por-crimenes-de-su-competencia/

Bensouda, F. (2016). *Statement of ICC Prosecutor, Fatou Bensouda, on the conclusion of the peace negotiations between the Government of Colombia and the Revolutionary Armed Forces of Colombia—People's Army*. International Criminal Court. Retrieved March 1, 2025, from https://www.icc-cpi.int/news/statement-icc-prosecutor-fatou-bensouda-conclusion-peace-negotiations-between-government

Birdsall, A. (2016). But we don't call it 'torture'! Norm contestation during the US 'War on Terror'. *International Politics, 53*(2), 176–197. https://doi.org/10.1057/ip.2015.42

Boehme, F. (2017). 'We chose Africa': South Africa and the regional politics of cooperation with the International Criminal Court. *International Journal of Transitional Justice, 11*(1), 50–70. https://doi.org/10.1093/ijtj/ijw024

Brandt, M., & Kaplan, J. A. (1995). The tension between women's rights and religious rights: Reservations to CEDAW by Egypt, Bangladesh and Tunisia. *Journal of Law and Religion, 12*(1), 105–142.

Campbell, J. (2016, October 21). *South Africa's possible withdraw from the International Criminal Court*. Council on Foreign Relations. Retrieved March 1, 2025, from https://www.cfr.org/blog/south-africas-possible-withdraw-international-criminal-court

Carvajalino, J., & Davidovic, M. (2023). Escaping or reinforcing hierarchies? Norm relations in transitional justice. *International Studies Review, 25*(3). https://doi.org/10.1093/isr/viad022

CICC. (2016). *Reaction: South Africa ICC withdrawal move*. Coalition for the International Criminal Court. Retrieved March 1, 2025, from https://www.coalitionfortheicc.org/news/20161024/reaction-south-africa-icc-withdrawal-move

Clinton, W. (1999). *Transcript: Clinton addresses nation on Yugoslavia strike. March 24, 1999*. BBC. Retrieved March 1, 2025, from https://edition.cnn.com/ALLPOLITICS/stories/1999/03/25/clinton.transcript/

Deitelhoff, N., & Zimmermann, L. (2019). Norms under challenge: Unpacking the dynamics of norm robustness. *Journal of Global Security Studies, 4*(1), 2–17.

Deitelhoff, N., & Zimmermann, L. (2020). Things we lost in the fire: How different types of contestation affect the robustness of international norms. *International Studies Review, 22*(1), 51–76. https://doi.org/10.1093/isr/viy080

Easterday, J. (2015). Beyond the 'shadow' of the ICC: Struggles over control of the conflict narrative in Colombia. In C. De Vos, S. Kendall, & C. Stahn (Eds.), *Contested justice: The politics and practice of International Criminal Court interventions* (pp. 432–455). Cambridge University Press.

Ellis, J. (2007). *Honoured in the breach: The response of international law to breaches of rules*. SSRN. https://doi.org/10.2139/ssrn.1414545

Engle, K. (2016). A genealogy of the criminal turn in human rights. In K. Engle, Z. Miller, & D. Davis (Eds.), *Anti-impunity and the human rights agenda* (pp. 15–67). Cambridge University Press.

Espinosa, M. J. C. (2005). The judicialization of politics in Colombia: The old and the new. In R. Sieder, R. Schiolden, & M. A. Angell (Eds.), *The judicialization of politics in Latin America* (pp. 67–103). Palgrave.

García Iommi, L. (2020). Whose justice? The ICC 'Africa problem'. *International Relations, 34*(1), 105–129. https://doi.org/10.1177/0047117819842294

García Iommi, L. (2023). Nothing changed after Rome: Continuity in state support for the International Criminal Court. *Journal of Human Rights, 22*(1), 16–30. https://doi.org/10.1080/14754835.2022.2157206

Gholiagha, S., Holzscheiter, A., & Liese, A. (2020). Activating norm collisions: Interface conflicts in international drug control. *Global Constitutionalism, 9*(2), 290–317. https://doi.org/10.1017/S2045381719000388

Han, Y., & Rosenberg, S. (2021). Claiming equality: The African Union's contestation of the anti-impunity norm. *International Studies Review, 23*(3), 726–751. https://doi.org/10.1093/isr/viaa065

Hansen-Magnusson, H., Vetterlein, A., & Wiener, A. (2018). The problem of non-compliance: Knowledge gaps and moments of contestation in global governance. *Journal of International Relations and Development, 23*(3), 636–656. https://doi.org/10.1057/s41268-018-0157-x

Henderson, C. (2022). Between formalism and instrumentalism. The United States and international law governing the use of interstate force. In L. García Iommi & R. W. Maass (Eds.), *The United States and international law. Paradoxes of support across contemporary issues* (pp. 81–101). University of Michigan Press.

Hillebrecht, C., Huneeus, A., & Borda, S. (2018). The judicialization of peace. *Harvard International Law Journal, 59*, 279–330.

Hunter, Q., Mataboge, M., & De Wet, P. (2015). How Zuma and ministers plotted Omar al-Bashir's escape. *Mail & Guardian*. Retrieved March 1, 2025, from https://mg.co.za/article/2015-06-18-how-zuma-and-ministers-plotted-omar-al-bashirs-escape/

ICC. (2009). *Warrant of arrest for Omar Hassan Ahmad Al Bashir* (ICC-02/05-01/09-1). Retrieved March 1, 2025, from https://www.icc-cpi.int/court-record/icc-02/05-01/09-1

ICC. (2010). *Second Decision on the Prosecution's Application for a Warrant of Arrest* (ICC-02/05-01/09-94). Retrieved March 1, 2025, from https://www.icc-cpi.int/court-record/icc-02/05-01/09-94

Kallander, A. A. (2021). *Tunisia's modern woman: Nation-building and state feminism in the global 1960s*. Cambridge University Press.

Kratochwil, F. (1989). *Rules, norms, and decisions: On the conditions of practical and legal reasoning in international relations and domestic affairs*. Cambridge University Press.

Krivenko, E. Y. (2009). *Women, Islam and international law: Within the context of the convention on the elimination of all forms of discrimination against women.* Brill.

Labuda, P. (2013). The International Criminal Court and perceptions of sovereignty, colonialism and pan-African solidarity. *African Yearbook of International Law, 20*(1), 299–330. https://doi.org/10.1163/22116176-90000149

Lucenti, F., Ducci, C., & Lee, P. K. (2025). Conceptualising the Responsibility to Prosecute norm as a cluster: Impunity for war crimes in Sri Lanka. In Lucenti, F., Ducci, C., Wunderlich, C., & Lantis, J. S. (Eds.), *Contestation in prism: The evolution of norms and norm clusters in contemporary global politics* (pp. 87–105). Springer.

Marcos, A. (2016, October 6). *Miles de personas marchan en Colombia para que se apruebe el acuerdo de paz.* El Pais. Retrieved March 1, 2025, from https://elpais.com/internacional/2016/10/06/colombia/1475712809_874532.html

Mashhour, A. (2005). Islamic law and gender equality: Could there be a common ground?: A study of divorce and polygamy in Sharia Law and contemporary legislation in Tunisia and Egypt. *Human Rights Quarterly, 27*, 562–596.

Naqvi, Y. (2018). *Amnesties and the ICC, The Peace and Justice Initiative.* Retrieved March 1, 2025, from http://www.peaceandjusticeinitiative.org/implementation-resources/amnesties-and-the-icc

Nathan, L. (2010). Interests, ideas and ideology: South Africa's policy on Darfur. *African Affairs, 110*(438), 55–74. https://doi.org/10.1093/afraf/adq058

NATO. (2022, May 17). *Kosovo air campaign (March–June 1999).* Retrieved March 1, 2025, from https://www.nato.int/cps/en/natohq/topics_49602.htm

Onishi, N. (2017, March 8). South Africa reverses withdrawal from International Criminal Court. *The New York Times.* Retrieved March 1, 2025, from https://www.nytimes.com/2017/03/08/world/africa/south-africa-icc-withdrawal.html

Orchard, P., & Wiener, A. (2022). Norms and norm contestation. In P. Mello & F. Ostermann (Eds.), *Routledge handbook of foreign policy analysis methods* (pp. 51–66). Taylor & Francis.

Panke, D., Grundsfeld, L., & Tverskoi, P. (2025). Regional organisations, exit threats, and contestation of community norms. In F. Lucenti, C. Ducci, C. Wunderlich, J. S. & Lantis (Eds.), *Contestation in prism: The evolution of norms and norm clusters in contemporary global politics* (pp. 45–63). Springer.

Park, S., & Vetterlein, A. (2010). *Owning development: Creating policy norms in the IMF and the World Bank.* Cambridge University Press.

Parliamentarians for Global Action. (2024). *Colombia and the Rome Statute.* Retrieved March 1, 2025, from https://www.pgaction.org/ilhr/rome-statute/colombia.html

Peace Accord. (2016). *Colombia: final agreement to end the armed conflict and build a stable and lasting peace.* Retrieved March 1, 2025, from https://www.refworld.org/legal/agreements/natlegbod/2016/en/121520

Putin, V. (2014, March 18). Address by President of The Russian Federation. President of Russia. Retrieved March 1, 2025, from http://www.en.kremlin.ru/events/president/news/20603

Radio Tamazuj. (2015, August 7). *Zuma defends allowing Bashir to evade arrest.* Retrieved March 1, 2025, from https://radiotamazuj.org/en/news/article/zuma-defends-allowing-bashir-to-evade-arrest

Rees, N. (2000). The Kosovo crisis, the international response and Ireland. *Irish Studies in International Affairs, 11*, 55–70. https://www.jstor.org/stable/30001912

Reuters. (2015, September 1). *South Africa lawmakers reject bid to impeach Zuma over Bashir saga.* Retrieved March 1, 2025, from https://www.reuters.com/article/idUSKCN0R14G5/

Select Committee on Foreign Affairs. (1999). Memorandum by the foreign and commonwealth office, "Kosovo: History of the crisis. Select Committee on Foreign Affairs, Fourth Report, Minutes of Evidence, House of Commons. Retrieved March 1, 2025, from https://publications.parliament.uk/pa/cm199900/cmselect/cmfaff/28/9111803.htm

Tunisian Constitution. (1959). Retrieved March 1, 2025, from https://www.google.com/url?sa=t&source=web&rct=j&opi=89978449&url=https://www.wipo.int/wipolex/en/legislation/detai

ls/7201&ved=2ahUKEwjst_24hdyGAxUrD1kFHWptOxkQFnoECBMQAQ&usg=AOvVaw3XMj4A5xmLZH1qVSi6xNbY

United Nations. (2006). *Declarations, reservations, objections and notifications of withdrawal of reservations relating to the CEDAW* (CEDAW/SP/2006/2). Retrieved July 1, 2024, from https://www.un.org/womenwatch/daw/cedaw/reservations.htm

United Nations. (2014). Tunisia: Withdrawal of the declaration with regard to Article 15(4) and of the reservations to Articles 9*(2),* 16(c), *(d), (f), (g), (h) and 29 (1) made upon ratification* (C.N.220.2014.TREATIES-IV.8). Retrieved March 1, 2025, from https://treaties.un.org/doc/Publication/CN/2014/CN.220.2014-Eng.pdf

United Nations Committee on the Elimination of Discrimination Against Women. (2000). *Combined third and fourth periodic reports of Tunisia, August 2* (CEDAW/C/TUN/3-4). Retrieved March 1, 2025, from https://www.google.com/url?sa=t&source=web&rct=j&opi=89978449&url=https://www.un.org/womenwatch/daw/cedaw/cedaw27/tun3-4.pdf&ved=2ahUKEwi-0NT3ityGAxUonokEHX10CYYQFnoECBAQAQ&usg=AOvVaw1KYMO5I9ixqgKi8ti3jbUI

United Nations Secretary General Press Release. (1999). *Secretary-General deeply regrets Yugoslav rejection of political settlement; says Security Council should be involved in any decision to use force* (SG/SM/6938). Retrieved March 1, 2025, from https://press.un.org/en/1999/sgsm6938.doc.htm

United Nations Security Council Press Release. (1999a). *NATO action against Serbian military targets prompts divergent views as Security Council holds urgent meeting on situation in Kosovo* (SC/6657). Retrieved March 1, 2025, from https://press.un.org/en/1999/19990324.sc6657.html

United Nations Security Council Press Release. (1999b). *Security Council rejects demand for cessation of use of force against federal republic of Yugoslavia* (SC/6659). Retrieved March 1, 2025, from https://press.un.org/en/1999/19990326.sc6659.html

United States. (1990). *U.S. reservations, declarations, and understandings, Convention against torture and other cruel, inhuman or degrading treatment or punishment* (Cong. Rec. S17486-01). Retrieved March 1, 2025, from http://hrlibrary.umn.edu/usdocs/tortres.html

Universal Rights Group. (2019). *Lifting religion-based reservations to the core international human rights conventions as a means of strengthening women's rights at the national level: A guide for women's rights groups.*

Urueña, R. (2016). Playing with fire: International criminal law, transitional justice, and the implementation of the Colombian peace agreement. *AJIL Unbound, 110*, 364–368. https://doi.org/10.1017/aju.2017.13

Washington Post. (1999a, March 29). U.S. Policy in the Balkans. Retrieved March 1, 2025, from https://www.washingtonpost.com/wp-srv/national/talk/archive/nsc0329.htm

Washington Post. (1999b, May 18). *Air campaign ignites anti-U.S. sentiment.* Retrieved March 1, 2025, from https://www.washingtonpost.com/wp-srv/inatl/longterm/balkans/stories/anger051899.htm

Whippman, D. (2001). Kosovo and the limits of international law. *Fordham International Law Journal, 25*(1), 129–150. https://ir.lawnet.fordham.edu/ilj/vol25/iss1/5

Wiener, A. (2014). *A theory of contestation*. Springer.

Wiener, A. (2017). Agency of the governed in global international relations: Access to norm validation. *Third World Thematics: A TWQ Journal, 2*(5), 709–725. https://doi.org/10.1080/23802014.2017.1359064

Winston, C. (2018). Norm structure, diffusion, and evolution: A conceptual approach. *European Journal of International Relations, 24*(3), 638–661. https://doi.org/10.1177/1354066117720794

Wojciak, P. (2014). *International Criminal Court to keep close watch on Colombia peace process.* Colombia Reporters. Retrieved March 1, 2025, from https://colombiareports.com/international-criminal-court-keep-close-watch-colombia-peace-process/amp/

Yoo, J. (2003). *Memorandum for William J. Haynes IT, General Counsel of the Department of Defense*. US Department of Justice, Office of Legal Counsel. Retrieved March 1, 2025, from https://www.aclu.org/documents/memo-regarding-torture-and-military-interrogation-alien-unlawful-combatants-held-outside

Chapter 9
Hidden Transcripts and Normative Transformations

Simone Tholens

Norm(ative) Configurations and Contestation

Norms research in International Relations (IR) has a long pedigree of thinking about contestation. This edited volume captures new approaches to how international norms may decay, disappear, be made irrelevant, ignored, strengthened, or transformed in ways that realign its original normative shape and intent. Building on what the editors of this project identify as interlinkages between norms and wider norm clusters (Wunderlich et al., 2025, Chap. 1), this chapter explores relational theories of normative transformation (Hofferberth & Weber, 2015; Pratt, 2022). Furthermore, I reflect on the conditions that produce what this volume is mainly concerned with: normative transformations that undo or change certain constellations of normativity, and in particular those that appear to maintain normative hegemony, but which face such enduring 'low-cost' contestation that they metamorphosise into 'something else'. In other words, this chapter seeks to capture transformation without anyone explicitly declaring change, or the art of non-change as produced through incremental and indeed often hidden moves.

A relational account of norm change requires critical reflections on three aspects of norms research. First, the ontological scope is relocated from norms to normative configurations. This requires accepting that the starting point is not 'norms' but continuously (re)assembled and thus emergent configurations of normativity. In other words, it requires moving away from what Donna Haraway (1988, p. 582) has called the 'god trick' of fixing singular norms to be studied, and rather arguing that norms always are temporally contingent reflections of normative dispositions.

S. Tholens (✉)
John Cabot University, Rome, Italy

European University Institute, Florence, Italy
e-mail: simone.tholens@eui.eu; simone.tholens@johncabot.edu

F. Lucenti et al. (eds.), *Contestation in Prism*, Norm Research in International Relations, https://doi.org/10.1007/978-3-031-83639-8_9

To take a processual view of norms, rather than treat them as fixed 'things' (Krook & True, 2012; Laffey & Weldes, 1997), requires a move that Pratt (2022) has defined as de-reification of norms. Following the critique that a focus on norms as discrete social entities reifies norms—i.e. a discursive move that objectifies their existence—Pratt proposes to de-reify their use by adopting an epistemological approach that conceives of normativity in practice. By moving away from norms as objects, he proposes 'normative configurations' as a way of retaining the normative as a site of struggle over meaning but which ontologically does away with the singularity of 'norms' (Pratt, 2022, p. 52).

Similar arguments describing a processual and relational view of normativity can be found in critical constructivist studies. For example, Hofferberth and Weber (2015, p. 80) in their critique of constructivist norms research, in particular their point that the 'norm research literature is steeped in a peculiar inconsistency: Although they introduce norms as contingent social phenomena, sometimes emphasising explicitly that their meaning is intersubjectively constructed, the ensuing research designs and empirical studies picture them as stable things with fixed and unequivocal content'. David McCourt (2016) also identifies how the limitations in constructivism's main interest in norms, identities, and culture can be overcome by thinking about what he defines as New Constructivism, harnessing the promise in practice and relationality approaches to global politics. Taken together, these perspectives support the argument that contestation is simply a part of normativity-making, not a reaction or opposition to a specific norm (e.g. Wiener, 2004, 2014), nor to fixed 'norm clusters' (e.g. Lantis & Wunderlich, 2018; Winston, 2018).

Secondly, this approach denotes an ontological shift that opens up to the situational as opposed to a preoccupation in norm contestation studies towards normative transformation as outcome. For example, the theoretical distinction between change and decay (e.g. Deitelhoff & Zimmermann, 2020) is problematic, as it becomes a normative move of the researcher to measure *normness*. As Pratt observes in his study, norms don't necessarily get replaced or abandoned. Percy and Sandholtz (2022) similarly argue that norms rarely die, and rather we see an evolution in the normative scope. As the authors write 'a change in the reference-relation between the articulable principles or values associated with a [normative configuration] and the situational ways in which it informs right, virtuous, and appropriate conduct' (Percy & Sandholtz, 2022, p. 951). Here, a pragmatist view of action as part of practice emerges, where a disentanglement of normativity concerning one set of practices effectively produces a transformation in the very normative configuration simply through the doing and saying taking place. Pratt's frame of normative transformation *is* helpful to unlock the capacity for norms research to reach beyond tracing a 'phantom ontology' of norms. But the pragmatism of Dewey and Shatzki, as inspiring Pratt, downplays the subversive force of the dominated, the hierarchies of sociality embedded and embodied in normative configurations, and the calculus involved in crafting narratives of domination. This is why normative transformation is in need of an account of resistance to be complete.

Third, building on a relational account of normative transformation, I argue that resistance practices in the form of struggles between 'public' and 'hidden transcripts' exist within and throughout international practices and that capacity for normative change resides in communities of resistance that transcend binary views of international versus national, public versus private, and norm giver versus norm taker. This raises the intriguing proposition that the very same agents can be both entrepreneurs and antipreneurs, as per Bloomfeld's (2016) typology, depending on the role they perform in a given community. Inconsistencies in rhetoric—by states, by issue organisations, by private actors, and by individuals—are expressions of the transcript struggles that are constantly underway in international social life. Hidden transcripts, specifically, exist across communities of practice and are written at an offstage arena of politics that are fragmented and hidden from view, often even from the multiplicity of participants themselves. In transnational politics, resistance practices will be visible both at particular moments where the built-up pressure disrupts the calm surface of silence and consent and in equal measure through everyday speech acts or insurrectional practices. An account of transcript struggles is thus not just a more forceful take on norm contestation. Rather, hidden transcripts are embodiments of lived experiences and alternative lifeworld and they co-exist with dominant normative configurations—be they liberal, good, or otherwise. To understand normative transformations requires an understanding of their nature; how they operate; and how they, under certain conditions, may produce change and transformative dynamics in the public script.

In the next section, I outline how hidden transcripts, of special interest in this chapter, can resolve some of the challenges related to transformation for norms research, and how they provide an onto-epistemology that is deeply relational and simultaneously offers avenues for thinking about power in transnational relations.

Public Versus Hidden Transcript Struggles

As an ontological move, normative contestation is a way of shedding new light on how seemingly established and formally agreed upon, possibly even institutionalised, normative configurations transform and change in international social life. Adding to the rich repertoire of this project, I suggest highlighting how concealed resistance and official discourse in the form of 'public' transcripts inform behaviour and shape the normative configuration. In keeping with the edited volume's lexicon (Wunderlich et al., 2025, Chap. 1), we can observe how norm contestation through largely unarticulated 'hidden' transcripts may lead to shifts in norms and norm clusters. Whether it does so, though, remains contingent on context. My concern with hidden transcripts as a type of non-articulated or subtly articulated counter-narratives rests with the observation that normative configurations are not void of hierarchies: they are enactments thereof, and the repertoires available to transformers are influenced by their relative position within them. But this must not lock us in structural-materialist analyses of determinism and should rather act as a starting point for a more relational account of normativity in practice.

These arguments build on a rich theoretical foundation. Early perspectives on hidden transcripts were developed in a post-Marxist and Gramscian tradition, where oppressed subordinate groups such as peasants, slaves, or serfs were seen as resisting dominant elite narratives and structures. These varieties of offstage discourses and practices that would at times be enacted could provoke a 'rupture in the performance' of the public transcript (Scott, 1990, p. 4). Expanding on his earlier work on everyday forms of resistance in peasant communities as 'Weapons of the Weak', political anthropologist James Scott's (1985) thinking about hidden transcripts was influenced by his ethnographic studies of rice farming societies in Malaya, in which he observed how both elites and 'subordinate groups' performed a 'public transcript', while different 'hidden' scripts were collectively written 'offstage'. This public performance, he observed, was ritualistic in the sense that it was designed to conceal an alternative arena of politics that would contradict the public transcript (Scott, 1990, p. 12).

Scott's interest rested in seeking to discern 'how the hidden transcripts of various actors are formed, the conditions under which they do or do not find public expression, and what relation they bear to the public transcript' (Scott, 1990, p. 13). For him, it is not a question of if but how such hidden transcripts would rupture the performance. He argues, '[t]he public transcript is, to put it crudely, the self-portrait of dominant elites as they would have themselves seen. Given the usual power of dominant elites to compel performances from others, the discourse of the public transcript is a decidedly lopsided discussion [...]. It is designed to be impressive, to affirm and naturalize the power of dominant elites, and to conceal or euphemize the dirty linen of their rule' (Scott, 1990, p. 18).

This view of the public transcript comes close to post-structural, and especially feminist, critical IR theory that has worked extensively on how discourses shape and legitimise behaviour and produce subjectivities in and through its performativity (e.g. Butler, 2011; Hansen, 2000). It is for our purposes important to note the relationship between norms and discourses, as they form part of an ideational ecosystem that can be reinforcing but can also pull in different directions. Either way, in many instances, discourse analyses, drawing mainly on Foucauldian concepts of governmentality and knowledge power, often paradoxically stick with the 'lopsided' account of power in the interest of unravelling taken-for-*grantedness* and naturalisation of power. If we are to grasp how they transform, however, we also need to allow for more fine-grained perspectives on their resistance. This leads to the question: How do offstage discourses intertwine with public proclamations, formal institutionalisation, and perceptions of expectations attached to certain identities? In this respect, Scott demonstrates how hidden transcripts are formed by both speech acts and practices. Mapping this 'realm of possible dissent' (Scott, 1990, p. 20) is required to reveal how hidden transcripts—whether through everyday forms of contestation of the public narrative, or through the occasional insurrection, namely the 'rupture in the performance' (Scott, 1990, p. 4)—act as 'sequestered social sites' (Scott, 1990, p. 120) where resistance can be nurtured and given meaning. In such offstage sites, will we gain insights into how hidden transcripts are collectively written.

This is not inconsequential, but since normative configurations are saturated with normative claims and associated expectations of sanctions for deviant behaviour—as already emphasised by March and Olsen's (1998) concept of the logic of consequences, we can assume that hidden transcripts exist in 'sequestered social sites' also in relation to international norms. In order to make the struggles between public and hidden transcripts relevant for investigating normative transformations, and thus to take seriously that normativity is intrinsically intertwined with interests and identities, we need to couple the framework with a more precise account of situationing. The next section offers an explication of the role that the hidden transcripts play in order to 'write' alternative normative scripts with the capacity to transform intersubjective configurations, including in international life.

Normative Transformation in and through Hidden Transcripts

This edited book is concerned with how contestation critically examines the development, scope, strength, and resiliency of norm architectures. I introduce a framework to show how hidden transcripts can be employed to investigate how transformation can take place in ways that are hidden or concealed from plain view. Having established that norms are best treated as constantly evolving and transforming normative configurations and that change therefore becomes a matter of capturing reinterpretations, practices, and 'petit arrangements' (Gravier, 2020) along the margins of solidified normativity, the next step is to unpack how hidden transcripts operate: How they become visible through ruptures in the public transcript and how we can study them methodologically in IR context. This speaks to the question whether norm clusters may show resiliency despite widespread contestation of specific norms within them. However, it will also show how norm clusters may appear robust because practices deviate at a non-articulated level. The potency of hidden transcripts is precisely that they allow for the ritualistic performance of normative configurations while gradually shifting or re-situationing the discourse at a subtle level which may or may not burst out into the open. It is in this re-situationing that both continuity and change in behaviour can be detected.

The chapter also builds on earlier attempts at developing insight into hidden transcripts. For instance, in her study of how EU member states resist norms about deeper defence integration at home after having actively promoted them in Brussels, Cross (2015) introduced the notions of hidden and public transcripts to analyse how formally committed norms continued to be contested domestically. She did so by reference to different value spaces internationally and domestically, as per the Weberian understanding of value spheres as expressions of different rationalities that pertain to the different spaces or domains that humans occupy. Cross' concern was to understand how value spheres at home would set states up against their own commitment internationally, and how varieties of hidden transcripts in EU member states would seep into official texts and the public transcript via subtle resistance practices (Cross, 2015, p. 86). While her study in many ways replicates the rationalist levels of analysis or two-level game models, it is a good starting point for thinking about hidden narratives at work in IR. Importantly, she too highlights Scott's (1990, p. 88) point that the hidden transcripts are often in public view, but in a 'veiled or disguised form'. In other words, we can begin looking for hidden transcripts as they are folded into normative configurations in plain sight.

If established normativity, including highly institutionalised normative configurations, is conceived of as public transcripts, then they also embody their constitutive hidden transcripts. Scott argues, 'Each participant will be familiar with the public transcript and the hidden transcript of his or her circle, but not with the hidden transcript of the other' (1990, p. 15). This is to some extent the case also in international life, but with moderation: awareness of the hidden transcript of 'others' may exist across, even if often in juxtaposition mode to that of 'self'. As Cross (2015) shows, many EU member states' hidden narratives reflect ontological security positions that were co-produced by its opposition: as she notes, 'Spain's hidden transcript of resistance comes from its feeling of being ignored by the key players' (p. 97), while in the case of the UK, 'the hidden transcript of norm resistance at the domestic level is based in part on British criticism of other member states for inaction' (p. 96). Differently, the French hidden transcript is described as 'carr[ying] an element of blame' vis-à-vis the other EU members (Cross, 2015, p. 98). These circles resemble 'communities of practice' as they have been popularised in IR, first by the work by Adler and Pouliot (2011), Bueger and Gadinger (2018), and then by its capitalisation, the Communities of Practice (CoP) (Bicchi, 2022). In these Bourdieusian-inspired approaches, 'transnational guilds' are formed upon loyalty as practised by a professional ethos and code (Bigo, 2016).

We may thus observe hidden narratives at a variety of sites and across traditional political science boundaries. It is in such a multi-scalar networked social context that hidden transcripts may transform normative configurations, so that they may turn into something else than what they at some points were. In line with the volume's concern with how contestation critically examines the evolution of norm architectures, I highlight a three-step framework that can be employed to empirically investigate how hidden transcripts, practised both among dominating and dominated, and their persistent force produce transformation.

Identify the Public Transcript

Goffman's frontstage is a useful metaphor when capturing the dramaturgy enacted through public transcripts, and how they relate to a normative configuration at a given moment. When treating a normative configuration as a performance, the emotive and situational dimensions come to the fore. The public transcript is performed by different groups, and its naturalisation sits in the shared belief that there is something taken-for-granted at the core of the system. Yet any normative configuration is dependent on a performance of naturalisation, suppressing alternative claims. Drawing on Scott's lexicon, we can identify affirmation, concealment, euphemism, and appearance of unanimity as processual modes of performing public transcripts.

Modalities of Hidden Transcripts

The second part of the framework concerns modalities of hidden transcripts, not as secret or unknown, but as alternative bodies of truth that exist along the margins of public discourse, but which are not quite invited into direct contact with such. This frontier is breached when hidden transcripts burst into the official realm. This does not mean that it changes accordingly; in fact, we can observe that states often commit to international normative configurations with inherent ambiguity. Governments know they are not unitary actors and work under the assumption that margins of interpretation allow for sufficient openness to isolate critique with varieties of constituents. The logic here is that commitments made by governments are in themselves not norms, but express emergent configurations of normativity, and that their protagonists are aware of the limits, and even perhaps calculate on making concessions to constituents with hidden narrative repertoires. Take, for instance, commitments to climate change as a normative configuration. Despite high level claims, meetings, and commitments, governments know that their pledges will be resisted by a range of different actors such as oil and gas companies, by indigenous communities whose land might be sequestered to exploit the renewable energy potential, and by bureaucracies in their effort to resist cumbersome change. Such communities of resistance to normative configurations are often formally supportive of the inter-governmental commitments but will activate repertoires of resistance to adjust and transform these into something else.

In Wiener's (2014) view, these are contestations in the form of meaning in use, which may result in strengthened norms through processes of legitimation and shared understanding of their meaning. From a perspective of seeing hidden transcripts as subversive resistance repertoires, the view changes. In-built ambiguity is more active than what Wiener acknowledges, and in the emergent normative configuration there is a realisation of dissident voices. The performativity of public scripts thus becomes about ritualising and neutralising dissent, since alternative voices become welcomed and accepted, if mainly in a sanitised form. This mechanism of turning critique into acceptable forms of multiplicity through intentional ambiguity is important for an understanding of how hidden transcripts can find ways to engage with the public transcript as in the form of 'dribbling your mind out by the sly' as identified by Scott (1990). Whether this will weaken or strengthen norm robustness is not the central question. Rather, such inherent ambiguity should be seen as designed to absorb critique and accommodate brief and toothless manifestations of hidden transcripts by conceiving of their protagonists as 'grudging conscripts to the performance' (Scott, 1990, p. 15). This chapter therefore further contributes to the aims of the volume by showing yet a different, and understudied, form of subtle contestation.

Institutionalisation of normative configurations, moreover, allows for platforms where hidden transcripts come into contact with public transcripts in direct ways. As such, Deitelhoff and Zimmerman's (2020) distinction between applicatory and justificatory contestation collapses, because they are part of the same repertoires of resistance, and the same group might alternate between performing the public transcript and practising their hidden one. Whereas some communities will take the opportunity to address validity claims against the existence of the normative configurations (e.g. claiming that 'the ICC is racist'),[1] others will operate in their wake and address 'applicatory' adjustments to practice (e.g. arguing that the Court's mandate does not cover X, Y, and Z). Others may launch an attack on the very existence of the institution. These two forms—mirroring Adler-Nissen and Pouliot's (2014) 'thin' and 'thick' contestations—are part of the same transformative forces that while seemingly attacking or contesting specific normative configurations are expressions of alternative worldviews that co-exist with public transcript and may gradually transform these organically. Here it should become clear that contestation can equally be the articulation of positions, and hence not necessarily contestation, but advocacy of particular worldviews. This might be a helpful way forward to think about the world beyond liberal versus non-liberal scripts (Zürn & Gerschewski, 2021). Instead, we could think of it as variously contextualised struggles to articulate political visions from the position of global liminality.

A separate process dynamic at work, however, offers the possibility for more staged drama. Public controversies and scandals allow for venues to solidify and systematise hidden transcripts; indeed, crises may provide opportunities for more forceful and systematic expression of the hidden transcript. This view, akin to the 'dangerous but gratifying full blast', as in the analogy provided by Scott (1990), sees crises as moments where normative configurations can be openly challenged with less risk of consequences in the form of penalties than under conditions of stability. One example of this might be seen in the moratorium against the use of indiscriminate weapons in war, and the ban on cluster munitions specifically. While many states have not signed the Convention on Cluster Munitions (CCM), considerable debate over the use of such indiscriminate weapons has taken place, in particular, in regard to the long civil war in Syria. However, as the Ukraine war has dragged on, and ammunition shortages became part of public discourse, the US decided to provide the Ukrainian armed forces with such cluster munitions in the summer of 2023. Since neither the US nor Ukraine, nor Russia for that matter, had signed the CCM, it was normatively interesting to observe how they justified their action, referencing the dramatic events unfolding on the battleground in Ukraine, and their own intentions to adhere to the normative configuration by justifying its military advantage and highlighting how US cluster munitions have a much lower 'dud rate'

[1] On accusations against the ICC that it adopts a 'neo-imperialist' approach, see also Lucenti et al. (2025, Chap. 5).

than the Russian. The war against Ukraine therefore offered an opportunity for the exposure of a hidden transcript that seeks an alternative interpretation of why, when, and how cluster munitions can be deployed in war, producing a re-situationing of the normative configuration in this issue area. The effect is a likely transformation of the normative configuration, with some initially strong supporters of the CCM, such as Norway, being deliberately late in their rather mild condemnation of the US decision to supply Ukraine with such capabilities, implicitly accepting such a transformation. Lingering hidden transcripts have thus burst into the public transcript by way of the opportunity provided by crises and shifted the terms of the debate of its very existence.

From Hidden Transcripts to Normative Transformation

Normative configurations, their performances, and the hidden transcripts that constantly seek to rearrange them are always emergent. This contingent nature is a premise but also poses challenges when looking for normative transformation. Thus, as highlighted in this chapter, by adopting a relational view of such change, we also need to understand change as situational. This means that transformation occurs by shifts in context—by relocating the normative contents in accord with a new set of conditions, via new technologies, and through new constellations of networks. Pratt (2022) identifies three mechanisms for such change: convention reorientation, technological revision, and network synthesis. Without going into their detail, what is important for this chapter is the focus on how subtle resistance transcripts work in and through emergent normative configurations. This means that both continuity and change are equally important processes and that the subtle transformations are best captured by analyses of the emergence of alternative scripts, which gradually replace or partially substitute discourse, and the way existing institutions are given new tasks, purposes, or scope of membership. I will return to these in the final part of this chapter.

Hidden Transcripts and the Transformation of Euro-Mediterranean Normativity

To empirically illustrate the conceptual framework of this analysis, the transformation of the Euro-Mediterranean community model of policy interaction as a geospatial and normative configuration lends itself well. In the twenty years between 2003 and 2023, the Euro-Mediterranean community model of relations institutionalised and solidified and then gradually stagnated and changed into something else, yet did not 'die'. Tracing parts of these processes with a focus on hidden transcripts adds to theories of varieties of contestation and norm change in international politics.

Identifying the Public Transcript: The Emergence of a 'Community Vision' for the Med

Since the launch of the Euro-Mediterranean Partnership (EMP) in 1995, there has been a proliferation of bilateral and multilateral agreements between the EU and the MENA countries that have reinforced, if not driven entirely, the notion of a concerted EU foreign and security policy. The overall effect of this invention has been described as the EU turning the Middle East and North Africa into its 'Borderlands', with the core extending its influence on the external periphery, creating a 'buffer zone', a 'ring of friends', and a 'hub-and-spoke' relationship with what lies beyond the 'empire' (Del Sarto, 2009, 2015). In this way, the EU structured its external relations based on distinct ambitions, policies, and institutions, and it provided a public transcript to accompany them. This frame largely reflects the 'wider Europe' construct frequently featured in policy documents from the period around the launch of the European Neighbourhood Policy (ENP) in 2004. Yet, critics charge that this 'geospatial fantasy' (Mamadouh, 2022) of the Mediterranean, which in many ways evokes orientalist desires, connects to colonisation in constructing the European integration project according to a conception of its relationship with the post-colonial other (e.g. Hansen & Jonsson, 2014; Onar & Nicolaïdis, 2013; Pace & Roccu, 2020).

In identifying the 'public transcript' in constructing the Euro-Mediterranean community model, I should first emphasise the predominance of asymmetric relationships, based on 'hub-and-spoke' modes of interaction, where the EU exports its own system of integration to non-membership countries, either through the transfer of parts of the *Acquis Communautaire* or with reference to the European Commission (EC) model of integration based on the principle of convergence. While this is a misnomer to the extent that it is not official policy to impose EU law on non-EU states, the early 2000s increasingly witnessed the *acquis* becoming the basis for relations across sectors and geographical areas. This extensive body of law was increasingly utilised as a reference point in ENP policy documents, reflecting the logic of rule export within the context of 'wider Europe'. For example, when referring to the establishment of an EU-Mediterranean Energy Community, the EC (2011, p. 10) makes clear that 'this community should cover relevant parts of the EU's energy legislation with a view to promoting a real and reliable convergence of South Mediterranean partners' energy policies with EU.' In addition, with reference to the new generation of Deep and Comprehensive Free Trade Agreements (DCFTAs) that was proposed to Neighbourhood countries after the 2011 Arab Uprisings, the EC (Commission, 2011, p. 9) indicates that 'beyond the mere elimination of import duties, these agreements should foster, in a progressive manner, closer integration between the economies of our Southern Mediterranean partners and the EU single market and would include actions such as regulatory convergence'. While the *acquis* is not always explicitly mentioned, references to the 'governing of the internal market' and 'creating convergence' based on extending the EU patterns of governance are prevalent in Euro-Mediterranean policy documents.

Obviously, such a 'neo-imperial' (Zielonka, 2006) approach was always contested, and a significant portion of this contestation was a part of the public transcript. Indeed, there were some who did not love the liberal overtures of Europe, and these in many ways confirmed the official transcript by their very unconforming nature. For instance, a rejection of the claim to competence over the rules governing a 'Euro-Mediterranean community' can be seen in those countries that did not sign an Association Agreement (AA) under the ENP, i.e. Syria and Libya. The generally considered uncooperative nature of these states, in particular, after 2011 and their descent into civil war, would not in itself pose a challenge to the public transcript—which is based on certain characteristics of cooperative behaviour and built on existing 'pyramids of preferences' that went back to the initial Global Mediterranean Policy of the mid-1970s (see Bicchi, 2007). However, those states that did sign AAs with the EU instead contested the public transcript by not implementing the Action Plan (AP), rendering the AA something like a normative umbrella, irrelevant to the daily engagement between the EU and the specific MENA state but structuring references to community building. As highlighted above, the ways in which variations of contestation are present in the public script are both interesting and important when unpacking narratives of domination and control.

Beyond the general framework of 'EU-Neighbourhood relations' official endorsement of the public transcript, in which convergence means MENA countries adopting EU rules in diverse policy fields, can be seen in the signing up of a number of regional and bilateral agreements and their formal participation in their supporting institutions. Individual EU member states also contributed to the normative reconfiguration underway, by engaging in bilateral relations with the respective MENA countries, contesting the EU's competence area in foreign policy. The resulting situation was ambiguous: on the one hand, there was clearly friction in the daily practices defining interactions in the realm. On the other hand, stakeholders on both sides of the Mediterranean appeared to live quite well with this ambiguity, where the EU claimed authorship of the official script, but where everyone knew the contested nature of said script (see Gravier, 2020 and the 'petits arrangements'). This shows how parts of the normative configuration are formally adhered to, but re-situated in practice, over time pulling the normative figuration in new directions.

Euro-Mediterranean Energy Community

Energy reappeared on the agenda of EU policymakers during the early-mid 2000s, after decades in the shadow of European affairs. Increased consumption and decreased production of energy on the European continent had created a situation whereby Europe's energy independence had dropped. Awareness of the vulnerability of European energy markets became particularly pertinent after the 2006 Gazprom crisis, in which gas was withheld on its journey from Russia to Europe via Ukraine. Subsequent EU communications addressed the need for the Europeanization of energy policy and for a rapid completion of the internal market in energy across

Europe. The Lisbon Treaty of 2009 included for the first time a chapter on energy, and thus transferred significant competencies in the field of energy from the member states to the European Community, evident in the establishment of a Directorate General for Energy (DG ENER).

But during a critical period between 2011 and 2015, there was, and remains so to this day, very little evidence pointing to any real integration of the energy systems north, south, and east of the Mediterranean, despite the upsurge in activities. These activities have been focused on technical infrastructure projects, on renewable energy and energy efficiency in the South, and on incremental steps towards developing common grid codes and those technical harmonisation processes needed to trade energy, mainly through the Mediterranean Association of Energy Regulators (MEDREG) and Transmission System Operators (Med-TSO) networks. However, initiatives in both the EMP and ENP frameworks have so far largely failed to institutionalise EU-MENA Energy integration. This applies both to the traditionally protectionist hydrocarbon sectors—oil and gas—and to Renewable Energy and electricity, where EU-backed industry mega-plans (e.g. Desertec, MEDGRID, the Mediterranean Solar Plan) repeatedly failed to garner sufficient investment and traction.

Given that the energy market is partly driven by sovereign states and partly by private actors therein, the EU is engaged in transcript struggles both internally and externally. The external dimension witnessed a number of policy documents outlining the challenges and priorities, and in the 2011 Communication *EU Energy Policy: Engaging with Partners beyond Our Borders*, the EU spelled out its interest in 'secure, sustainable and competitive' energy. This corresponds to the priorities often observed as 'the European approach' in the field of energy: (1) a need for energy security, mainly through infrastructure development; (2) a focus on the creation of renewable energy and energy efficiency in the Southern countries; and (3) market liberalisation, specifically through unbundling of the ownership structures in domestic markets and through an independent regulator model.

Particularly interesting for this analysis of identifying the normative configuration in this area is the EC Communication *A Partnership for Democracy and Shared Prosperity*, in which the EC announced its commitment to 'establish an EU-South Mediterranean Energy Community' (European Commission, 2011, p. 10). Identifying the strategic relevance of supplies from and transit through the Mediterranean region, and referring to the possibility of extending the Energy Community Treaty that was already in place with Eastern and South-Eastern neighbours, the 2011 Communication stated that 'this community should cover relevant parts of the EU's energy legislation with a view to promoting a real and reliable convergence of South Mediterranean partners' energy policies with EU policy' (European Commission, 2011, p. 15). According to EC Communications, an Energy Community should therefore be based on regulatory convergence with the EU *Acquis Communautaire*, much in the same vein as the pre-existing Energy Community (EnC) with Southeast Europe. The EnC was a highly institutionalised, and top-down instrument aimed predominantly at pre-accession countries or countries with such ambitions. The fact that the same name was applied to energy cooperation in the MENA region is hardly coincidental; it is an effective way of performing a public transcript by reference to a well-anchored existing institutional framework.

Modalities of Hidden Transcripts: Dissident Voices, Outbursts, and The Euro-Mediterranean Energy Community

How then can we best understand this grinding away at the official normative configuration on integration in the Euro-Mediterranean, and in the energy sector specifically? Direct, or thick, contestation, i.e. refusal to accept the competence claim laid out by the EU, does occur in the cases where MENA countries do not participate in 'Euro-Mediterranean' energy cooperation frameworks, do not forge energy partnerships, or do not in any way accept energy as a policy area in their bilateral relations with the EC. This has been the case for Libya, a net-exporting country, as well as for Syria, which is an important transit country for oil and gas from the Gulf countries. There are also great regional differences, and while in general the MENA countries lack rule-based integration, they are deeply inter-dependent in terms of energy markets. This is particularly the case in the field of gas, where infrastructure, long-term contracts, and market shares point to inter-dependency and integration between the North and South Mediterranean. This is driven through bilateral relations often by former colonial ties, and while the EU has been involved in regional—south-south—integration projects—notably the Euro-Arab Mashreq Gas Market Project and the Maghreb Electricity Market Integration Project—there is very little integration across all energy sectors in the region. However, and of key interest to uncovering hidden transcripts, even those countries that seemingly refuse the EU's claim to competence in the field of energy often participate in Euro-Med energy events. Thick contestation of EU competence in the energy realm is, arguably, gradually being eroded, as each country is being co-opted into the frameworks of cooperation. For example, Algeria signed in July 2013 a memorandum of understanding to develop energy cooperation with the EU, indicating that it will follow the path of connecting to the EU via conventional mechanisms, albeit a path of a broad and non-committing nature. This is not to say that such countries accept the entire package of EU regulations in the area—far from it—but it does indicate that contestatory practices take on more concealed characteristics.

This second, and less costly, form of contestation emphasises the opposition to the order of priorities, or to the relative position of the actors involved, but maintains some level of commitment to energy 'integration' EU style. Interactions in the EU-MENA energy realm are mainly composed of several so-called capacity building events, which are instructive with regard to detecting patterns of interaction and practices of contestation. These events are usually structured around the main discourses identified as EU policy priorities: energy security versus infrastructure, regulatory convergence versus integrated energy market, and renewable energy versus energy efficiency. Author participation in one such capacity building event in Venice, Italy, in 2013 revealed different sets of discussions around the idea of creating but also extending the Energy Community concept. Friction occurred, for example, when the speaker from the Energy Community (EnC) introduced the experience of the EnC in the Western Balkans. Several of the participants intervened to express scepticism about the functioning of the EnC in the Balkans, and about its applicability in the MENA region. In the coffee break, the participant from Algeria states his response to this idea: 'creating such a community is not my interest', he said (Fieldnotes 1, see Table 9.1). Moreover, a speaker from a European consortium on Renewable Energy garnered enthusiasm and applause when he addressed the participants—all engineers or economists from MENA countries:

> You don't have to get together politically to share and cooperate on energy and electricity—remember that Europe was connected on electricity before it was so political! In fact, there should be a Nobel Peace prize for electricity, and electrical engineers can be more diplomatic than diplomats. You guys don't need another instrument from Europe to do this. You can do what you want with the process (Fieldnotes 3, see Table 9.1).

In the next intervention, a Union for the Mediterranean (UfM) representative pointed out that the UfM had received its mandate from its members to support the implementation of the Mediterranean Solar Plan, and so it was now rather unfair to be criticised for respecting the member states' intentions. Yet, also he used a curious formulation: 'We are now facing how to create an Energy Community, as the EC calls it in the Communications' (Fieldnotes 3, see Table 9.1). He did not seem completely confident with this term. He then quickly added that the intention was 'not to propose international legislation—no one would accept a unified system of this kind—but to try to highlight the advantages of coordination on a regional level, as it is better to share the concerns and challenges coming from similar problems' (Fieldnotes 3, see Table 9.1). Such framing of the 'convergence' model in terms of interest-based rationality, rather than imposition of EU rules, is a commonly observed strategy used by protagonists of the EU model of integration, participatory observation shows. A similar form of hidden transcripts bursting to the surface can be seen in critical interventions in 'EU-Mediterranean' energy events. As one participant in one of these events said:

> A community is more a place to say no, than to favour investments. So, we don't need any more institutions. We need only MEDREG and MEDTSO, and the rest should be left to the free market. We shouldn't give the officials in Brussels the chance to sign something nonsensical! (Fieldnotes 2, see Table 9.1).

Table 9.1 List of fieldnotes

#	Position	Date
1	Author participatory observation in Euro-Mediterranean energy event	Venice, May 2013
2	Author participatory observation in Euro-Mediterranean energy event	Rome, May 2013
3	Author participatory observation in Euro-Mediterranean energy event	Florence, September 2013

In summary, hidden transcripts observed to 'burst' were part and parcel of the process that led to the failure to reach a commitment to the Mediterranean Solar Plan (MSP) and the Mediterranean Energy Community, during the December 2013 Union for the Mediterranean (UfM) Ministerial Meeting on Energy. Nevertheless, the EU's insistence on pursuing the institutional integration path continued unabated, and in 2014 the EC proposed the creation of three thematic platforms—on gas, electricity, and renewable energy and energy efficiency—and to subsume these initiatives under the Union for the Mediterranean, continuing its approach of integration based on—EU—institutions.

From Hidden Transcripts to Normative Transformation: The Enduring Character of the Euro-Mediterranean Community Model

So far, I have identified a set of practices encompassing the public transcript of a Euro-Mediterranean energy community, and the hidden transcripts as they were enacted through participation in network meetings during 2013–2014. What remains is to trace the process whereby hidden transcripts and transcript struggles produced changes to the normative figuration of a Euro-Mediterranean energy community model of interaction.

The 'wider Europe' transcript has gradually been replaced by narratives of a 'geopolitical' Union, flanked by a Mediterranean 'ring of fire'. The early post-Arab Uprising enthusiasm for support to democratic transitions and a deeper engagement in the region, a persistent feature of the community model of Euro-Mediterranean relations, was challenged by alternative scripts that key security threats—such as, migration, terrorism, energy security—were to take centre stage in the regional frame. The hidden transcript of many MENA states also contributed to this transformation: the fossil exporting, (semi-) authoritarian states of the region were partly contributing to such a new frame. Stability and investment gradually transformed rule convergence as a normative configuration.

But it is also significant how, despite transcript changes, many interaction platforms and networks have remained. One example is in the workings of MEDREG. The Association of Mediterranean Energy (Electricity and Gas) Regulators started as a voluntary working group in 2006, and became a permanent regional organisation in 2007, supported and financed by the EC through its DG Energy and DG Near. It has been noted that MEDREG is a voluntary association, based on mutual gains and aiming for regulatory harmonisation strategies and roadmaps for convergence, rather than imposition of any external regulatory framework. Participation in MEDREG is highlighted as fostering informal contact and 'bottom-up' exchange among regulators, who in this way create networks and mutual interest in energy cooperation. However, while MEDREG is in part a networked model of integration, it is also a product of EC priorities in the field of EU-MENA energy integration.

First of all, it is funded by the EU. Secondly, it is based on the participation of regulators, who, according to MEDREG, should be independent, and with clear powers and competences. The current situation in almost all MENA countries today is one whereby the 'regulator' is not independent and is without power and competence to oversee and implement fair competition in the domestic energy market. In fact, establishing such an independent 'market watchdog' function is a core aspect of the EU's own internal energy market, and therefore a stated aim rather than a reality of MEDREG. Thirdly, in November 2014, MEDREG signed a memorandum of understanding with the European Commission and the Mediterranean Association of Transmission System Operators (Med-TSO), pledging to establish a Euro-Mediterranean Platform on Regional Electricity Markets, which works in the direction of the establishment of a Mediterranean Energy Community. This commitment to the Mediterranean Energy Community points to increasing collusion between formal, acquis-based energy 'integration' and the hitherto described 'bottom-up' network of practitioners. Taken together, the existence and current functioning of MEDREG indicate a situational change, whereby practices of participation and interaction are structured according to concepts and models originating from the EU's internal market but have progressively aligned with the same principles that are contested in the top-down political dialogue. Taken together, this is testimony to how non-independent regulators participate in events, and publish glossy reports, year after year since 2006, on how Euro-Mediterranean energy integration should be based on independent regulators and free market rules, without actually subscribing to any of that which the EU claims to be the governing rules for energy integration. This outcome is thus best described as normative transformation, where EU rules are formally written and repeated, yet where power is exerted in the collusion of subversive and everyday practices between MENA and European energy stakeholders.

Conclusion

This chapter outlines a framework for thinking about norm transformation through the workings of hidden transcripts. In line with this volume's starting point that the diversification of the norm contestation literature has offered ample evidence of the complex transformations of normative configurations, it drew on this framework to analyse the case of attempts to create Euro-Mediterranean relations as per a 'community' model of integration. After a decade of optimism around this way of conceptualising the Middle East and North Africa as part of a 'southern neighbourhood' where norms, rules, and values could diffuse, the lack of uptake and a more 'geopolitical' world after 2014 meant that this normative configuration was increasingly abandoned. But rather than declare the Euro-Mediterranean community model for 'dead', the chapter highlights how it came from somewhere, was contested most prominently through hidden transcripts, and has been transformed into 'something else'. Many of the institutions and initiatives still exist, but the chapter argues, they have been situated within new discourses, and embedded in new normative arrangements.

The normative configuration in this case was only rarely explicitly contested. The countries in the designated Southern Mediterranean entertained, with a few exceptions, this normative configuration—or this 'geospatial fantasy' as Mamadouh (2022) has called it—and engaged in participation, negotiation, and discursive mimicking. There were, as shown elsewhere, rather rare to observe cases of 'thick' contestation (Adler-Nissen & Pouliot, 2014; Del Sarto & Tholens, 2020). Rather, we could observe a wide range of 'thin' contestation practices, each of which would pull at the normative configuration, and eventually transform its very normative significance. Where the Euro-Mediterranean community would in 2011 connote a rule-exporting European 'core', flanked by a rule-importing Southern Mediterranean 'periphery', this same construct a decade later meant cooperation on infrastructure and 'partnership' based on collaboration with governments on various aspects of the migration and refugee governance portfolio, with only minor significance extended to governance in other political areas. Rather than describe this shift as one from liberal norms to 'realpolitik', prevalent in public debates, this analysis has argued that this is evidence of a normative transformation and that this process has mainly been driven by the workings of hidden transcripts, mobilised 'in the shadows', and only intermittently burst out into the open.

The value of exploring the work of hidden transcripts and its impact on normative change rests in their capacity to exist alongside public transcripts and gradually transform these, mainly through behavioural contestation rather than discursive—even if the odd 'outburst' does take place. Hidden transcripts are not a mechanism—they are rather the field which shapes and produces contestation practices, whether characterised by action or inaction, discursive or behavioural. It is therefore necessary to understand them in their subversive and legitimate nature, as well as in their capacity to endure. As they often constitute the actors that practice them, they tend to provide persistent frames of identification and positionality.

References

Adler, E., & Pouliot, V. (2011). International practices. *International Theory, 3*(1), 1–36. https://doi.org/10.1017/S175297191000031X

Adler-Nissen, R., & Pouliot, V. (2014). Power in practice: Negotiating the international intervention in Libya. *European Journal of International Relations, 20*(4), 889–911. https://doi.org/10.1177/1354066113512702

Bicchi, F. (2007). *European foreign policy making towards the Mediterranean*. Palgrave.

Bicchi, F. (2022). Communities of practice and what they can do for International Relations. *Review of International Studies, 48*(1), 24–43. https://doi.org/10.1017/S0260210521000528

Bigo, D. (2016). Sociology of transnational guilds. *International Political Sociology, 10*(4), 398–416. https://doi.org/10.1093/ips/olw022

Bloomfield, A. (2016). Norm antipreneurs and theorising resistance to normative change. *Review of International Studies, 42*(2), 310–333. https://doi.org/10.1017/S026021051500025X

Bueger, C., & Gadinger, F. (2018). *International practice theory*. Palgrave.

Butler, J. (2011). *Gender trouble: Feminism and the subversion of identity*. Routledge.

Cross, M. K. D. (2015). The European Defence Agency and the member states: Public and hidden transcripts. *European Foreign Affairs Review, 20*(2/1), 83–102.

Deitelhoff, N., & Zimmermann, L. (2020). Things we lost in the fire: How different types of contestation affect the robustness of international norms. *International Studies Review, 22*(1), 51–76. https://doi.org/10.1093/isr/viy080

Del Sarto, R. A. (2009). Borderlands: The Middle East and North Africa as the EU's southern buffer zone. In D. Bechev & K. Nicolaidis (Eds.), *Mediterranean frontiers: Borders, conflicts and memory in a transnational world*. I.B. Tauris.

Del Sarto, R. A. (2015). Normative empire Europe: The European Union, its borderlands, and the 'Arab Spring'. *Journal of Common Market Studies, 54*(2), 215–232. https://doi.org/10.1111/jcms.12282

Del Sarto, R. A., & Tholens, S. (2020). *Resisting Europe: Practices of contestation in the Mediterranean Middle East*. University of Michigan Press. https://doi.org/10.3998/mpub.9965409

European Commission. (2011). *A partnership for democracy and shared prosperity with the Southern Mediterranean* (COM (2011) 200 final). https://eur-lex.europa.eu/LexUriServ/LexUriServ.do?uri=COM:2011:0200:FIN:en:PDF

Gravier, M. (2020). Petits arrangements avec l'Empire: Reflections on imperial power at its fringes. In R. A. Del Sarto & S. Tholens (Eds.), *Resisting Europe: Practices of contestation in the Mediterranean Middle East* (pp. 25–46). University of Michigan Press. https://doi.org/10.3998/mpub.9965409

Hansen, L. (2000). The little mermaid's silent security dilemma and the absence of gender in the Copenhagen School. *Millennium, 29*(2), 285–306.

Hansen, P., & Jonsson, S. (2014). *Eurafrica: The untold history of European integration and colonialism*. Bloomsbury Academic.

Haraway, D. (1988). Situated knowledges: The science question in feminism and the privilege of partial perspective. *Feminist Studies, 14*(3), 575–599.

Hofferberth, M., & Weber, C. (2015). Lost in translation: A critique of constructivist norm research. *Journal of International Relations and Development, 18*, 75–103. https://doi.org/10.1057/jird.2014.1

Krook, M. L., & True, J. (2012). Rethinking the life cycles of international norms: The United Nations and the global promotion of gender equality. *European Journal of International Relations, 18*(1), 103–127. https://doi.org/10.1177/1354066110380963

Laffey, M., & Weldes, J. (1997). Beyond belief: Ideas and symbolic technologies in the study of international relations. *European Journal of International Relations, 3*(2), 193–237.

Lantis, J. S., & Wunderlich, C. (2018). Resiliency dynamics of norm clusters: Norm contestation and international cooperation. *Review of International Studies, 44*(3), 570–593. https://doi.org/10.1017/S0260210517000626

Lucenti, F., Ducci, C., & Lee, P. K. (2025). Conceptualising the Responsibility to Prosecute norm as a cluster: Impunity for war crimes in Sri Lanka. In F. Lucenti, C. Ducci, C. Wunderlich & J. S. Lantis (Eds.), *Contestation in prism: The evolution of norms and norm clusters in contemporary global politics* (pp. 87–105). Springer.

Mamadouh, V. (2022). In the shadow of the European neighbourhood: Political geographies of EU–Middle East relations. In D. Bouris, D. Huber, & M. Pace (Eds.), *Routledge Handbook of EU–Middle East Relations* (pp. 137–146). Routledge.

March, J. G., & Olsen, J. P. (1998). The institutional dynamics of international political orders. *International Organization, 52*(4), 943–970.

McCourt, D. M. (2016). Practice theory and relationalism as the new constructivism. *International Studies Quarterly, 60*(3), 475–485.

Onar, N. F., & Nicolaïdis, K. (2013). The decentring agenda: Europe as a post-colonial power. *Cooperation and Conflict, 48*(2), 283–303.

Pace, M., & Roccu, R. (2020). Imperial pasts in the EU's approach to the Mediterranean. *Interventions, 22*(6), 671–685.

Percy, S., & Sandholtz, W. (2022). Why norms rarely die. *European Journal of International Relations, 28*(4), 934–954. https://doi.org/10.1177/13540661221126018

Pratt, S. F. (2022). *Normative transformation and the war on terrorism*. Cambridge University Press.

Scott, J. C. (1985). *Weapons of the weak: Everyday forms of peasant resistance*. Yale University Press.

Scott, J. C. (1990). *Domination and the arts of resistance: Hidden transcripts*. Yale University Press.

Wiener, A. (2004). Contested compliance: Interventions on the normative structure of world politics. *European Journal of International Relations, 10*(2), 189–234. https://doi.org/10.1177/1354066104042934

Wiener, A. (2014). *A theory of contestation*. Springer. https://doi.org/10.1007/978-3-642-55235-9

Winston, C. (2018). Norm structure, diffusion, and evolution: A conceptual approach. *European Journal of International Relations, 24*(3), 638–661.

Wunderlich, C., Lucenti, F., Ducci, C., & Lantis, J. S. (2025). Contestation in prism: An introduction. In F. Lucenti, C. Ducci, C. Wunderlich, & J. S. Lantis (Eds.), *Contestation in prism: The evolution of norms and norm clusters in contemporary global politics* (pp. 1–21). Springer.

Zielonka, J. (2006). *Europe as empire: The nature of the enlarged European Union*. Oxford University Press.

Zürn, M., & Gerschewski, J. (2021). Sketching the liberal script. A target of contestations. *SCRIPTS Working Paper No. 10*. https://www.scripts-berlin.eu/publications/working-paper-series/Working-Paper-No_-10-2021/SCRIPTS_Working_Paper_10_WEB.pdf

Chapter 10
Conclusion: A Multifaceted Understanding of Norm Contestation

Flavia Lucenti, Cecilia Ducci, Carmen Wunderlich, and Jeffrey S. Lantis

This volume has explored a wide range of illustrative examples of different types of norm contestation at work. The driving goal of this project has been to offer a substantial advancement to IR norm scholarship by widening the theoretical lens to capture the multiple facets of norm contestation. To this end, chapters have examined the implications of contestation for norm life cycles in different issue areas and institutional contexts. It focuses the attention on the relationship between contestation, norm clusters, norm robustness, and norm cluster resiliency, zooming in on norm structures and norm linkages (Deitelhoff & Zimmermann, 2020; Lantis, 2017; Lantis & Wunderlich, 2018, 2022; Orchard & Wiener, 2024; Wiener, 2014, 2018; Zimmermann et al., 2024). The result is progress towards a richer and more multifaceted understanding of norm robustness, coupled with the dynamism of the concept of norm clusters (Lantis & Wunderlich, 2018, 2022; Winston, 2018).

In this concluding analysis, we point to the theoretical innovations advanced in the volume and then draw together powerful lessons from the evidence of the contributions in a structured comparison of the results. The chapter surveys key findings and compares insights from the individual contributions and in relation to

F. Lucenti (✉)
Department of Political Science, LUISS Guido Carli University, Rome, Italy
e-mail: flucenti@luiss.it

C. Ducci
Department of Political and Social Sciences, University of Bologna, Bologna, Italy
e-mail: cecilia.ducci2@unibo.it

C. Wunderlich
Department of Political Science, University of Freiburg, Freiburg, Germany
e-mail: carmen.wunderlich@politik.uni-freiburg.de

J. S. Lantis
The College of Wooster, Wooster, OH, USA
e-mail: jlantis@wooster.edu

F. Lucenti et al. (eds.), *Contestation in Prism*, Norm Research in International Relations, https://doi.org/10.1007/978-3-031-83639-8_10

broader research questions that have led our project. The chapter also identifies remaining research puzzles and limitations that might help pave the way for future research.

Theoretical Contributions: What Is Contestation in Prism?

Building on critical perspectives and advancements of contestation theory by Wiener (e.g. 2007, 2008, 2009, 2014) and Deitelhoff and Zimmermann (2019, 2020), our volume offers a multidimensional and critical account of contestation types, processes, and outcomes, or what often really constitutes the life cycle of norms. Specifically, we argue that there are many dynamics involved in the perpetuation of normative standards, as any norm is inextricably interlinked with other norms in broader normative constellations (Lantis & Wunderlich, 2018, 2022; Percy & Sandholtz, 2022). At the same time, we acknowledge that in such a complex system, the agents, strategies, and practices of contestation may be more layered and subtle than is sometimes assumed. Thus, our analogy of 'contestation in prism' is meant to capture these dynamics—reminiscent of when white light passes through a prism and is refracted into its spectral components, producing a rainbow of colours.

Building on the existing literature in the field, and the questions that guided our research as outlined in the introduction (Wunderlich et al., 2025, Chap. 1, p. 1), we identify four different dimensions through which we grasp relevant outcomes of norm contestation. First, rather than focusing on individual norms, we investigate the effects of contestation on norm clusters. In line with Lantis and Wunderlich (2018), we contend that norms do not exist in a vacuum but are usually interlinked with other similarly aligned norms or broader normative structures (see also Lantis & Wunderlich, 2022). Norm clusters also reflect 'an intrinsic tripartite structure' (Winston, 2018, p. 640) of the norm itself, in terms of problems, values, and behaviours. This exposes the norm to more contestation, as it can also be contested in terms of its inner founding principles. By combining these approaches, we provide a more comprehensive picture of norms' structure while adding a further layer of complexity to the research on norm dynamics in that we consider clusters as existing both inside and outside the norm (Wunderlich, 2023; for a recent empirical illustration combining both models, see also Zhang, 2024).

Second, the volume looks at the complex practices of contestation employed by diverse sets of norm challengers, ranging from discursive and behavioural (Stimmer & Wisken, 2019; Wiener, 2014) to reactive, proactive, and interpretive (Orchard & Wiener, 2024; Wiener, 2017), applicatory and validity (Deitelhoff & Zimmermann, 2020; Trenta, 2021; Wolff & Zimmermann, 2016), hard and soft (Johansson-Nogués et al., 2020), and overt or subtle contestation (Drubel & Mende, 2023; Schmidt & Sikkink, 2019). It also covers the concept of 'norm withdrawal' in different forms, as an exit strategy or as an expression of a hierarchy between norms that allows norm challengers to disengage from the norm(ative) principle, which they consider less desirable.

Third, we recognise that different sets of norm challengers, including norm entrepreneurs (Finnemore & Sikkink, 1998, p. 895; Wunderlich, 2020) and 'norm antipreneurs' (Bloomfield, 2016, p. 311; Bloomfield & Scott, 2016; Panke & Petersohn, 2016), can be active in the international system. Norm agents can be state or non-state actors and operate at different scales, from local to global. The chapters in this volume explore how norm agents sometimes position themselves relative to the Liberal International Order (LIO) and have different impacts on norms. Some may see themselves as part of it, acting as members or even defenders of its main institutions and organisations, or they may feel they are outside of it, promoting what we define as a form of contestation 'from within' the LIO (Börzel & Zürn, 2021; Dian & Dugar, 2022; Ducci & Lucenti, 2022; Newman & Zala, 2018; Wiener, 2004). In this respect, our contribution departs from the prevailing view in the literature that challenges to norms come mainly from outside the LIO.

Fourth, we explore the ways in which norm systems appear to adapt to contestation, often continuing to expand or alternatively being weakened. We therefore seek to assess whether a norm's embeddedness in a cluster allows it to better withstand challenges as suggested by the concept of 'norm cluster resiliency' (Lantis & Wunderlich, 2018), thus not only avoiding decay but strengthening the norm cluster itself. In addition, this model allows that contestation in networked norm connections may have spillover effects on other norms or principles in the cluster, compromising the robustness of the norm or affecting the cluster as a whole, leading to its potential disintegration.

Revisiting Theories of Contestation Through Norm Linkages

In this section, we discuss the empirical evidence from a variety of issue areas related to the debate about whether being embedded in a cluster enables norms to better withstand the challenges posed by contestation. It reviews the main contributions emerging from the chapters of the volume, highlights similarities and differences between them, and points out some of the limitations that still exist in the literature.

Contestation and Norm Clusters

Chapters to this volume offer different perspectives on the types of norm clusters and norm linkages that face contestation, including differences related to the content or policy field and to the respective norm cluster concept in use. For example, human rights norms are the most recurring focus in the volume, addressed by Knapp and Fritzler (2025, Chap. 4), Lucenti et al. (2025, Chap. 5), Badell (2025, Chap. 7), and García Iommi (2025, Chap. 8). Knapp and Fritzler (2025, Chap. 4) examine challenges to the Responsibility to Protect (R2P), which they see as part of a 'wider protection cluster'. Transcending the narrow dichotomy of 'norm entrepreneurs' vs. 'norm antipreneurs', they argue that states can strategically engage in norm clusters by shifting positions and shaping contestation discourses. In the case of R2P, this allows for a redefinition, or at least a partial substitution of this norm with other norms from the protection cluster to which the norm of the R2P belongs. Nevertheless, rather than negatively affecting the resiliency of the cluster as a whole, it only impinges on the R2P norm within it. Similarly, Lucenti et al. (2025, Chap. 5) address the norm of the Responsibility to Prosecute. Although they acknowledge that this norm is also inserted in what they call a broader 'humanitarian norm cluster', which also includes R2P, in their analysis, they opt to conceptualise the Responsibility to Prosecute as a norm cluster itself. In line with Winston's (2018) tripartite structure, they identify two fundamental principles at work: universal jurisdiction and complementarity. Whilst the norm is firmly anchored in such a set of cohesive principles, these may render the Responsibility to Prosecute vulnerable to more contestation. As the authors discuss, the contesting practices performed by defiant regimes, such as Sri Lanka, impinge on the robustness of the Responsibility to Prosecute precisely by challenging its core principles.

Other authors take a slightly different approach to this question. For example, Badell (2025, Chap. 7) shifts the discussion on gender equality norms and, in particular, Sexual and Reproductive Health and Rights (SRHR) in the European Union (EU). He finds that despite opposition from the governments of Hungary and Poland in particular, but also Italy and Malta, the 'gender equality norm cluster' within the European normative context guarantees a mechanism of protection against contestation of SRHR. Therefore, the author contends that it is only by recognising the normative links of the SRHR norm within the gender equality cluster that we can understand how the latter has acted in terms of resiliency despite the contestation efforts within the EU. Human rights norms are also examined by García Iommi in her study on the impact of norm withdrawal—as a form of contestation—on norm clusters. This chapter empirically delves into gender equality norms, non-impunity, and norms regulating the use of force. According to the author, clusters of norms in principle reduce the likelihood of norm withdrawal by increasing the costs of non-compliance, but do not eliminate it because at the same time they establish a larger set of legal obligations for agents. Contrary to existing scholarship (Lantis & Wunderlich, 2018; Percy & Sandholtz, 2022), which expects similar norms to become intertwined with institutionalisation to create particularly resilient systems, García Iommi questions this effect of norm clusters in the case of norm withdrawal. Interestingly, Lucenti et al. (2025, Chap. 5) who also use Winston's concept find similar internal contestation dynamics.

Chapter contributions also address specific types of security norms within larger clusters. This is the case in chapters by Lantis (2025, Chap. 2), Huelss (2025, Chap. 6), and Tholens (2025, Chap. 9). Lantis explores the nuclear non-use norm in the context of a broader cluster of nuclear non-proliferation norms that provide support in the face of contestation. Although Lantis acknowledges that contestation involves applicatory challenges as well as deeper questions about the validity of norms designed for security threats and responses, he credits norm clusters for 'their ability to absorb, diffuse, and redirect the energy of contestatory challenges toward reinforcement of existing norms' (Lantis, 2025, Chap. 2, p. 24). Huelss' chapter on the contemporary development of norms for Artificial Intelligence (AI) deals with the practical uses of setting standards for the appropriate application of AI in a military context within the protection of a legal norm cluster. Huelss expresses concern that the resiliency of this cluster and the robustness of the norms it contains—with specific reference to the International Humanitarian Law and International Human Rights Law norms—may be increasingly affected by the (mis)use of AI tools, with implications for security. Tholens' chapter is perhaps more optimistic, arguing that interconnected norms can be more resilient and that normative configurations supporting Euro-Mediterranean cooperation help to tackle important matters, such as energy security. Finally, Panke et al. (2025, Chap. 3) analyse clusters of community norms that define membership rights and obligations and that way function as an integral element of a Regional International Organisation (RIO)'s cohesion.

Types of Contestation

Contributors to this volume identify a wide range of forms and types of norm contestation across different issue areas. Broadly speaking, these fall into three categories. First, there are authors who mainly deal with types of contestation that have been established in earlier studies, especially the differentiation between applicatory and validity contestation (Deitelhoff & Zimmermann, 2020), and combine them with interactions between norms within clusters. Focusing on challenges by governments against international norms, Lantis (2025, Chap. 2) addresses the significance of applicatory and validity contestation in threats by state leaders to consider the use of nuclear weapons. Badell (2025, Chap. 7) stresses the shift from applicatory to validity contestation in the EU context regarding SRHR norms. He charts how debates focused on application helped to create a permissive consensus in support of the norm in the EU but eventually led to an escalation of contestation towards validity contestation. Interestingly, Badell links the 'radicalisation' of contestation to the viability of an outside alternative norm—due to the shift in US policy—and explains how their policies moderated when this outside alternative fell away. This also speaks to findings by Zimmermann et al. (2024, p. 254, emphasis in original), who find that with regard to the historical norm once permitting slave trade, 'the demise of slave trading was brought about by linking the norm to *alternative* norm clusters'. Lucenti et al. (2025, Chap. 5) recognise additional variations on these themes in their exploration of discursive and behavioural contestation as reflective of both applicatory and validity contestation related to the Responsibility to Prosecute with respect to war crimes committed during the Sri Lankan civil war. They argue that behavioural contestation, in particular, was carried out by establishing 'home-grown mechanisms' of accountability that were ultimately aimed at contesting the principle of complementarity subtending the Responsibility to Prosecute norm.

Second, some authors study variations in the scope, intensity, and content of contestation. Knapp and Fritzler (2025, Chap. 4) recognise the significance of applicatory contestation by Canada and Sweden to the R2P, highlighting their shift from norm entrepreneurship to competitor entrepreneurship. But they also emphasise that there are variations in the intensity, scope, and content of contestation practices, and identify patterns of 'soft contestation'. These manifest themselves in the neglect and substitution of individual components of the norm cluster to facilitate policy implementation while at the same time maintaining a supportive attitude overall. While such a 'pragmatic approach' could strengthen the subsidiary norms—and thus change the shape of the overarching norm cluster—the authors warn that gradual soft contestation could undermine the robustness of R2P in the long term. Ultimately, although contestation would not have a negative effect on the overarching norm cluster, it would probably shift the meaning- in- use of the R2P within it (see also Zimmermann et al., 2024, p. 258). Huelss (2025, Chap. 6) calls for more variation in how we understand contestation, including recognising new practices of using and interacting with yet unregulated emerging technologies. In a thoughtful exploration of AI, Huelss also acknowledges the existence of a hidden layer of 'non-public' and non-deliberative' contestation provoked by AI-driven decisions, which can be assessed as types of subtle norm contestation. In a similar vein, Tholens (2025, Chap. 9) describes hidden transcripts as a type of contestation that is not assimilated into public discourses but emerges more often at their margins. Tholens focuses on the struggle over the meaning of normative transformation by reasoning about the existence of social hierarchies embedded in normative configurations. In the conceptual framework she outlines, applicatory and validity are not distinct types of contestation, but part of the same spectrum of resistance that can affect both the application and the existence of underlying norms. Thus, by adopting a post-Marxist and Gramscian critical approach, Tholens observes what she defines as 'thin' contestation practices that actors at the 'periphery'—vs. the 'European core'—have contested mainly in a covert way.

Third, two studies focus on contestation in the form of 'norm withdrawal' but reach different conclusions on the subject and on the definition of the concept itself. Panke et al. (2025, Chap. 3) cover the role of RIOs as community-based organisations that champion clusters of community norms outlining membership rights and obligations. Starting from the assumption that these systems are almost constantly confronted with different forms of contestation, the authors assess how, in an attempt of institutional reform, states contest RIOs by threatening to withdraw their membership. This is seen by the authors as the 'nuclear option' (Panke et al., 2025, Chap. 3) of contestation by member states but, as the authors substantiate in their empirical research, the RIOs' cluster of community norms acts as a guarantee of resiliency in the face of norm withdrawal. If the threat of withdrawal serves as an ultimate strategy of contestation for member states, the threat of entrenchment, when used by IOs against those who challenge existing norms, serves to contain member states' contestation. Thus, as also Badell (2025) explains (Chap. 7), in this case, exit from IOs or expulsion from the normative community can be perceived as a symbolic ostracism. Conversely, García Iommi (2025, Chap. 8) argues that norm withdrawal is a more regular occurrence, which does not necessarily signal the demise of a collective but may rather even increase the legitimacy of a norm. Hence, norm withdrawal occurs when a norm enjoys a high degree of validity. She claims that norm withdrawal occurs when actors seek to establish a legitimate exception for themselves *vis-à-vis* a norm by pointing to other norms with competing prescriptions. Norm withdrawal can thereby lead the actor to prioritise one norm over another and create conflicting normative structures, including within clusters of norms.

Types of Contesting Agents

The chapters in the volume look at the role of a variety of agents of contestation, ranging from state to non-state actors, such as political leaders, but also IOs and RIOs, like the EU and other regional actors. Agents can act as 'norm entrepreneurs' or 'norm antipreneurs' depending on how they position themselves in relation to the norms in question. Knapp and Fritzler (2025, Chap. 4), for example, describe contestation and norm diplomacy relative to the R2P norm and the unconventional role of Canada and Sweden as not only norm entrepreneurs but also agents contesting the same norms they initially helped promote. While these two states were pioneers in the development of R2P, they have since retreated from this leadership, moving from a position of norm entrepreneurship to competitor entrepreneurship. However, Knapp and Fritzler affirm that binary role descriptions of norm support or norm challenge do not capture the subtlety of diverse positions in between, as it ignores the complexity of positionality and the ongoing evolution of normative debates. In this respect, Knapp and Fritzler's contribution proposes that the valuable theoretical lessons from studies of contestation lie in a broadening of our way of understanding of contestation (see also Wunderlich, 2022). Their study also emphasises that contestation does not only come from outsiders or challengers to the LIO, but from those acting within it, even if through more subtle forms of contestation. A similar process is acknowledged by Badell (2025, Chap. 7), who investigates contestation driven by both states and a regional organisation, the EU, which are traditionally seen as guarantors of certain international norms. In the context of gender equality and SRHR, the author argues that EU member states and the EU in general are among the main promoters of such norms. At the same time, however, some of these member states have been involved in contesting practices against SRHR, both in terms of applicatory and validity contestation. Ultimately, it is the entrepreneurship of norm supporters, who constitute a mostly dominant in-group', that re-enforces the legitimacy of the contested norms. Panke et al. (2025, Chap. 3) similarly assess the role of RIOs as entrepreneurs of community norms, preventing withdrawal mechanisms by their member states when these act as norm antagonists. Still coherent with a regional perspective, Tholens (2025, Chap. 9) observes the impact of institutionalised and solidified Euro-Mediterranean community models relations over the past two decades and how they reproduce hidden transcripts.

Shifting from the state to the role of individuals as normative agents, Lantis (2025, Chap. 2) addresses the significance of applicatory and validity contestation in threats by state leaders to consider the use of nuclear weapons. He describes how challenges by presidents Donald Trump and Vladimir Putin raise two-dimensional challenges to existing norms for the non-use and non-proliferation of nuclear weapons. Analogously, Lucenti et al. (2025, Chap. 5) cover the contesting practices of defiant regimes. They investigate the case of Sri Lanka's post-civil war governments as norm antagonists and how they affect the robustness and resiliency of the Responsibility to Prosecute norm and norm cluster. Finally, Huelss (2025, Chap. 6) pushes the question further, going beyond human agency to open the debate on the implications of norm challenge or compliance by potential AI-driven normative agents. His ontological approach to the subject of normative substance as normativity and to the normality of practices raises intriguing questions on the future of norm contestation studies, such as what do we do when AI-driven systems would be able to produce norms? Or what happens when machine learning starts to generate its own overt or covert challenges to the existing—human-made—international normative framework? It follows that the advent of AI-driven agency may therefore influence established concepts within norms research and challenge fundamental precepts of norm contestation theory.

How Contestation Shapes Clustered Norms

Contestation can have different effects on norms and state conduct in relation to norms. In particular, this volume asks how different forms of contestation affect the resiliency of norm clusters and, more or less directly, the robustness of individual norms. In contrast to existing arguments in norms research (Kutz, 2014; McKeown, 2009; Panke & Petersohn, 2012, 2016), none of the chapter authors argue that contestation leads to the absolute demise or death of norms, whenever they are involved in a cluster. Rather, the chapters describe variations of effects that often appear to be mitigated or at least contained by the presence of norm clusters, considering norm linkages complementary and reinforcing in nature. Lantis (2025, Chap. 2) explains that norm clusters provide a high level of resiliency for norm architectures and that applicatory and even validity contestation of nuclear non-proliferation norms can be moderated by cohesiveness and institutionalisation of norm systems. That model includes norm contestation or challenges that lead to an activation of clustered norm networks, dispersal of contestatory energy, and adaptation or new norm development. Panke et al. (2025, Chap. 3) find the applicatory scope of community norms as more frequently contested than their substantive content but recognise that different forms of contestations have different effects on the stabilisation, modification, or replacement of norms. Specifically, they see how RIOs' community norms result in the norms' stabilisation. Stabilisation occurs not only when the challenger state uses withdrawal threats to stabilise the community norm in question, but also when it pushes for the norm to be amended or replaced. This suggests that RIOs' clusters of community norms tend to be rather resilient and rarely changed by individual instances of member states threatening to withdraw from the RIO.

While most chapters in this volume consider that norm linkages are complementary and reinforcing in nature, others do see indicators that entire normative constellations are hampered. In the chapter by Lucenti et al. (2025, Chap. 5), for example, the authors indicate that the clustering of principles inherent in a norm may actually attract more contestation, rather than providing mechanisms for resiliency. If this same clustering is in fact 'used' by agents who pick and choose norm's underlying principles to justify their actions, this can ultimately have a negative impact on the norm. However, the authors do not consider a spillover effect on other related norms, but simply state the negative effect of contestation on the norm under study, which is assumed to be a cluster in itself.

Another interesting question that many of the chapters in this volume have grappled with was whether norm contestation could have spillover effects on the other clustered norms or principles integral to the norm clusters. More precisely, we ask whether and under which circumstances norm contestation could effectively create a 'reverse cascade' for normative systems. Authors' chapters reach mixed conclusions about the potential for these impacts. Knapp and Fritzler (2025, Chap. 4) acknowledge the positive impact of norm cluster spillover on the norm and argue that Canada and Sweden's 'soft contestation' of international humanitarian norms could potentially have a broader impact by undermining norm robustness through narrowing the conceptual scope of the R2P norm. However, they stress that these effects are limited and subtle. Other chapters admit that normative assemblages often can effectively contain the impact of contestation in the short term. Lantis (2025, Chap. 2), in particular, shows how this happens through stages including activation for accountability, dispersal, and adaptation. He claims that even in the direst circumstances, like threats of the use of weapons of mass destruction in conflict, the system appears to be more flaw-tolerant than many realists would acknowledge (see also Smetana & O'Mahoney, 2022). Badell (2025, Chap. 7) makes a similar argument in the fracturing of the EU normative community. As the author explains, even as Poland and Hungary escalated their contestation to SRHR, other EU countries put in place mechanisms of resiliency to reject the challenge. Here, a normative system worked to actively contain a potential spillover effect through the threat of a *de facto* expulsion of Hungary and Poland from the EU community. Hence, the resiliency of SRHR within the EU has been reinforced when some of its member states opted for a strategy of entrenchment, symbolically ostracising those who openly question the validity of the norm from the EU normative community.

Even when taken to the extreme of norm withdrawal, chapters point out that normative networks themselves would not be undermined by the impact of a potential spillover effect triggered by contestation practices. For García Iommi (2025, Chap. 8), norm withdrawal meant redefining the scope of the norm in accordance with a particular actor's expectations of the norm's behaviour. Yet, its impact on norm robustness and norm cluster resiliency can be significant, as already discussed.

While other actors' acceptance of norm withdrawal can foster norm robustness, rejection by the international community can undermine it. In turn, as is the case with other forms of contestation, the potential for norm withdrawal may sometimes increase the legitimacy of a norm, as García Iommi illustrates with examples. Indeed, what is at stake in this chapter is not the impact of a potential spillover effect of norm contestation on the other clustered norms and principles, but the capacity of the norm cluster to contain norm withdrawal. Panke et al. (2025, Chap. 3) reach similar conclusions, admitting that normative withdrawal in RIOs does not fundamentally undermine core norms, nor should it be expected to have dramatic spillover effects in other related normative linkages.

Theoretical Insights and New Questions

This study has presented a range of different perspectives towards the concept of contestation and its potential impact on the robustness and resiliency of broader norm constellations. The project began by identifying a prismatic focus on contestation—a recognition that the agents, strategies, mechanisms, and outcomes of contestation are often more subtle than sometimes assumed. We acknowledge numerous actors and dynamics at work in the perpetuation and change of normative standards. Chapters explore the role of norm clusters in relation to questions of resiliency and adaptability. This allows us to more fully capture the dynamics of norm evolution and devolution in a complex world. This exploration has also benefited from the participation of a new and diverse generation of norm scholars, who embrace the concept of contestation as an ontological innovation and draw on it to interpret contemporary global politics.

Chapters in the volume add value to the development of theory in this field by discussing variations on the traditional types and forms of contestation—including examinations of 'soft contestation' and norm withdrawal—and critically unpacking the development, scope, strength, and resiliency of norm architectures. In the process, we have welcomed conceptual and methodological advances in IR theory which have broadened the way we think about the role of institutions, structures, and processes in global politics. Furthermore, chapters in this volume offer valuable insights on the complexity of actors and processes in contestation, as well as the soft-moderating effects of norm clusters. On the one hand, they recognise the 'dual quality' of norms (Wiener, 2007, p. 49), as well as their malleability as 'works in progress' (Krook & True, 2012, p. 104), which acquire meaning in and through discursive practices. Indeed, the relative subtlety of the normative contests that our authors highlight, which are taking place all over the world and all the time, is itself a contribution to perspectives on norms. On the other hand, they recognise a diverse range of actors who are regularly challenging normative guidance. In some cases, norm contestation might be seen as 'predictable' when it is undertaken by determined leaders who seek to loudly challenge the international system. Vladimir Putin's threats of the use of nuclear weapons during the war with Ukraine are but one example of the types of highly visible norm challenges that can emerge. Challenges by Hungary and Poland to EU standards for SRHR and gender rights would appear to be similarly high-profile resistance to prevailing norms. But in other cases, countries that are often considered supporters of international norms, like Canada and Sweden, might take exception to the standards of international humanitarian law requiring humanitarian interventions. In extreme cases, as several chapters argue, governments may seek to withdraw from normative standards or requirements in discrete issue areas, with variable effects on the status of norm constellations. In such cases, even measures of norm robustness are not sufficient to fully capture norm strength, and even the dual features of validity and facticity miss the ways that resiliency allows us to delve into a more dynamic and stable relationship between norms and, above all, norm clusters and contesting practices.

In summary, this volume has demonstrated that contemporary politics are shaped by complex, multifaceted, and dynamic processes of contestation that yield different outcomes. Chapters show how many actors, including AI-driven systems, are seemingly in constant dialogue with norms, and characteristics of norm systems can help alter the outcomes of contestation. And this would seem to make it all the more urgent to develop new conceptual approaches and new empirical analyses of contemporary international politics. Only by doing so will norm contestation theory be able to still provide valid explanations for reading the complexity of today's world and of its normative structures.

References

Badell, D. (2025). Gender equality norm cluster in action: The resiliency of sexual and reproductive health and rights in the EU. In F. Lucenti, C. Ducci, C. Wunderlich, & J. S. Lantis (Eds.), *Contestation in prism: The evolution of norms and norm clusters in contemporary global politics* (pp. 125–142). Springer.

Bloomfield, A. (2016). Norm antipreneurs and theorising resistance to normative change. *Review of International Studies, 42*(2), 310–333. https://doi.org/10.1017/S026021051500025X

Bloomfield, A., & Scott, S. V. (2016). *Norm antipreneurs and the politics of resistance to global normative change*. Taylor & Francis.

Börzel, T., & Zürn, M. (2021). Contestations of the liberal international order: From liberal multilateralism to postnational liberalism. *International Organization, 75*(2), 282–305. https://doi.org/10.1017/S0020818320000570

Deitelhoff, N., & Zimmermann, L. (2019). Norms under challenge: Unpacking the dynamics of norm robustness. *Journal of Global Security Studies, 4*(1), 2–17. https://doi.org/10.1093/jogss/ogy041

Deitelhoff, N., & Zimmermann, L. (2020). Things we lost in the fire: How different types of contestation affect the robustness of international norms. *International Studies Review, 22*(1), 51–76. https://doi.org/10.1093/isr/viy080

Dian, M., & Dugar, G. (2022). A post-western world in the making. The conceptual framework. *Interdisciplinary Political Studies, 8*(2), 233–245. https://doi.org/10.1285/i20398573v8n2p233

Drubel, J., & Mende, J. (2023). The hidden contestation of norms: Decent work in the International Labour Organization and the United Nations. *Global Constitutionalism, 12*(2), 246–268. https://doi.org/10.1017/S2045381722000259

Ducci, C., & Lucenti, F. (2022). 'Contestation from within': US escalating aversion to the International Criminal Court and the non-impunity norm in the trump era. *Interdisciplinary Political Studies, 8*(2), 281–297. https://doi.org/10.1285/i20398573v8n2p281

Finnemore, M., & Sikkink, K. (1998). International norm dynamics and political change. *International Organization, 52*(4), 887–917. https://doi.org/10.1162/002081898550789

García Iommi, L. (2025). Exceptions as contestation: Understanding norm withdrawal. In F. Lucenti, C. Ducci, C. Wunderlich, & J. S. Lantis (Eds.), *Contestation in prism: The evolution of norms and norm clusters in contemporary global politics* (pp. 143–161). Springer.

Huelss, H. (2025). Contestation of normativity in military practices and the AI transformation. In F. Lucenti, C. Ducci, C. Wunderlich, & J. S. Lantis (Eds.), *Contestation in prism: The evolution of norms and norm clusters in contemporary global politics* (pp. 107–124). Springer.

Johansson-Nogués, E., Vlaskamp, M. C., & Barbé, E. (2020). *European Union contested.* Springer. https://doi.org/10.1007/978-3-030-33238-9

Knapp, A., & Fritzler, J. (2025). 'Soft contestation' of the responsibility to protect? Assessing Canada and Sweden's norm diplomacy. In F. Lucenti, C. Ducci, C. Wunderlich, & J. S. Lantis (Eds.), *Contestation in prism: The evolution of norms and norm clusters in contemporary global politics* (pp. 65–85). Springer.

Krook, M. L., & True, J. (2012). Rethinking the life cycles of international norms: The United Nations and the global promotion of gender equality. *European Journal of International Relations, 18*(1), 103–127. https://doi.org/10.1177/1354066110380963

Kutz, C. (2014). How norms die: Torture and assassination in American security policy. *Ethics & International Affairs, 28*(4), 425–449. https://doi.org/10.1017/S0892679414000598

Lantis, J. S. (2017). Theories of international norm contestation: Structure and outcomes. In *Oxford Research Encyclopedia of Politics*. Oxford University Press. https://doi.org/10.1093/acrefore/9780190228637.013.590

Lantis, J. S. (2025). Norm cluster resiliency in the face of contestation: Nuclear threats and international resolve. In F. Lucenti, C. Ducci, C. Wunderlich, & J. S. Lantis (Eds.), *Contestation in prism: The evolution of norms and norm clusters in contemporary global politics* (pp. 23–43). Springer.

Lantis, J. S., & Wunderlich, C. (2018). Resiliency dynamics of norm clusters: Norm contestation and international cooperation. *Review of International Studies, 44*(3), 570–593. https://doi.org/10.1017/S0260210517000626

Lantis, J. S., & Wunderlich, C. (2022). Reevaluating constructivist norm theory: A three-dimensional norms research program. *International Studies Review, 24*(1). https://doi.org/10.1093/isr/viab059

Lucenti, F., Ducci, C., & Lee, P. K. (2025). Conceptualising the responsibility to prosecute norm as a cluster: Impunity for war crimes in Sri Lanka. In Lucenti, F., Ducci, C., Wunderlich, C., & Lantis, J. S. (Eds.), *Contestation in prism: The evolution of norms and norm clusters in contemporary global politics* (pp. 87–105).

McKeown, R. (2009). Norm regress: US revisionism and the slow death of the torture norm. *International Relations, 23*(1), 5–25. https://doi.org/10.1177/0047117808100607

Newman, E., & Zala, B. (2018). Rising powers and order contestation: Disaggregating the normative from the representational. *Third World Quarterly, 39*(5), 871–888. https://doi.org/10.1080/01436597.2017.1392085

Orchard, P., & Wiener, A. (2024). *Contesting the world: Norm research in theory and practice.* Cambridge University Press.

Panke, D., & Petersohn, U. (2012). Why international norms disappear sometimes. *European Journal of International Relations, 18*(4), 719–742. https://doi.org/10.1177/1354066111407690

Panke, D., & Petersohn, U. (2016). Norm challenges and norm death: The inexplicable? *Cooperation and Conflict, 51*(1), 3–19. https://doi.org/10.1177/0010836715597948

Panke, D., Grundsfeld, L., & Tverskoi, P. (2025). Regional organisations, exit threats, and contestation of community norms. In F. Lucenti, C. Ducci, C. Wunderlich, & J. S. Lantis, (Eds.), *Contestation in prism: The evolution of norms and norm clusters in contemporary global politics* (pp. 45–63). Springer.

Percy, S., & Sandholtz, W. (2022). Why norms rarely die. *European Journal of International Relations, 28*(4), 934–954. https://doi.org/10.1177/13540661221126018
Schmidt, A., & Sikkink, K. (2019). Breaking the ban? The heterogeneous impact of US contestation of the torture norm. *Journal of Global Security Studies, 4*(1), 105–122. https://doi.org/10.1093/jogss/ogy036
Smetana, M., & O'Mahoney, J. (2022). NPT as an antifragile system: How contestation improves the nonproliferation regime. *Contemporary Security Policy, 43*(1), 24–49. https://doi.org/10.1080/13523260.2021.1978761
Stimmer, A., & Wisken, L. (2019). The dynamics of dissent: When actions are louder than words. *International Affairs, 95*(3), 515–533. https://doi.org/10.1093/ia/iiz019
Tholens, S. (2025). Hidden transcripts and normative transformations. In F. Lucenti, C. Ducci, C. Wunderlich, & J. S. Lantis (Eds.), *Contestation in prism: The evolution of norms and norm clusters in contemporary global politics* (pp. 163–181). Springer.
Trenta, L. (2021). Death by reinterpretation: Dynamics of norm contestation and the US ban on assassination in the Reagan years. *Journal of Global Security Studies, 6*(4). https://doi.org/10.1093/jogss/ogab012
Wiener, A. (2004). Contested compliance: Interventions on the normative structure of world politics. *European Journal of International Relations, 10*(2), 189–234. https://doi.org/10.1177/1354066104042934
Wiener, A. (2007). The dual quality of norms and governance beyond the state: Sociological and normative approaches to 'interaction'. *Critical Review of International Social and Political Philosophy, 10*(1), 47–69. https://doi.org/10.1080/13698230601122412
Wiener, A. (2008). *The invisible constitution of politics: Contested norms and international encounters*. Cambridge University Press. https://doi.org/10.1017/CBO9780511490408
Wiener, A. (2009). Enacting meaning-in-use: Qualitative research on norms and international relations. *Review of International Studies, 35*(1), 175–193. https://doi.org/10.1017/S0260210509008377
Wiener, A. (2014). *A theory of contestation*. Springer. https://doi.org/10.1007/978-3-642-55235-9
Wiener, A. (2017). A theory of contestation - a concise summary of its argument and concepts. *Polity, 49*(1), 109–125. https://doi.org/10.1086/690100
Wiener, A. (2018). *Contestation and constitution of norms in global international relations*. Cambridge University Press. https://doi.org/10.1017/9781316718599
Winston, C. (2018). Norm structure, diffusion, and evolution: A conceptual approach. *European Journal of International Relations, 24*(3), 638–661. https://doi.org/10.1177/1354066117720794
Wolff, J., & Zimmermann, L. (2016). Between banyans and battle scenes: Liberal norms, contestation, and the limits of critique. *Review of International Studies, 42*(3), 513–534. https://doi.org/10.1017/S0260210515000534
Wunderlich, C. (2020). *Rogue states as norm entrepreneurs*. Springer. https://doi.org/10.1007/978-3-030-27990-5
Wunderlich, C. (2022). Blinded by delight?: A plea for de-moralising the scholarship on norm entrepreneurs. *European Review of International Studies, 9*(3), 363–388.
Wunderlich, C. (2023). Normcluster und Normkomplexität. *ZIB Zeitschrift für Internationale Beziehungen, 30*(2), 160–171. https://doi.org/10.5771/0946-7165-2023-2-160
Wunderlich, C., Lucenti, F., Ducci, C., & Lantis, J. S. (2025). Contestation in prism: An introduction. In F. Lucenti, C. Ducci, C. Wunderlich, & J. S. Lantis (Eds.), *Contestation in prism: The evolution of norms and norm clusters in contemporary global politics* (pp. 1–21). Springer.
Zhang, Q. (2024). Prevention as a norm cluster? Mapping China's contestation on atrocity prevention. *International Affairs, 100*(1), 241–260. https://doi.org/10.1093/ia/iiad224
Zimmermann, L., Deitelhoff, N., Lesch, M., Arcudi, A., & Peez, A. (2024). *International norm disputes. The link between contestation and norm robustness*. Oxford University Press.

Index

F. Lucenti et al. (eds.), *Contestation in Prism*, Norm Research in International Relations, https://doi.org/10.1007/978-3-031-83639-8

The manufacturer's authorised representative in the EU is Springer Nature Customer Service Centre GmbH, Europaplatz 3, 69115 Heidelberg, Germany. If you have any concerns regarding our products, please contact ProductSafety@springernature.com

Printed and bound by CPI Group (UK) Ltd, Croydon, CR0 4YY
30/09/2026
02225598-0003